DIALOGUE GAMES

LAURI CARLSON

The Academy of Finland

DIALOGUE GAMES

An Approach to Discourse Analysis

D. REIDEL PUBLISHING COMPANY

DORDRECHT : HOLLAND / BOSTON : U.S.A.

LONDON : ENGLAND

Library of Congress Cataloging in Publication Data

Carlson, Lauri, 1952–
   Dialogue games.

   (Synthese language library ; v. 17)
   Bibliography: p.
   Includes indexes.
   1. S Discourse analysis. 2. Conversation.
3. English language–Discourse analysis. 4. Game
theory. I. Title. II. Series.
P302.C35   1982   401'.41   82–13318
ISBN 90–277–1455–X (hbk)
ISBN 90–277–1951–9 (pbk)

Published by D. Reidel Publishing Company,
P.O. Box 17, 3300 AA Dordrecht, Holland.

Sold and distributed in the U.S.A. and Canada
by Kluwer Academic Publishers,
190 Old Derby Street, Hingham, MA 02043, U.S.A.

In all other countries, sold and distributed
by Kluwer Academic Publishers Group,
P.O. Box 322, 3300 AH Dordrecht, Holland.

First published in 1983 in hardbound edition

TABLE OF CONTENTS

PREFACE

This essay constitutes yet another approach to the fields of inquiry variously known as discourse analysis, discourse grammar, text grammar, functional syntax, or text linguistics.[1]

An attempt is made to develop a fairly abstract unified theoretical framework for the description of discourse which actually helps explain concrete facts of the discourse grammar of a natural language.[2] This plan is reflected in the division of the study into two parts. In the first part, a semiformal framework for describing conversational discourse is developed in some detail. In the second part, this framework is applied to the functional syntax of English.

The relation of the discourse grammar of Part II to the descriptive framework of Part I can be instructively compared to the relation of Tarskian semantics to model theory. Tarski's semantics defines a concept of *truth* of a sentence in a *model*, an independently identified construct. Analogously, my rules of discourse grammar define a concept of *appropriateness* of a sentence to a given *context*. The task of the first Part of the essay is to characterize the relevant notion of context.

Although my original statement of the problem was linguistic — how to describe the meaning, or function, of certain aspects of word order and intonation — Part I is largely an application of various methods and results of philosophical logic. The justification of the interdisciplinary approach is the simplicity and naturalness of the eventual answers to specific linguistic problems in Part II.

Part II of the monograph provides new definitions to such traditional text linguistic concepts as discourse coherence and cohesion, discourse topic and subject, theme and rheme, and given and known information. Applied in rules of discourse grammar to data from actual and constructed discourse examples, the new definitions explain previous observations and unearth new facts about English sentential connectives and stylistic rules of word order.

The research reported here started out from the coincidence of two independent influences. The topic of discourse grammar was suggested by Mark Liberman's MIT lectures on intonation in 1978. He made me realize that the meaning of certain intonational and grammatical contrasts is essentially organizational: without adding factual information, they serve to direct the flow of information in discourse.

Jaakko Hintikka, in a talk given in Groningen in 1978, gave me the clue to what it is that such textual means organize. His outline of a description of dialogue as a game has been transformed through years and rewritings into the dialogue games described in this essay. I think he would agree that the prototype is barely recognizable from the finished product.

As soon becomes obvious to a reader of this essay, it owes its greatest intellectual debt to the work of Jaakko Hintikka. It would not be wild exaggeration to consider this monograph but an application of his ideas in the fields of philosophical logic, philosophy of language, and linguistics. This essay, in its entirety, constitutes a recognition of his formative influence on my thinking. Of course, he is not accountable for my failures to appreciate what I have learned from him.

I have also greatly benefited from the advice and criticism of my teachers at MIT, in particular, Mark Liberman, Ken Hale, James Higginbotham and my advisor, Paul Kiparsky. Paul Kiparsky not only suggested major theoretical improvements but also gave practical advice and encouragement.

Susumo Kuno at Harvard taught me most of what I know about functional syntax. My good personal friend, Esa Saarinen, constantly encouraged me to push forward with my lonely work. Among other supportive as well as instructive friends, I especially thank Janet Pierrehumbert, Nick Ostler, David Nash, Jane Simpson, Ken Safir, David Pesetsky, and Annie Zaenen.

I am deeply grateful to my parents for everything they have done for me. Most of all, I want to thank my wife, Seija, who made it possible for me to carry on writing, and my son, John, who made it necessary to finally put a stop to it.

My research has been supported by research assistantships in the Academy of Finland and at the Massachusetts Institute of Technology and by scholarships from the Asla-Fulbright Foundation, Oskar Öflunds Stiftelse, Heikki ja Hilma Honkasen Säätiö, and Suomen Kulttuurirahasto.

LAURI CARLSON

INTRODUCTION

1. DISCOURSE ANALYSIS

The present work is an essay in discourse analysis. By discourse, in a wide sense, can be understood any sustained stretch of speech (sequence of individual sentences). Discourse analysis in a wide sense, then, concerns "all those relations among linguistic entities which are statable ... in terms of wider spans than those which fall within the limits of the sentence".[1] This delimitation sets off discourse analysis (and discourse grammar) from traditional (sentence) grammar: as James Harris put it in 1751, "the longest extension with which Grammar has to do, is the Extension here consider'd, that is to say, a sentence. The great Extensions (such as Syllogism, Paragraph, Sections, and complete works) belong not to grammar but to Arts of higher order; not to mention that all of these are but Sentences repeated."[2]

The *subject* of discourse analysis, then, is discourse. What sets it off from other disciplines treating of the same subject, such as rhetoric, stylistics, poetics, or literary criticism, is the topical *question* it addresses.

In the words of Labov ([23], p. 252), "the fundamental problem of discourse analysis is to show how one utterance follows another in a rational, rule-governed manner — in other words, how we understand coherent discourse." The problem, in brief, is to explain *what is coherent (i.e., well-formed) discourse*. For illustration, I quote Coulthard ([6], p. 7):

Discourse, then, does not consist simply of a string of grammatically well-formed utterances or sentences. The following examples from Labov (1970) are grammatically unexceptional yet noticeably odd:[3]

A: What is your name?
B: Well, let's say you might have thought you had something from before but you haven't got it any more.
A: I'm going to call you Dean.

A: I feel hot today.
B: No.

In both examples B's contribution obviously breaks rules for the production of coherent discourse. One of the fundamental aims of discourse analysis is to discover these rules, but an even more fundamental question is the nature of the units whose structure and occurrence the sequencing rules will describe.

My approach to discourse analysis, the *dialogue game approach*, constitutes a particular attempt at an answer to the fundamental problems posed by Labov and Coulthard.

In my approach, the fundamental unit of description of discourse is a theoretical construct called a *dialogue game*. This construct admits the following characterization of well-formedness of discourse:

> A discourse is coherent if it can be extended into a well-formed dialogue game.

The problem of characterizing coherent discourse is thus reduced to the task of describing a certain class of games.

2. LANGUAGE-GAMES

The idea of comparing language to a game goes back, of course, to Ludwig Wittgenstein. "No one will deny that studying the nature of the rules of games must be useful for the study of grammatical rules, since it is beyond doubt there is some sort of similarity between them."[4] As the slogan goes, "The use of a word in the language is its meaning. The grammar describes the use of words in the language. So it has somewhat the same relation to the language as the description of a game, the rules of a game, have to the game."[5]

The force of Wittgenstein's idea from the point of view of discourse analysis is not in the easy observation that language, like games, is an (at least partly) conventional, rule-bound activity. The language game idea is not just a restatement of the structuralist view of language as a calculus governed by conventional rules.

Rather, its strength lies in the following points. First, Wittgenstein's language games serve to connect a calculus to a form of life. Language games are what establishes the link between language, conceived as a calculus, to the reality interpreted, described and transformed by it.[6] It is "the whole, consisting of language and the actions into which it is woven"[7] that constitutes a language game: "here the term 'language-game' is meant to bring into prominence the fact that the speaking of a language is part of an activity, or a form of life."[8] A similar point has been emphasized by Labov as the first and most important step in the analysis of discourse: it is essential "to distinguish *what is said* from *what is done*; that is, discourse analysis must be concerned with the functional use of language."[9]

Second, the game comparison brings out the *goal-directed* character of language use, recently emphasized by Paul Grice in his work on the logic of conversation.[10] The importance of the notion of the aim or purpose of a game was dawning on Wittgenstein in the following paragraphs of *Philosophical Grammar.*

But it might be asked: Do I understand the word just by describing its application? Do I understand its point? Haven't I deluded myself about something important?

At present, say, I know only how men use this word. But it might be a game, or a form of etiquette. I do not know why they behave in this way, how language meshes with their life.[11]

We said that when we understood the use we didn't yet understand the purpose of the word "perhaps". And by "purpose" in this case we meant the role in human life.[12]

To master a language game it does not suffice to know its admissible moves, but one has to understand its *point*, its internal aim, or rule of winning:

What constitutes winning and losing in a game (or success in patience)? It isn't, of course, just the winning position. A special rule is needed to lay down who is the winner.

How do I know if someone has won? Because he is pleased, or something of the kind? Really what the rule says is "you must try to get your pieces as soon as possible, etc." In this form the rule connects the game with life.[13]

The internal aim of a game must not be confused with the external purpose of playing the game. Wittgenstein makes this point in a comparison of a language game to a pianola:

You might then say that the sense of the signs is not their effect but their purpose. But consider this, that we're tempted to think that this purpose is only a part of the larger purpose served by the pianola. – This purpose, say, is to entertain people. But it's clear that when we spoke of "the sense of the signs" we didn't mean part of *that* purpose. We were thinking rather of the purpose of the signs within the mechanism of the pianola. – And so you can say that the purpose of an order is its sense, only so far as the purpose can be expressed by a rule of language. "I am saying 'go away' because I want you to leave me alone", "I am saying 'perhaps' because I am not quite sure."[14]

Wittgenstein appends to this insight an important warning. The internal aim of a given game may be externally motivated:

Are the rules of chess arbitrary? Imagine that it turned out that only chess entertained and satisfied people. Then the rules aren't arbitrary if the purpose of the game is to be achieved.[15]

Nevertheless, such a practicality, even if true, has no place in the definition of the game:

"The rules of a game are arbitrary" means: the concept 'game' is not defined by the effect the game is supposed to have on us.[16]

By the same token, it is only the notion of the internal, conventional aim of a language game that is linguistically significant, for

Language is not defined for us as an arrangement fulfilling a definite purpose.[17]

This warning will be taken into account in Chapter II.

3. GAME THEORY

Wittgenstein did not intend to develop his idea into a systematic theory of language-games.[18] On the contrary, he did not think such a project feasible: the very notion of a game seemed to him to defy precise definition.[19]

Now there is a very precise definition of a game (of strategy) in the mathematical theory of games developed by John von Neumann and Otto Morgenstein [30].[20]

Central concepts in this theory are the concepts of a *strategy, payoff*, and *solution* of a game. A game is determined by specifying each player's strategies in the game, and the payoff (gain or loss) for each player at each play of the game (choice of strategies for each player). A solution of a game is the specification of optimal strategies in the game: strategies which maximize each player's payoff in the game subject to his strategic options.

The concepts of strategy and payoff can be considered refinements of the concepts of *rules* and *aims* of a game: the rules of a game specify the admissible moves in it for each player, and these in turn constrain the players' strategic options in the game. The aim of the game determines the players' preferences over different turns the game might take, which preferences may be numerically represented by a payoff function.

The concept of a solution of a game can be considered a mathematical explication of the informal concept of *rationality*. A rational agent is one who uses the most efficient means available to him to further his goals, i.e., one who follows his optimal strategies. The main virtue (and occasional weakness) of game and decision theory is its ability to explicate this key concept of goal-oriented action.

4. APPLICATIONS OF GAME THEORETICAL IDEAS

The concepts and results of game theory have already been used to sharpen the informal idea of language game in a theory of natural language semantics developed by Jaakko Hintikka and his associates. This application is known as Hintikka's *game theoretical semantics*.[21] Hintikka's semantics is a version of model-theoretic semantics. A key concept is that of the truth of a sentence at a possible world or model.

The leading idea is to define the truth of each sentence S of [a fragment of English] by reference to an associated semantical game G(S). This game is a two-person, zero-sum game. The truth of S means that one of the players [the proponent of the sentence] has a winning strategy in G(S). The falsity of S means that the other player [the opponent of the sentence] has a winning strategy in G(S). Certain sentences of our fragment − or of a mild extension of it − will have to be thought of as unanalyzable (atomic) ones, and their truth-values are assumed to be determined unproblematically. At each stage of the game an English sentence is being considered, beginning with S. I win a play of G(S) if it ends with a true atomic sentence, lose if it ends with a false one. In a sense, G(S) may thus be considered as an attempt to verify S, as far as [the proponent is] concerned, against the schemes of a recalcitrant [opponent.] [22]

G(S) is fixed by a set of rules which specify for any sentence whether a move is to be made by the proponent or the opponent and which kind of move is to be made; in each non-terminal move, a sentence is picked in accordance with these rules with respect to which the game is then continued. The sentences chosen are progressively reduced in complexity; after a finite number of moves an atomic sentence results, and no further move is possible.[23]

What makes game theoretic semantics a genuine semantics in the sense of Wittgenstein, Morris and Tarski is the character of the activities which the players are occupied with in the course of the moves of the game. The players do not just swap sentences, but actually have to go out to the world and look for the right sorts of individuals and relations to exemplify their claims. Language games with quantifiers, for instance, involve the nonlinguistic activities of seeking and finding actual objects of different descriptions. On the other hand, what makes game theoretic semantics genuinely game theoretical is the fact that the semantical games are mathematical games. The existence of a well-defined truth value for sentences of the fragment of English is a corollary of the von Neumann and Morgenstern theorem that two-person zero-sum games with perfect information have a value (an equilibrium in pure strategies).

Game theoretical ideas have been applied in logic and the philosophy of language by others as well.[24]

In a number of recent publications, Hintikka has been developing a theory of information-seeking dialogues with potential applications in the philosophy of science and in proof theory. Although these ideas have influenced my approach, the two lines of work are largely independent.[25]

5. DIALOGUE GAMES

The dialogue games I set out to develop in the present essay differ from the semantical games of Hintikka in a number of important respects. The comparison is easiest to organize following the usual format of the game theoretical description of a game.

First, there is the number of players. Dialogue games will range from the general case of an *n*-person conversation through two-person dialogues to the monologue of a lone player. 'Dialogue', as a technical term, will not be restricted here to its usual meaning of a two-person exchange, but covers all of the above mentioned cases.

Next comes the question of the *strategies* of the players. Moves in a dialogue game will consist of complete sentences put forward by dialogue participants and addressed to other participants of the dialogue. Unlike the semantic games, the successive sentences put forward in a dialogue game need not be related to each other structurally or lexically. Nothing like the subformula property implicit in the semantical games need hold.

The dialogues considered here are *question-answer dialogues*: the only admissible moves consist of declarative and interrogative sentences. Consequently, the dialogue games considered here are what Hintikka ([15], p. 81) calls 'indoor games': the activities the players are involved in are activities of reception, processing, and transmission of information. This limitation is a practical one rather than a matter of principle. There is no reason why the present games could not be enriched for instance by including moves by the rules of the semantical games.

An extension of the dialogue games to sentences of imperative mood would obviously necessitate extending the players' strategy sets by various practical activities. Such extensions will be left for another occasion.

Next comes the question of the *aims* of the game. In the present work, one particular choice of internal aim has been made. My dialogue games are *cooperative activities of information exchange*: the players strive to achieve a common understanding on a true and informative answer to some problem or question on the basis of observation and considered opinion.

This delimitation of aims is not in any way unique (though it may be in some sense quite fundamental). It would be possible (and probably rewarding) to let the aims of conversation vary systematically and register its effects on conversational coherence.

Finally, the concept of a *solution* (rational game strategy) inherent in the game idea provides room for a Gricean *logic of conversation*.[26] Grice's main point is that conversational implicatures ought to fall out from a general characterization of the aims and means of linguistic exchanges together with assumptions of the rationality of the participants. The dialogue game framework can be looked upon as a systematic development of this general idea. Gricean 'maxims of conversation' become part of the aims of a dialogue game.

6. LOGIC AND RHETORIC

The above delimitation of the aims of dialogue connects our approach to the traditional art of *rhetoric*. Rhetoric, according to Aristotle, "may be defined as the faculty of considering the possible means of persuasion in reference to any subject whatever."[27] Now the aim of the players of my dialogue games is to convince themselves and each other of the optimal answer to the topic of inquiry that interests them. Rhetoric, therefore, has its place as a theory of optimal strategy in dialogue games.

Aristotle's most important contribution to the art of rhetoric is his insistence on the central position of logic in rhetoric. Rhetoric, for Aristotle, is essentially an application of dialectic: "arguments are the only thing that properly belong to the art, everything else is merely accessory".[28] This insight of Aristotle finds full recognition in the present work. My description of dialogue games essentially draws on methods and results obtained in the fields of deductive, inductive, epistemic, and erotetic logic.

7. CONTEXT

Another thing that distinguishes dialogue games from the semantic games is increased explicitness about the context of discussion. An essential consideration in planning one's conversational strategy concerns what one's audience already knows and what it wants to know. Such considerations place my dialogue games squarely in the domain of linguistic *pragmatics*, the study of "the relations of signs to interpreters".[29] According to a recent statement, "Pragmatics is concerned with the ways in which the interpretation of syntactically defined expressions depends on the particular conditions of their use in *context*",[30] with the weight of the definition obviously on the notion of context.

Context, in the present work, is explicated by a description of a *dialogue game situation*. This is essentially a possible worlds representation of what players of a dialogue game have on their minds at a given stage of the game.

Pragmatic rules of interpretation, say, rules for words like 'perhaps' and for the subjunctive mood will make reference to dialogue context, thus explicated.[31]

My possible worlds representation of players' information in a dialogue game leads to a major departure from the received notions of game theory. As a result of it, my dialogue games are not a special case, but rather a generalization, of the game theoretic notion of a game in extensive form. In consequence, the game theoretic notions of strategy, outcome, and solution are not directly applicable to dialogue games. I have not worked out how these notions should be generalized so as to approach a definition of rational game strategy in a dialogue game. I believe that such a generalization can be given; in any case, the received definitions apply in the special case where dialogue games do reduce to games in the sense of game theory.

These shortcomings, with the concomitant absence of an explicit definition of a dialogue game from this work provide the reason for calling the present essay an *approach* to discourse analysis rather than a fully spelled-out theory.

8. PLAN OF THE WORK – PART I

The disposition of the work roughly follows the traditional division of rhetoric into *invention and arrangement* of arguments on the one hand and *style and delivery* on the other hand.

Thus, the first Part of the essay is concerned with the structure and logic of dialogue. The first chapter 'Aims of the Game' starts with an informal statement of the aims of dialogue as a list of putative conversational maxims. These maxims turn out to constitute desiderata for a familiar decision-theoretic approach to inductive logic. As explained in an Appendix, this approach can be used to give a refined explication of the aims of the game in the form of an epistemic utility function. The inductive rule of acceptance based on the epistemic utility function can then be considered as part of a solution of a dialogue game.

The second Chapter 'Propositional Attitudes' develops a representation of the propositional attitudes of the players in a dialogue game. The representation is a fairly straightforward application of Hintikka's semi-syntactic *model set* semantics for epistemic logic. The problem of "logical omniscience" is avoided by leaving it up to the players to worry about the logical consistency of their propositional attitudes.

The third Chapter 'Questions' analyzes the critical notion of an answer to a question. This analysis is an elaboration of Hintikka's work on the semantics and pragmatics of questions.

The fourth Chapter 'Dialogue Game Rules' considers what strategies players can use to communicate their propositional attitudes to others. A number of important types of conversational move are described.

The fifth Chapter 'Structure of Dialogue' studies the contribution of the representations and rules of the previous chapters to the structure of a conversation.

The sixth Chapter 'Logical Game Rules' outlines a system of natural deduction for a fragment of English, based on the rules of Hintikka's semantical games.

The seventh Chapter 'Logic of Dialogue' shows how the rules of the previous chapter can be used by the players to test their assumptions for consistency and to examine their logical consequences.

The eighth Chapter 'Question-Answer Dialogues' applies the dialogue game framework to the analysis of the interrogative mood. The leading idea here goes back to Wittgenstein; more recently, it has been developed by Stenius (1967). The idea is that dialogue games can be taken to constitute a theory of meaning for sentential moods. To explain what the interrogative mood means, one has to describe the language games in which it is at home. The findings of this Chapter seem to vindicate Wittgenstein's warning:

If you do not keep the multiplicity of language-games in view you will perhaps be inclined to ask questions like: "What is a question?" – Is it the statement that I do not know such-and-such, or the statement that I wish the other person would tell me ...? Or is it the description of my mental state of uncertainty? [32]

The dialogues studied in this Chapter rule out any too facile answers to Wittgenstein's question.

9. PLAN OF THE WORK – PART II

The second Part of the essay is concerned with questions coming under the traditional heading of *style*. As Aristotle put it,

Our next subject will be the style of expression. For it is not enough to know what we ought to say; we must also say it as we ought; much help is thus afforded towards producing the right impression of a speech. The first question to receive attention was naturally the one that comes first naturally – how persuasion can be produced from the facts themselves. The second is how to set these facts out in language. [33]

Linguistic stylistics has been characterized as the study of contextual

conditions of choice among paraphrases (logically equivalent expressions).[34]
If we define discourse grammar as the study of the dialogue function of
words and grammatical constructions, discourse grammar becomes part of
stylistics. Differences of function in a dialogue contribute to choices among
logically equivalent stylistic variants. The second Part of this essay is devoted
to the study of the dialogue function of a selected number of words and
constructions in English.

As was pointed out earlier, the right choice of primitives is a more fundamental question than the precise formulation of rules in terms of those
primitives. If the primitives are well chosen, the rules can be expected to
come out simple and elegant. In this essay, three discourse grammatical
primitives are introduced: the notion of *topic* of a dialogue, the concept of
thematicity, and the notion of a *dialogue subject*. The characterization of
these notions is the main task of this Part of the essay.

This part is structured as follows. In the first Chapter 'Discourse Grammar',
I lay out my main theses in discourse analysis and discourse grammar. First
and foremost is my answer to the fundamental problem of discourse analysis,
quoted in the beginning. The second thesis asserts the autonomy of discourse
grammar from sentence grammar, and the modularity of discourse grammar.

In the second Chapter 'Connectives', I examine the functional constraints
and differences among a number of natural language connectives. It turns out
that these constraints and differences can be stated naturally in terms of the
notions of dialogue games. The dialogue game approach is compared to and
contrasted with generative semantics.

The third Chapter 'Old and New Information' is devoted to the concepts
of *theme* and *rheme*. These notions are defined as properties of constituents
of sentences relative to a dialogue context. Essentially, a constituent is
thematic if it repeats a constituent from dialogue context and rhematic
otherwise. The notions of theme and rheme are put to use in a number of
rules of dialogue grammar for word order and topicalization.

The fourth Chapter 'Given vs. Known Information' contrasts thematicity
with syntactic subordination. Certain aspects of the notion of presupposition
are discussed. Discourse rules for cleft sentences are formulated.

The fifth and last Chapter 'Aboutness' starts with a review of some of the
text linguistic tradition. The intuitive notion of 'aboutness' is distinguished
from the notion of givenness, leading to the recognition of a notion of
dialogue subject. Dialogue subjects are what dialogues are *about*, in one of
the senses of the versatile proposition. The notion of dialogue subject is put
to use in rules of dialogue grammar for anaphora and dislocation phenomena.

In the traditional order of things, the discussion of style should be followed by a discussion of delivery. Omitted from this work is a series of chapters on discourse intonation. Preliminary research on the topic appears in Carlson [4].

PART I

DIALOGUE GAMES

CHAPTER 1

AIMS OF THE GAME

1. FUNCTIONS OF LANGUAGE

Language is a tool for thinking and telling. Its two main functions are representation and processing of information about the environment, and information transferral between users (communication).[1]

For the individual user, the capacity of representative thought is an important tool for guiding and organizing action. Isn't it just their superior capacity of representing the environment, processing such representations and realizing them again in the environment that gives humans their edge over other animals? Studying the situation, comparing different contingencies open in it and steering one's action to suit them involve a capacity of representative thought.

This connection of language as a means of representation with practical action motivates some basic requirements of well-formedness of anyone's representative thought, his beliefs about the status quo and his plan about possible alternatives to it.

First of all: *Think consistently*. There are two parts to the requirement of consistency. First, a theory or a plan of action must be at least in principle feasible, otherwise it has no chance of being realized. This principle may be called the maxim of *satisfiability*. Second, one ought to follow through the consequences of one's ideas. Theories and plans must be examined thoroughly to see what will follow if they are realized. This principle could be called the maxim of *cogency*.

Second: *Believe what is true*. Realistic plans must be based on a correct representation of the status quo. Knowledge is power! We may call this maxim the *maxim of truth*.

Deriving these maxims from practical considerations has the advantage of explaining their relativity. It is not impossible, nor even unusual, for people not to follow them. Except being violated because of human imperfection, they may relax when they are not needed. No matter if small children hold inconsistent beliefs about imaginary characters. It is not likely to cause them or anyone else any harm, and it keeps them (and others) entertained.

The above maxims of thought make no reference to the social function of

3

language. Indeed, the function of language in information transfer seems to presuppose a capacity of information representation in the communicating subjects, which shows the capacity of thought conceptually prior to the capacity to communication.

Genetically, it has been maintained for long times, the two functions are reciprocal. Popular speculation on the phylogenetic origin of language has derived language from the need of cooperation, or coordination of action toward common goals, among a number of individuals. Whatever the historical value of such speculation, it does suggest a 'transcendental deduction' for a further conversational maxim.

In analogy with the individual case, one may consider a group of individuals as a collective agent whose aim is to agree on aims and means to achieve them. This simple analogy immediately suggests an intersubjective analogue for the maxim of consistency. Just as an individual has to agree with himself about his aims and means, a number of cooperating agents had better agree with each other on their interests and acceptations. Else no consistent common plan of action is likely to be followed.

This condition can be formulated as the conversational *maxim of agreement*: one of the conventional aims of communication is achieving a common understanding among the participants of the exchange.

An explication of the concept of common understanding is in order. What we have in mind is an arbitrarily interable loop of propositional attitudes as exemplified by the iteration in (1):

(1)   Every player accepts that p
         Every player accepts that every player accepts that p
         Every player accepts that ... that every player accepts that p
         etc.[2]

A point that should be appreciated about the representation of arbitrarily iterable loops like (1) is this: although the set of sentences in (1) is infinite, it is satisfiable in a finite model, actually in a system of possible worlds with just one sole possible world consisting of nothing else than p. It suffices to let that possible world alone constitute the field of all players' accessibility relations; the truth of all the sentences in (1) follows. A possible worlds representation of propositional attitudes will enable a finitary representation of such apparently infinitary notions as (1) in the theory of dialogue.

The general aim of agreement is to a degree independent of the choice of means of arriving at an agreement, leaving room for further preferences about those means. A friendly discussion and a fierce debate may both aim at common agreement. (They would be no need to dispute if there were no interest in achieving agreement: why not just leave each other alone?) There is just a difference as to whose opinion should preferably prevail.

Again, we do not have an absolute maxim. Counterexamples can be expected to come from cases where cooperation − a common understanding and a common plan of action − is not sought. If one is out to get the others, lies and deceit are called for. Their intention is precisely to create a hidden disagreement between the beliefs of the interlocutors. Agreement is not sought either when language is used to offend. At best, one wants to give the other side "a piece of one's mind", whether or not they accept it. At worst, the intention to offend may overrule all of the maxims: whatever will cause offense will do, whether acceptable, true, or even consistent. But note that these violations of the conversational maxims would not have the effect they do if they were not interpreted against the background of the maxims.

Now all of the foregoing goals can be trivially reached in a discussion if all players agree in having no beliefs at all: then all that they believe is true and consistent and everyone has just the same beliefs. Surely then the foregoing aims are not exhaustive; far from it, they only represent boundary conditions for a more fundamental goal, namely *search for information*. As Aristotle once put it, man by nature desires to know.[3] Typically, however, the participants of a communication situation are not motivated by a boundless hunger for knowledge, but they are interested in some particular *problem* or *topic*. I shall represent such topics of a discussion by means of *questions*. The participants of an information sharing dialogue will do their best to satisfy their curiosity with respect to the topical question of a dialogue they are involved in: i.e., ceteris paribus prefer adopting a (partial or complete) answer to the topical question to remaining agnostic to it. Let us term this preference the *maxim of information*.

2. AIMS VS. MEANS

The different epistemic aims of dialogue discussed in the previous section are ideally in no conflict with each other. There is an ideal situation where every one of them is optimally satisfied, viz. when all players in agreement accept a complete true answer to each topical question of the dialogue.

If the discussants were so ideally equipped that they could immediately recognize true answers and knew that others were equally capable, no discussion or deliberation would be needed to attain the ideal situation. Each player would be justified in presuming that the maxims are satisfied at the outset.

That such a situation remains an ideal is what motivates dialogue in the first place. Players cannot be assumed to hold true, consistent, compatible and complete answers to the topic of discussion at the outset. Some players may know what others do not; players may fail to recognize inconsistencies in their assumptions, or hold consistent but divergent points of view.

Such failures from omniscience can be corrected by discussion. Privileged information may be made public; inconsistencies may be brought out by logical argument, and agreement may be reached by an exchange of opinions.

The limitedness of individual players' means of attaining the ideal end point of the game is what motivates the multiplicity of conversational maxims, too. If the maxim of truth could be followed without impediment, other maxims would be satisfied without extra effort. But since the maxim of truth is hard to realize in practice, one may be forced to choose among a number of feasible compromises which realize one or another aspect of the ideal situation. For instance, adopting some hypothesis at the risk of error or even inconsistency may be better than indecision; or reaching a consensus may be necessary for cooperation, whatever the price in terms of other maxims.

The problem of mixing the different maxims of dialogue so as to define a consistent preference relation over alternative outcomes is a complex question. Different assignments of relative weight to different maxims can be made to reflect different personal traits of character; for instance, a conservative prefers old views over new ideas, an individualist puts little premium on agreement, and a skeptic values certain truisms over uncertain information.

More systematically, different weightings can again be externally motivated by assumptions about the external goals of a dialogue. A social converstion on matters of small importance may put more value on agreement than on literal truth; a scientist interested in extending his knowledge may risk being wrong more willingly than someone whose life or economical situation depends on his guess.

As a special case, one might concentrate on finding a basis for choosing between alternative hypotheses that would fit the *aims of rational inquiry*: how to choose what to believe when the evidence is inconclusive, so as to maximize one's expectancy of reliable information.

When is it rational to accept a sentence? There are three traditionally recognized methods that will be considered: *observation, deductive inference* and *inductive decision*.

In any simple-minded account of rational inquiry, observations form the rock-bottom of knowledge. In more refined accounts, observations can also be refuted; yet there are certain preferences as to what to keep and what to throw out in case of a conflict, and observations tend to be pretty high in this reliability ordering. In our account, observations will be represented as Nature's revelations to other players. Nature being truthful and reliable, her contributions can be accepted by other players at their face value. If the refinement is needed, observations may be assigned probabilities which reflect their reliability: if one is hard of hearing, the reliability of hearsay is accordingly lowered.

Clearly, a player can add to his set of assumptions any logical entailments of those assumptions without fear of violating his epistemic maxims. If the premises are true, so are the consequences; and no new inconsistencies can be created which were not already implicit in the assumptions. To the contrary, a player could not deny any entailment of what he already accepts without falling into inconsistency, and failing to accept them would go against the maxim of cogency.

But it stands to reason that a rational dialogue participant can sometimes accept sentences that are not implied by what he already knows or believes or observes. Otherwise, how could anyone tell anybody anything new? However, a rational dialogue participant cannot just swallow anything that he may be told by anybody even supposing that what he is told is consistent with what he already knows (or believes). For one thing, he has to have some method of choosing what to believe when several players tell him incompatible things. More than that, a rational dialogue participant can be assumed to be open to change his own mind when presented with reliable contradicting evidence. Such considerations indicate that a rational player must be provided with some method of weighing plausible arguments when the truth of a matter is not immediately obvious.

3. GAMBLING WITH TRUTH

This approach to solving the preference logical problem takes us in the middle of the discussion of rules of acceptance in inductive logic.[4] This discussion is especially germane for our point of view, for it construes the problem of inductive acceptance as a game (or decision) theoretical problem. Here is how:

The inductive decision situation is described as a one-person game against Nature. Nature chooses, unbeknownst to the other player, the actual "state of nature" concerning the problem setting at hand. The player has to choose a hypothesis among a given set of alternative hypotheses so as to maximize his preferences over the alternative outcomes of the game (determined by the two players' choices). The game is described by (i) a specification of the problem situation (the players' strategy sets), (ii) the second player's preferences over the outcomes (Nature is assumed to be a disinterested partner); and (iii) the second player's state of information about Nature's moves. The solution of the game is a rule that determines the second player's optimal strategy, i.e., his rational choice of hypothesis in the problem situation.

In accordance with our formulation of the maxim of information, this approach restricts inductive decision making to a rather narrowly defined sort of problem situation. It assumes as given an exhaustive class of mutually exclusive alternatives, which can be thought as a set of alternative *complete answers to a topical question*. These alternative answers represent the depth (and width) of the inquirer's present interest in the problem he is trying to solve: the alternatives are each definitive with respect to his cognitive interests and they exhaust the range of alternatives that he is considering at the moment. The complete answers thus can be thought of as representing Nature's alternative moves in the problem situation at hand: it is up to Nature to decide which one of them is true.

The class of relevant complete answers to the initial problem induces a class of *partial answers* to it, these being all the logically distinct disjunctions of some of the complete answers. As a limiting case, the disjunction of all the complete answers may be taken to represent the starting point of the problem, or the *presupposition* which the inquirer already accepts. The class of all the (complete or partial) answers to the initial question then constitute the second player's range of strategy choices: his task is to accept one of them as his best bet.

The next step toward a game theoretical solution of the inductive decision problem is to describe the decision maker's utilities over alternative outcomes.

As it happens, the epistemic maxims we have singled out nicely match desiderata used in inductive logic. It is assumed that a rational inductive decision rule satisfies the following conditions of *consistency* and deductive *cogency*:

(1)   The set of sentences acceptable by a rational rule of inductive acceptance is consistent

(2)   Any logical consequence of a set of acceptable statements is likewise an acceptable statement: or, the set of acceptable sentences is closed under logical consequence.

Furthermore, it is assumed that a decision maker's utilities over alternative outcomes of an inductive decision problem are determined by some mixture of the preferences registered by the maxim of truth and the maxim of information. The main problems in defining an appropriate utility function to this effect concern the characterization of informativeness and the adjudication of the relative weights of the two maxims.

In an Appendix, I describe the essentials of Levi's [46] and Hilpinen's [42] solutions to these problems. The upshot of their proposals is a probabilistic rule of inductive acceptance which recommends the rejection of a hypothesis if its epistemic utility stays below a given threshold. The rule weighs the probability of a hypothesis against its informativeness subject to an adjustable parameter which represents the investigator's lack of caution. If the index is set to 0, the utility of an answer equals its truth value. The weight of information vanishes and the epistemic utility function is based exclusively on the maxim of truth. Higher values of the index reflect less cautious inductive attitudes, varying from player to player with personality and occasion. Naturally enough, some situations warrant more caution than others: compare for instance casual conversation and professional advice.

For definiteness, I shall assume some version of such a probabilistic decision procedure to form part of the statement of the player's optimal strategies in a dialogue game.

4. THE MAXIM OF AGREEMENT

The above solution to the preference logical problem pays no attention to the maxim of agreement, the only genuine maxim of conversation among our putative maxims of dialogue. It only concerns the question of optimizing a rational enquirer's chances of forming correct and informed opinions about some question he is interested in.

In a way, this is not at all surprising. It is natural to assume that a rational decision maker is one who cannot be *persuaded*, but at best *convinced*: in other words, he never prefers agreement when it would imply abandoning a position which is epistemically optimal as defined by reference to the maxims of rational inquiry alone. Other dialogue participants' arguments can make him change his mind only through changing the epistemic utilities of different alternative hypotheses. A rational dialogue participant thus treats other people's opinions and arguments only as so much more evidence for or against a position. If an interlocutor is a reliable source of information, he is willing to go along with him; if the person is likely to be wrong, he prefers to convince him.

But even if other maxims override the maxim of agreement, it does not make the maxim superfluous. A player of a dialogue game still prefers agreement over disagreement; the other maxims just decide what opinions he wants everyone to agree upon.

It is important to realize that my maxims of dialogue say absolutely nothing about the external question what initially motivates players to wonder about certain questions, and what motivates them to enter or not to enter a given dialogue game (just as the rules of chess do not specify why one should play chess).

Given that players do wonder about certain questions, and that they do agree to play dialogue games on them, the game rules explain what else they are committed to do and believe.

Assume someone asks someone a question. Is the addressee committed to answer it? Only if he agrees to enter into a dialogue game whose topic is the question proposed. If he does not and, say, just stares, turns his back or pretends not to hear, the game does not even get started: it takes two to carry a conversation. Of course, as a rule, people are cooperative and polite; if they have no overriding interests, they oblige. However, they are not obliged to by our maxims. Whether they will or will not enter a conversation is a matter external to the rules of dialogue games, and depends on what external interests and obligations the players have.[5]

CHAPTER 2

PROPOSITIONAL ATTITUDES

1. INFORMATION SETS

A third central consideration in the game theoretical description of any game concerns the players' knowledge of the game situation at each stage of the game. If each player knows what the actual game situation is at each stage of the game, we have a game of *perfect information*: else the game is one of imperfect information.

The game theoretical description of a game of imperfect information can be illustrated by a simple inductive decision problem of the sort discussed in the previous chapter. Such a decision problem can be described as a one-person game, or rather, a game against Nature as a disinterested partner. The first move of the game is by Nature, who chooses the right answer to the decision problem. Say the problem is to decide whether it will rain today. The presupposition — and the weakest answer — is that it may or it may not. There are two alternative complete answers: that it will rain, or that it will not. Nature decides on the outcome, of course, unbeknownst to the decision maker. The decision maker has the next move. His aim is to make an educated guess about the weather, given some probabilities over Nature's alternatives. His alternative moves are the different predictions he can make: he may say it will rain, that it won't, or that it may or may not, passing the question. His payoff over the alternative guesses depends on the information value of each guess and the actual "state of Nature". The game can be represented as the following tree:

(1)

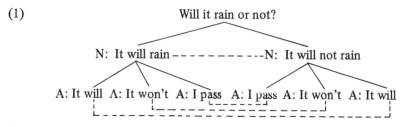

The decision maker's state of information at each game situation is depicted by his information sets, described in the figure by dotted lines. Each

11

information set includes game situations which, though they are distinguishable to an objective observer, the player cannot tell apart when he is at one
of them. In (1), the decision maker does not know Nature's move when he is
making his own, though he can of course tell what answer he has his money
on himself.

Now dialogue games are obviously games of imperfect information: is it
not their main function to make people's information about each other's
assumptions less imperfect.

However — and this is of crucial importance — players in a dialogue
game can suffer an even more radical imperfection in their knowledge of the
actual game situation: more often than not, players are not only imperfectly
informed but downright *misinformed* about the real game situation, including
the truths of the matter, their interlocutors' aims and attitudes, possibly even
their own state of mind. This more radical imperfection takes us out of the
bounds of standard game theory to the less developed field of games with
misperception.[1]

Standard games in game theory, whether perfect or imperfect in information, satisfy the following condition (actually, an analogue of the reflexivity
condition of epistemic logic): at each game situation, the actual situation is a
member of every player's information set at that situation. Even if a player
does not know exactly where the game is at, at least he is not totally off
the mark.

Which is what players in a dialogue game often are. In order to do justice
to this eccentricity of players' information in dialogue games, we cannot any
more make do with the simple device of concentric information sets. Instead,
we have to as it were allow each player his own representation of the game to
serve as the guide in strategy choice. Among other things, this will require a
redefinition of established strategic notions as well, in particular, the whole
question of rationality (determination of optimal strategies as the solution of
the game) will come up to reconsideration.[2] However these notions are to be
extended to dialogue games, we shall try to ensure that they will be proper
extensions of the corresponding concepts of standard games: dialogue games
will reduce to standard games when the reflexivity assumption holds.

So let us start pondering how to generalize the game theoretic notion of
information set.

Of course, the description of a game as one of perfect or imperfect information depends on the aims òf the game. If players in a dialogue game want
to find out facts, the game situations must distinguish false sentences from
true sentences. If the players are only interested in agreement, game situations

will be essentially different only when players agree or disagree, whatever the facts. In each case, the game will be one of imperfect information if there remain essentially different game situations which players cannot distinguish from each other.

It is clear from our statement of the aims of the players of a dialogue game that an objective description of a game situation must distinguish at least

(i)   Whether a given answer to a topical question is true or not

and

(ii)   Whether any given player accepts a given answer to the topical question or not.

Further, it is assumed that players may have imperfect (even incorrect) information about game situations which differ with respect to (i) and (ii).

Our representation of a typical dialogue game situation ought to have, then, at least the following properties. It determines for each player a set of sentences which represent the assumptions the player accepts at the stage of the game (as answers to topics of discussion or as background assumptions). Among the players, we include a designated "silent partner" called Nature. Nature is supposed to hold the right answers to all questions the other players are interested in. This assumption allows us to subsume (i) as a special case under (ii).

In particular, it should be possible to read from the representation what each player assumes the others to assume, and so on indefinitely. Fortunately, there already exists a framework for representing iterated propositional attitudes in the epistemic and doxastic logic developed by Jaakko Hintikka [61–72]. In the following few sections, I propose to turn Hintikka's semantics for epistemic logic into a description of a dialogue game situation that avoids some of the drawbacks of standard developments of possible worlds semantics.

2. THE PROBLEM OF LOGICAL OMNISCIENCE

Perhaps the most serious single objection to a possible worlds semantics for propositional attitudes involves the so-called problem of logical omniscience.[3] The problem concerns the validity of the following epistemic analogues of alethic modal logic:

(2) $\dfrac{\vdash p}{\vdash A \text{ knows that } p}$

(3)   A knows that $(p \ \& \ q) \equiv$ A knows that p & A knows that q

On the assumption that (2)–(3) are valid truths about knowledge, a possible worlds semantics for knowledge suggests itself. In it, 'A knows that' is translated into a universal quantifier over a range of possible contexts of reference, or possible worlds. In this case, the universal quantifier is naturally thought of as ranging over such conceivable situations, or alternative states of affairs, as are compatible with everything A knows — in other words, such possible circumstances which would not force A to revise his knowledge.

As the logic for an idealized epistemic notion like

(4)   It follows from what A knows that p

the principles (2)–(3) seem uncontroversial. Unfortunately, the idealized concept (4) seems far removed from the everyday epistemic concept of knowing: the words "it follows from what" make a huge difference. If the rule of necessitation (2) were true of everyday knowers, who would need logicians, as even the remotest results of logic would be obvious to everyone. (2) and (3) together imply another principle of logical omniscience (known as the rule of regularity in modal logic):

(5) $\dfrac{\vdash p \supset q}{\vdash A \text{ knows that } p \supset A \text{ knows that } q}$

(5) is hardly true of even the keenest intellect: even Sherlock Holmes at his dull moments fails to draw an essential inference. Denser types may be unable to see even the simplest consequences of what they know. Clearly, (2)–(5) at best pertain to a quite idealized sense of knowing, something like the geometrical knowledge which Plato ascribes to the serf boy in the *Meno*, or the tacit knowledge of grammar Chomsky ascribes to his competent speaker in the *Aspects*.

However, as Hintikka already argued in his *Knowledge and Belief*, this does not make the idealized concept (4) devoid of interest. (4) does represent an important idealization, the logic of knowing for a perfectly logical person. It is significant that we take a person's ability to follow the consequences of what he knows as a measure of his *intelligence* rather than his *learning*. Furthermore, whatever one infers from what he knows is accepted as something he knows without further argument: we do act as if the inferential knowledge "had already been there" in the person's head. Such aspects of the everyday concept of knowledge can be explained if (4) is a correct idealization of the everyday concept of knowledge.

Following this train of thought, we can construe the epistemic principles (2)–(3) as representing *norms* or *constraints* on epistemic inference rather than surefire inference tickets. At the very least, epistemic logic distinguishes inferences that fail because of human obtuseness from ones that fail for reasons of principle, such as

(6)   A knows that p or q;
       therefore A knows that p or A knows that q.

We shall see how this point will be accommodated in our dialogue semantics for epistemic notions.

3. MODEL SETS AND MODEL SYSTEMS

One important point about Hintikka's epistemic logic ought not to be missed: its insights into reference and quantification in epistemic contexts are conceptually independent of the assumption of logical omniscience. All that is involved in the former insights is the idea of *modality as referential multiplicity*: the idea that each epistemic context involves a multiplicity of possible contexts or points of reference on which the truth of individual sentences and the reference of referring expressions may depend.[4]

It is therefore worth inquiring whether the former insights could be kept while relaxing the assumption of logical omniscience. For this purpose, we have to see where the assumption of logical omniscience exactly comes into the picture.

The first thing to realize about Hintikka's semantics for epistemic logic is that it is not literally a possible worlds semantics at all. Possible worlds do not enter it as a set of unanalyzed semantic primitives. Rather, the job of possible worlds is done by partial syntactic *descriptions* of worlds, consisting of sets of sentences Hintikka calls *model sets*.[5]

What makes model sets a very useful logical tool is their position as a bridge between semantic and proof theoretical ideas. Semantically, a model set can be looked upon as the shortest syntactic description of a possible world which is guaranteed to have an extension into a complete theory of some model or other.

Syntactically, they give us a very simple and natural proof procedure. To prove that a given set of sentences is consistent, it suffices to show that it can be extended into a model set.

Hintikka's semantics for propositional attitudes is an extension of the methods of model sets to modal logic. The main new feature compared to the extensional case is that, owing to the multiplicity of contexts of reference introduced by modalities, a whole set of model sets may have to be constructed to show a set of modal sentences consistent, one model set for each different type of context (model or possible world) that needs to be considered.

Such structured sets of model sets are called by Hintikka *model systems*. A simple set of rules for constructing model systems suffices for a quantified version of the epistemic logic characterized by (2)–(3).[6]

4. IMPOSSIBLE POSSIBLE WORLDS

We are now in a position to explain how Hintikka's epistemic logic comes to embrace the principles of logical omniscience (1), (2), (5). What is at fault is that every model set that goes into an epistemic model system satisfies model set conditions which guarantee its logical consistency.

That this assumption is what validates the principle of logical omniscience is easy to see. According to the possible worlds translation rule for *A knows that*, A could fail to know some logical consequence of what he knows only if that consequence could be false, for all he knows, i.e., its negation could be embedded into some model set alongside with everything he does know. But then such a model set would be logically inconsistent and hence certain to violate the extensional model set conditions.

In other words, what is at fault is the requirement that all the epistemic contexts compatible with what someone knows can be extended to full consistent descriptions of possible worlds, worlds in which all the same laws of logic hold as in our own. To put it in the form of a slogan, logical omniscience follows from the assumption that all *epistemically possible worlds* (contexts compatible with what someone knows) *are also logically possible worlds*.

If one thinks of possible worlds as serious alternatives to the real world, this assumption may seem unavoidable: how could a real world contain contradictions? Taking a less absolute position, considering a possible world any structure with an associated interpretation of a language in that structure, it is easy to imagine otherwise. There are then several ways of making sense of the idea of an "impossible possible world". One may let the interpretation of a language be deviant at an impossible world: '*p* and not *p*' is a contradiction only if the meanings of '*p*', 'and', and 'not' are the standard ones. Alternatively, one may allow a model to change imperceptibly as one proceeds in evaluating sentences with respect to it: this also would create an impression of a contradictory world.[7]

In the syntactic approach to model theory we have been considering of late, one can just continue to consider sets of sentences as their own models: a model for an impossible world is simply a contradictory set of sentences, one not closed under model set conditions.

The results of this relaxation are disastrous for completeness theorems: the modal logic determined by such a semantics has in the extreme case no interesting structure at all. But that is a move in the right direction when the everyday semantics of knowledge (and even more, that of belief) is concerned. People do have contradictory beliefs, and that has to be recognized in any realistic semantics of belief sentences. What is important, though we lose a logic, we still have a semantics. The essential insight of possible worlds semantics of modality as referential multiplicity is retained: the emphasis in "several possible worlds" is not on *possible* but on *several*. Hintikka's insights into quantifying in and in the *de dicto-de re* distinction are not lost. What is more, we can see epistemic logic arise again as a limiting case of the more general semantics, when all epistemic alternatives happen to be logically consistent.

5. ASSUMPTION LISTS AS 'SMALL WORLDS'

The reader may have started to guess the relevance of the above discussion to the dialogue game approach. The starting insight is that the assumption lists involved in the dialogue games are nothing but other sets of sentences. What we plan to do is reinterpret the assumption lists of the dialogue games as epistemic contexts of reference of a sort, a sort of "small possible worlds". One appealing upshot of this idea will be that the logical consistency of such "possible worlds" will be up to the players themselves: keeping one's set of assumptions in harmony with a set of model system conditions will be part of the aim of the game. A player's success in a dialogue game will depend on his ability to think consistently, i.e., to make sure that no hidden contradictions are buried in the assumptions he entertains.

Another advantage is that our standard description of a dialogue game situation will be a familiar sort of structure, i.e., a model system as already known and extensively studied in possible worlds semantics.

The essential step that has to be made is to replace the unique set of assumptions assigned to a player so far with a whole class of such sets of assumptions, as partial descriptions of such alternative epistemic states of affairs that he is prepared to face: these sets of sentences will do for us the work of the several possible worlds of possible worlds semantics.

The original set of assumptions which represented the player's actual acceptations will now be the intersection of all the alternatives he is prepared for: they are the sentences that he expects to find true whichever epistemic alternative turns out to be correct.

Note that we cannot define the set of the alternative epistemic states of affairs for a player conversely as the set of all maximal extensions (complete theories) consistent with the player's beliefs, for these beliefs, and the alternatives themselves, may be inconsistent to start with. The set of alternatives must be taken as a primitive notion. We do not want to put any ready-made constraints of completeness and consistency on the epistemic states of affairs describing a player's mental state (epistemic attitude). It is just the fact that they are "small worlds", not closed under logical consequence, that allows the player to entertain them as real alternatives.

The standard form of description of a dialogue game situation will now be simply a generalized epistemic *model system*: a set S of (possibly inconsistent) assumption lists, on which there are N binary alternativeness relations defined, one for each player in the game and a designated alternative singled out as Nature's list of assumptions. Nature's alternativeness relation can, if needed, be defined as the identity relation: in each situation, Nature knows everything there is to know.

Any given player's epistemic alternatives in a game situation are then simply the assumption lists accessible from Nature's list of assumptions by that player's accessibility relation.

The assumption of imperfect information in the dialogue games now means that a player, in general, cannot distinguish between model systems which keep his own alternativeness relation invariant; he cannot tell what Nature's assumptions are nor does he generally know with any precision how the other players' accessibility relations actually look like.

Relative to such a description of a typical game situation, we can formulate the following simple truth definition for acceptance:

(7)   Player *P accepts* sentence S at the alternative A iff S is included in the intersection of P's epistemic alternatives to A.

The term 'accept' is used here as a noncommittal cover term for a number of related propositional attitudes: if true and backed by appropriate evidence, acceptance counts as knowledge; if suitably steadfast, as belief; if its object is a question rather than a statement, acceptance counts as interest or wonder.

I sHfall occasionally use these or other more colloquial words intending the present technical sense.

As is implicit in the above, an important novelty about (7) is that it is designed to be *independent of the grammatical mood of S*: we shall be speaking indiscriminately about accepting or rejecting questions as well as declarative sentences.[8]

The intersection condition in (7) ensures that P has to actually consider or entertain S at A in order to (actively) accept S: S must occur in one and in all of P's epistemic alternatives. A player may fail to accept a sentence for several different reasons. It may be that he accepts the denial of S; if he is consistent, S will be absent from his epistemic alternatives. Or perhaps he has just not thought about S: both S and its denial are absent from his assumptions. Or P may be entertaining S but does not include it in every epistemic alternative of his: for instance, its denial may be also considered a live possibility.

To spell out explicitly the weaker (though not quite dual) notion of entertaining a sentence, I introduce the definition

(8)   Player P *admits* sentence S at the alternative A iff S is included in the union of P's epistemic alternatives to A.

6. AN EXAMPLE OF A DIALOGUE GAME SITUATION

To make it easier to visualize a dialogue game situation, let us draw an example. We shall consider the following situation. Three applicants are examined for a certain position, say they are girls trying to get elected as the Dallas Cowboys cheerleaders. They are told beforehand that at least one of them is going to pass the exam — but possibly more, even all. Each applicant can watch the others doing the tests and can tell whether they will pass or not. But it is impossible to tell what the judges are thinking when one is going through one's own number.

After everyone has done the tests, each girl is anxious to know if she passed: all that she knows is that the other two did.[9]

This game situation can be depicted by the diagram of (9).

The seven groups of three sentences constitute the epistemic alternatives in the game situation. The actual situation, or Nature's alternative, is the center one: all girls were accepted. The network of arrows connecting the lists describe the accessibility relations for each player. Each girl's information set consists of Nature's alternative together with that alternative which is connected to Nature's alternative with a bidirectional arrow labeled by the girl's initial.

(9)

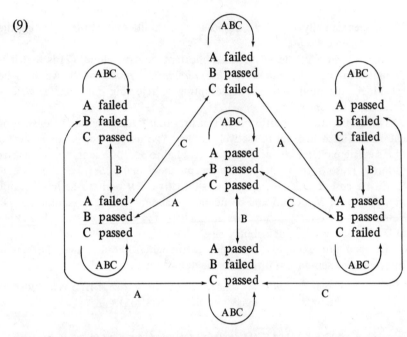

Thus interpreted, the diagram (9) tells everything the girls know and don't know about the outcome. For instance, A does not know if she passed or failed: she cannot tell between the two alternatives in her information set. But A knows that B and C know whether A passed. Furthermore, she knows, or can infer, that neither B nor C are sure of their personal success, for she knows B to know that C passed, and C to know that B did. (Only if a girl had seen both of her competitors eliminated could she be sure of winning.)

What is even subtler, A can't be sure that *B* can exclude the possibility that C already recognizes herself as the winner. For all that A knows, B may already know that A has flunked, and not knowing her own fate, B may fear that C has been able to draw the obvious conclusion.

All this rather subtle information is reflected in a concise form in the diagram (9).

7. THE AIMS OF THE GAME REVISITED

The possible worlds description of a dialogue game situation as a model system allows a reformulation of the aims of a dialogue game. The starting point is the assumption that Nature, as a designated player, is ideally situated with respect to the informational aims of the dialogue. She always satisfies the maxims of consistency, information, and truth to an ideal degree. To wit:

(i)   Nature is consistent, i.e., satisfiable and cogent. Her assumptions are closed under logical inference and she agrees with herself.

(ii)   Nature is informative. Her list of assumptions includes every true topical question in the dialogue; she has a complete answer to every one of them; she only has one epistemic alternative.[10]

(iii) Nature is truthful. Her list of assumptions contain only true sentences.

Then the first three dialogue maxims can be condensed into one maxim: *Try to agree with nature*. The maxim of consistency implies that the player imitates nature by trying to keep his assumption lists closed under the logical game rules and rejecting alternatives which contain contradictory assumptions. The maxim of information implies that the player aims at a minimum number of completely answered epistemic alternatives, and the maxim of truth implies that he tries to zero in on Nature's alternative in doing so.

The remaining maxim of conversation, the maxim of agreement, is also ultimately aimed to simplify the outcome of the game. According to it, players prefer for everyone to end up adopting identical positions. Eventually, such sharing of information will diminish the number of epistemic alternatives, approaching Nature's designated alternative as a limit.

CHAPTER 3

QUESTIONS

1. INDIRECT QUESTIONS

The possible worlds analysis of epistemic notions derives particular interest from the insight it gives into the logic of questions. It is easy to give indirect question complements of 'know' simple and revealing analyses in the language of Hintikka's epistemic logic.[1] Consider the paradigmatic question types below:

(1)   A knows whether he won (or not).
(2)   A knows whether he (won) or B (won) or C won.
(3)   A knows who won.
(4)   A knows who wants tea and who wants coffee.
(5)   A knows who wants what.

Hintikka observes that these question types have simple paraphrases in terms of the construction *A knows that p* plus some logical (propositional and quantificational) apparatus. Thus the simple *sentential* (yes-no) *question* (1) can be paraphrased in either of the ways

(6)   A won and A knows that (he won) or
         A did not win and A knows that (he did not win).
(7)   If A won A knows that (he won) and
         if A did not win A knows that (he did not win).

It is easy to see that the disjunctive paraphrase (6) is logically equivalent to the conjunctive (or conditional) paraphrase (7). Note that the naturalness of both paraphrases is directly confirmed by grammatical fact: the disjunctive form of (6) is in evidence in the optional tag *or not* in (1), while the conditional paraphrase (7) motivates the use of *if* in the place of *whether* in the more colloquial locution

(8)   A knows if he won.

Similar paraphrases are available for the choice question (2):

(9)   A won and A knows that (he won), or
         B won and A knows that (B won), or
         C won and A knows that (C won).

22

(10)   If A won, A knows that (he won), and
         if B won, A knows that (B won), and
         if C won, A knows that (C won).

This time the two paraphrases (9)–(10) are not automatically equivalent. The disjunctive paraphrase implies the conditional one only if *at most one* alternative is true (at most one player won), and conversely the conditional paraphrase implies the disjunctive one only if *at least one* alternative is true. We may call the last mentioned condition the *existential presupposition* of the disjunctive question, and the former condition its *uniqueness presupposition*. Using 'either-or' to indicate exclusive disjunction, (9)–(10) are equivalent on the combined presupposition that

(11)   Either A (won) or B (won) or C won.

It does seem that a disjunctive question like (2) often carries the sort of combined presupposition (11) that makes the two putative paraphrases (9)–(10) equivalent, though not always.

In retrospect, it is not difficult to recognize sentential questions as a special case of choice questions.

A *search question* (or wh-question) like (3) has analogous two paraphrases in terms of quantifying into a knowledge context:

(12)   Someone won and A knows that he won.
(13)   If anyone won, A knows that he won.[2]

Again analogously, the existential paraphrase (12) implies the universal one (13) only if *at most* one player won and the converse implication holds only if *at least* one player won. We may call

(14)   Someone won

the *existential presupposition* of the search-question (3) and

(15)   At most one won

the *uniqueness presupposition* of (3). Again, it is not uncommon for (3) to presuppose both of (14)–(15). But the tendency is not quite watertight. Some uses of question clauses suggest only one or another of the two paraphrases. An existential paraphrase is appropriate for a "for instance" sense such as in

(16)   A knows how he can win

which only says that A knows at least one winning strategy, whether or not he is aware of others. The existential reading is also encouraged by the subjunctive mood:

(17)   A knows who might help us.

(17) can very well mean that A knows at least one helpful individual, he need not be able to rattle off an exhaustive list. Yet there is no implication that there might not be more than one putative helper. In these examples, it is clear from context that the interest of the questioner is satisfied by any one example. This point may be quite explicit in the question too:

(18)   What is an example of a perfect number?

The semantics of (18) makes it quite clear that any one example will do.
   On the other hand, there are questions which have a 'list' sense, such as (4):

(4)   A knows who wants tea and who wants coffee.

Here, the obvious paraphrase is a universal one:

(19)   If anyone wants tea, A knows that he wants tea, and
         if anyone wants coffee, A knows that he wants coffee.

Conjunctive questions like (4) can actually be considered as instances of *multiple questions*, questions like (5), whose most natural paraphrase is (20):

(5)   A knows who wants what.
(20)   If anyone wants anything, A knows that he wants it.

The close relation of (4) to (5) is particularly evident when *what* in (5) ranges over tea and coffee: then (4) and (5) are actually equivalent.
   One way of looking at (4) is in fact to see in it a double question combining a search question (who?) with a choice question (coffee or tea?). There is even some temptation to rephrase (4) quite faithfully to this analysis as

(21)   Who wants coffee or tea?

The fact that (21) can mean the same as (4) is explained by noting that the choice connected with the disjunction *or* in questions is left to the answerer(s). From the point of view of the questioner of (21), *or* represents an opponent's move, i.e., becomes equivalent to *and*. (This phenomenon of duality switch is known in deontic logic as the free choice permission paradox.)[3]

It might seem that, however things might be with simple search questions, multiple ones at least only admit of a universal reading. This impression, I submit, is misleading.

Naturally, a multiple search question echoing a foregoing assertion does not expect a list as an answer:

(22)   "Ann was in trouble. All she really wanted was advice. She had found out something about somebody and wanted to know what to do about it."
"What had she found out about who?"
"I don't know. She wouldn't tell me." Rex Stout, *Not Quite Dead Enough*

However, (22) can be discredited on the grounds that A's previous claim amounts to a uniqueness presupposition, in which case, as we noted, the universal and existential readings coincide.

What is more to the point, I do not find a uniqueness assumption necessary to make sense of an incredulous question like

(23)   A: Was it not awful the way those people lied to each other?
B: What do you mean? Who did you think lied to whom?

B is challenging A to produce some examples: there is no implication that exactly one lie was told, if any, nor does B need a complete list to be convinced.

Another example comes from literature:

– What was Lawson doing in Gorsemere in that evening?
– He was being set up to be murdered, said Henry grimly, but he imagined that he had a date with Harry Heathfield to discuss the purchase of Lady Griselda. Heathfield had no appointment with Lawson, of course, but Pennington assured Lawson it was all arranged. In that way, he knew exactly where Lawson would be, at what time. (Moyes, *The Curious Affair of the Third Dog*, p. 211)

It seems to me that what the named Pennington accomplished by setting up the false appointment was determine *one* particular space-time juncture at which he could be sure to locate his victim. Here, it would be absurd to claim that Lawson's space-time coordinates were unique, nor does the story imply that Pennington was aware of Lawson's complete itinerary and timetable.

2. DIRECT QUESTIONS

The above paraphrases of indirect questions in terms of epistemic logic have
proved useful in the analysis of direct questions via the introduction of the
notion of the *desideratum* of a direct question. In Hintikka's analysis, a direct
question amounts to a request by the questioner that the addressee bring
about a certain epistemic state in the questioner (provided that the presupposition of the question is true): thus, e.g., the choice question

>   (24)   Is he mad or drunk?

can be paraphrased as

>   (25)   Assuming that he is either mad or drunk,
>   bring it about that:
>   I know that he is mad or I know that he is drunk.

Here the first line of (25) represents the *presupposition* of the direct question
(24), the second line its optative operator (its mood as a request), and the
third line represents its desideratum (the epistemic attitude the questioner
wants to be brought about). The appropriate desideratum may vary according
to need and circumstance: for instance, an examination question would have
as its desideratum that the examiner knows whether the *subject* knows the
right answer to the question (the examiner may know it already).

My analysis of the function of direct questions in dialogue can be construed
as an attempt to describe a semantics for the paraphrase (25) for (24) (and
similar pairs). In particular, the contribution of the interrogative mood
(represented by the imperative or optative operator of (25)) is described by
spelling out conditions of appropriate (rational) use of direct questions as
moves in dialogue games.

Similarly, the notion of the desideratum of a question will be absorbed in
the description of the dialogue game situations players aim at.

These analyses aim to do away with the syntactic concepts of optative
operator and desideratum in favor of a semantic account of the meaning
of questions. These syntactic concepts will therefore not play any explicit
role in the following discussion, useful as they are as an intermediary level
of abstraction.

An analysis of direct questions along the lines of (25) forces an important
distinction between *syntactic* conditions of answerhood and *functional* ones.
The linguistic form of each type of question suggests canonical linguistic
forms of answer to that type of question. But observe that the analysis of

the function of direct questions exemplified by (25) is quite independent
of such considerations. Functionally, anything can serve as an answer to a
question that fulfills its aim, i.e., brings about the truth of its desideratum.
We shall see that both aspects of answerhood are rather straightforwardly
and illuminatingly captured by the present analysis.

A rough characterization of the syntactically simple form of answer for
each type of question is easy to give. The syntactical *direct answers* to any
question are the several immediate subformulas of its *presupposition*, where
the presupposition of each type of question can be obtained by simply
dropping epistemic operators from the desideratum. This means that in
choice questions, direct answers consist of the disjuncts of the respective
presuppositions; while in search questions, direct answers consist of substitution instances of the existential presupposition.[4]

Thus for instance, the direct answers to a sentential question

(26)   Will he win?

will be the two disjuncts of its presupposition

(27)   He will win or he will not win.

It is easy to see why the syntactically direct answers to (26) are usually
functionally adequate answers to it, too. For the desideratum of (26)

(28)   I know that he will win or I know that he will not win

is satisfied by *letting the questioner know* either of the two direct answers:
either of

(29)   I know that he will win
(30)   I know that he will not win

imply the desideratum. If putting forward either of the direct answers to
(26) does suffice to bring about one of the states (29)–(30), that is all the
addressee will have to do. But note that even less may suffice, whatever is
enough to bring about (28) – for instance, a gesture. And conversely, more
may be needed, say if the questioner is deaf or doubts the addressee's words.
What is essential are the functional demands of answerhood as spelled out by
the desideratum.

Using the distinction between syntactically direct answers and functionally
sufficient answers, we may sharpen the pretheoretic notion of answerhood.
On the basis of syntax, we can distinguish direct answers from indirect
answers. An indirect answer can still be *decisive*, if it entails, with or without

other assumptions that the questioner accepts, a direct answer. Thus *Did he win?* is decisively if indirectly answered by *He lost*; the reply *He did not lose* in contrast, is likely to be indecisive in the absence of suitable background information. In the case of yes-no questions, it seems fair to say that a direct answer normally counts as a functionally sufficient or complete answer. We shall see that this is by no means true for search questions.

3. ANSWERS TO SEARCH QUESTIONS

For search questions, the notion of a *complete* (vs. *incomplete* or *partial*) *answer* splits into at least three different distinctions. We shall call them respectively *definiteness, exhaustiveness*, and *conclusiveness*.

To give an intuitive feeling of these three aspects of completeness, we may present an example dialogue for each of the corresponding species of incompleteness. For depending on the respect in which an answer falls short of being complete, the questioner's response is typically different:

(31) — What did you find?
      — I found a tool.
      — What tool did you find?
      — I found an awl.

(32) — What did you find?
      — I found an awl.
      — Did you find anything else?
      — No.

(33) — What did you find?
      — I found an awl.
      — What is an awl?
      — An awl is a tool.

In the first dialogue (30), the answer is indefinite. The corresponding notion of definiteness of an answer is not identical to the syntactic notion of definiteness. In syntax, one usually means by a definite noun phrase a proper noun, a demonstrative, relative, or personal pronoun, or a phrase whose determiner is either the definite article (*the*) or the genitive form of a definite phrase.

The present notion of definiteness is different. According to it, the definiteness of an answer depends on the *identity criteria* which the questioner is assuming in asking a question. For instance, the last line of (31) may well be a definite answer to the questioner's original question despite its indefinite form. This is the case if the questioner was only interested in the *kind* of thing found: as a name of kind, *an awl* is as definite as the questioner cares. The questioner's original desideratum could be formalized by using a special style of variables to quantify over kinds of things:

(34) (EX) I know that (Ex) you found x & $X(x)$.

Now in our sense, an answer is definite with respect to a search question if it identifies a unique value for the initial quantifier of the desideratum of the question within each epistemic alternative for the questioner.

Thus the definiteness of an answer is relative to the questioner's beliefs and interests, in particular, to the criteria of identity he uses to establish the range of the initial quantifier, and to his supply of background assumptions. The definiteness of an answer is thus clearly a pragmatic or context-dependent notion.

The follow-up question in the case of an indefinite answer is typically a repetition of the question accompanied by some clarification of the range of the initial quantifier of the desideratum. A simple way to convey the criteria of identity assumed is to use a sortal noun phrase as in (31). The identity criteria to be used then are those associated with the accompanying sortal noun phrase: for instance, it is clear in (31) that what is being quantified over are different (sorts of) tools.

Below, we shall refer to the just discussed notion of definiteness by the term 'dialogue definiteness'.

Exhaustiveness, which is checked for in dialogue (32), concerns quite another dimension. It has to do with the quantifier character of the question quantifier. If a question is intended as an existential one, e.g., as in

(35)   What is an example of a perfect number?

any definite and conclusive answer of course also exhausts the interests of the questioner. However, if a question is understood as a request for an exhaustive list, as in

(36)   Who wants tea and who wants coffee?

a single substitution instance may still fall short of exhaustiveness. An answer to a universally understood search question, say (36), is not exhaustive until it satisfies the desideratum, in the case of (36),

(37)   If anyone wants tea, I know that he wants tea, and
         if anyone wants coffee, I know that he wants coffee.

Hence an exhaustive answer must take into account every value of 'anyone' present in the universe of discourse for which the conditional clauses are satisfied.

Here, the follow-up question is a straightforward inquiry about further instances of the same sort.

Finally, in (33), we are dealing with what Hintikka has termed the *conclusiveness condition* of an answer. The problems connected with the conclusiveness condition are difficult enough to warrant a somewhat longer discussion. That will be undertaken in the following three sections.

4. CONCLUSIVENESS

The typical syntactically direct answer to a question like

(38)   Who won?

is a singular substitution instance of its presupposition

(39)   Someone won,

say,

(40)   A won.

When will an answer like (40) satisfy a questioner? Obviously not every definite answer to (38) will be found satisfactory, at least not

(41)   The winner won.

What is unsatisfactory about (41) is that the questioner is not made any wiser by the answer: he will not know who the winner is if he has to ask (38).

As it happens, this intuition is already accounted for by the principles of epistemic logic. For the desideratum of (38) is likely to be

(42)   I know who won.

On the other hand, all that an answer of the form (43) can accomplish is that the questioner comes to know it is true, i.e., he can truly say

(43)   I know that A won.

When does (43) suffice to imply the desideratum (42)? That is easy to see from the respective logical forms of (42)–(43) in epistemic logic:

(44) (Ex) I know that $p(x)$
(45)   I know that $p(a)$

The missing premise which justifies the step of existential generalization from (45) to (44) is, according to epistemic logic,

(46) (Ex) I know that $(x = a)$[5]

whose verbal rendition in the case at hand is

(47)   I know who A is.

This argument neatly shows why (41) fails to add anything to what the questioner already knows: for the missing premise that would make (41) a satisfactory answer is (48), nothing else than a reiteration of the original desideratum:

(48)   I know who the winner is.

We have shown, then, that the questioner of (38) will not be satisfied with (40) unless he has an answer to the follow-up question

(49)   Who is A?

A problem with this result is its apparent circularity: for any answer for (49) in turn, say

(50)   A is B.

prompts a further identity question

(51)   Who is B?

and so on *ad infinitum*, it would seem. Of course, the regress is stopped if the questioner actually knows who A is under some description or other. But if he does not, how can he ever be satisfied? In plainer words, how can new individuals ever be introduced to a questioner if he does not already know them? On a superficial reading of what Hintikka says of this question in *Knowledge and Belief*, it looks as if there is no way, for he says there (p. 150):

[The conclusiveness condition] involves the recognition of what may be called a logical *conservation principle*. [According to it] no sentence in which a bound variable occurs within the scope of one of the epistemic operators . . . will be implied by sentences at least one of which does not have this property. This fact may be thought of as [a] formalization of the rough intuitive principle that . . . a conclusion in which the identity of at least one individual is assumed to be known can be drawn only from premises at least one of which embodies the same assumption.

Yet it would seem that people can be introduced to someone's acquaintance by no less mysterious methods than providing enough descriptive information about them: if a person or thing is described to me with full enough detail, there will be a point when it is justified for me to say that I know who (or what) that person or object is as well as anybody.

Actually, the contradiction is only apparent. In order to see Hintikka's point in the above quote, we have to look at the semantics of the conclusiveness condition (47). Hintikka's semantics for (47) is simple enough in words, but it introduces quite intriguing conceptual problems. According to Hintikka, (47) is true if and only if 'A' names *one and the same individual* in all the epistemic alternatives of the questioner.

But when is an individual in one context of reference the same is one in another context of reference? This is known as the problem of cross-identification across possible worlds (rather than within one). In *Knowledge and Belief*, Hintikka notes that trans-world cross-identification is dependent on the identity criteria assumed in each case:

In practice it is frequently difficult to tell whether a given sentence of the form "*a* knows who *b* is" . . . is true or not. The criteria as to when one may be said to know who this or that man is are highly variable. Sometimes knowing the name of the person in question suffices; sometimes it does not. Often "acquaintance" of some sort is required. (p. 149)

The point of the previous quote seems clear now. As far as the logic of knowing who is concerned — i.e., formal relations of entailment between knowing who-sentences and other sentences of epistemic logic (or their natural language translations) is concerned, the conclusiveness condition is not easily improved on. In different contexts of use, sentences of the form (47) can be satisfied in different ways, all according to the criteria of identity applied. Because of this variability (and occasional vagueness) of trans-world identity criteria, and the consequent instability of the truth conditions of knowing who sentences, there are no formally valid relations of logical entailment from descriptive (de dicto) knowledge to identifying (de re) knowledge.[6]

This amounts to saying that there is no syntactic characterization of trans-world identity: no verbal definition of individual essence in effect. There is no more reason to expect there to be one than there is for assuming definability of identity even within a possible world.

In semantic terms, a properly cross-identified individual can be represented by a *world-line*: a (possibly partial) function from possible worlds to individuals in their domain.[7] Our syntactical analogue of such an individuating function would be a function from descriptions of possible worlds (i.e., sets of sentences) to descriptions of individuals in them (sets of sentences in which some particular name occurs prominently). This simplification already glosses over one source of difficulty for defining trans-world identity, as such a syntacticized world line cannot depend on unverbalized aspects of a possible world. Yet enough interesting complication remains for the simplification to be instructive.

For one thing, the description of a properly cross-identified individual may well depend on, and vary with, each context of reference. No one description need hold of an individual in all the contexts or possible worlds where it is found: an individual need not have any sort of essence which remains stable in every possible world, no real definition which picks it out no matter what. It follows, among other things, that to know who or what an individual is it is not necessary nor sufficient to know that some particular description applies to it.

Secondly, it also follows that one may find out who someone is by learning new information which is in no obvious sense *about* that individual. For such background information may suffice to rule out enough epistemic alternatives with the result that some individuating function which was only partially defined in one's epistemic alternatives becomes everywhere defined in the remaining alternatives. This is how it is that Sherlock Holmes can figure out the identity of the murderer by purely circumstantial evidence – say by eliminating all other candidates.

These observations already suffice to exclude any overly simplistic approach to refining Hintikka's criterion for knowing who. It becomes clear that it can be improved on only by analyzing questions case by case and ascertaining what the relevant criteria of identity are in each case. In the following few sections, we shall take up some such special cases.

5. *WHAT*-QUESTIONS

Despite their variability and occasional vagueness, genuine identity criteria can be expected to satisfy some minimal requirements of well-behavedness.

One plausible condition proposed by Hintikka is that individuals characterized by one and the same set of identity criteria cannot *split* or *merge* into one another: individuating functions based on the same criteria of identity must be identical if they intersect at all. In epistemic terms, well-known individuals cannot be confused with one another: if one knows who or what A and B are, one is bound to know whether A is the same as B or not.[8]

This requirement can be turned into a test of conclusive answerhood: a conclusive answer to a search question must enable the questioner to distinguish the object inquired about from any other objects which he already knows (relative to the same identity criteria).

Another, more superficial test suggested by Hintikka is appending the words "I do not know but" to an answer: the addition is not appropriate if the answerer considers the answer already conclusive.

Armed with these tests, we can make at least some of the most important distinctions among different criteria of identity. The most obvious – though little discussed – observation is that by far the most inquiries concern kinds of object rather than individuals.[9] For instance, the archetypal identity question

(52)   What is that?

typically asks for the *kind* of object pointed at rather than the individual specimen. Hence it can very well be conclusively answered by a syntactically indefinite noun phrase such as

(53)   It is an awl.

Indeed, it would sound quite odd to qualify (53) by "I do not know but". Note that an adjective or a non-sortal noun would command such a qualification:

(54)   I do not know, but it is sharp (a nuisance).

Now Hintikka's conclusiveness condition predicts that (53), if really inconclusive as an answer to (52), would elicit a generic follow-up question:

(55)   But what is an awl?

(55) is the question to ask if one is ignorant of the identity criteria of awls (the kind of tool), i.e., the criteria of application of the noun *awl*. Thus a fully conclusive answer to (55) in turn would be something like a dictionary definition of an awl, describing its main descriptive and functional characteristics in more familiar words.

The first mentioned identity test agrees with the above analysis. I can know in some conclusive sense what I just had in my pocket (i.e., a fountain pen) and what my neighbor holds in his hand (a fountain pen, too), without knowing whether he has my pen: what I do know is that it is the same *kind* of thing (a fountain pen) in each case.

On the other hand, we also realize that it is not a loose sense of cross-identifying individual pens that is involved here: for my knowledge does not allow the inference that his pen *is* my pen in any sense, however loose.

To clarify the distinction between definiteness and conclusiveness, note what might happen if (52) were answered by

(56)   (I do not know but) it is some tool.

The questioner might impatiently retort

(57)   I know that it is a tool, but what tool is it?

The retort clearly indicates that the questioner is after a sortal answer rather than an individuating one. What is wrong with (56) is not that the questioner would not know what tools are. What is wrong is that the answer is not definite enough. The questioner wants a more specific answer: the criteria of identity he assumes do not allowing identifying any two tools as the same sort of thing.

Though easily confused, definiteness and conclusiveness thus clearly concern different dimensions. Definiteness pertains to individuation within an epistemic alternative: the question is whether an answer succeeds to pick out a *unique* value for the question quantifier in each epistemic alternative in turn. Conclusiveness concerns cross-world identity: the question whether an answer succeeds to pick out the *same* value from all epistemic alternatives. Conclusiveness is thus a strictly stronger notion than definiteness.

We may summarize the observations made in this section as follows. The word *what* can frequently be replaced without change of meaning by *what kind of* (*thing*): accordingly, it can be definitely and conclusively answered by an indefinite noun phrase of the form *an X*, provided only the questioner knows what X's are (conclusiveness) and is prepared to identify any two X's as the same sort of thing (definiteness).

6. *WHO*-QUESTIONS

The generic interpretation is in evidence in *who*-questions too. For instance, the question

(58)   Who is the most powerful man in Finland?

can be conclusively answered by

(59)   The President

even if the questioner does not know who the President is. What he is asking for is an office or a social station rather than an individual person. Accordingly, an answer like

(60)   Kekkonen

is likely to elicit the further query

(61)   But who is Kekkonen?

asking the addressee to identify Kekkonen's position of power rather than to describe him as a private person. For instance, (59) will be a satisfactory answer to (61) if the questioner knows what sort of an office the President's office is.

The only difference here to previous examples is that the kind of person sought for is an exclusive one: just one actual person may exemplify it in any context of reference. In more fashionable terminology, the last example looks for an *individual concept* rather than for a common kind.

Perhaps the most trivial individual concept conceivable is one associated to a *proper name*. But as Hintikka noted, even a name may be a conclusive answer to a *who*-question in some contexts, e.g., in the context of a sports quiz. A contestant is considered to know who won some event or other if he come forward with the name of the person (and perhaps, his or her nationality). The conclusiveness condition here boils down to little more than the requirement that the answerer gets the name right (does not confuse it with other names). The sports context also provides an example of a who-question that can be satisfied by a syntactically indefinite answer: the question

(62)   Who won?

can be conclusively answered by

(63)   A Russian.

if the questioner is interested in nationalities rather than individuals.

A more idiosyncratic example of search for a kind of individual is found in Conan Doyle's story *The Adventure of Charles Augustus Milverton*. The story starts with Dr. Watson picking up a visiting card with the name, address, and profession of a certain Charles Augustus Milverton printed on it. His curiosity about the man is not satisfied by these facts: he asks his friend

(64)   Who is he?

Holmes answers,

(65)   The worst man in London,

and goes on to compare Mr. Milverton, rather unfavorably, to murderers and snakes. Even this does not yet satisfy Watson, who asks again

(66)   But who is he?

Now Holmes replies,

(67)   I'll tell you, Watson. He is the king of all blackmailers.

following up with a detailed description of Milverton's particular method of blackmail. This seems to constitute a conclusive answer for Watson, for in the sequel, he speaks of 'the fellow' as a familiar sort of figure.

It is rather clear what sort of sortal identity criteria Watson is operating here, given his friend's profession: he wants to find out what kind of person Mr. Milverton is that Holmes would have business with him: is he a client or a quarry, the victim or the perpetrator of some kind of crime or other. His card or character do not yet decide this question of identity.

Another example in which the intended conclusiveness condition is spelled out in so many words is the following one from Agatha Christie's *The Man in a Brown Suit*:

— Who is Colonel Race? I asked.
— That's rather a question, said Suzanne. He's pretty well known as a big-game hunter, and, as you heard him say tonight, he was a distant cousin of Sir Laurence Eardsley. I've never actually met him until this trip. He journeys to and from Africa a good deal. There's a general idea that he does Secret Service work. I don't know whether it is true or not. He's certainly rather a mysterious creature.
— What I want to know is, I said with determination, what has Colonel Race got to do with this? He's in it somewhere.

What the questioner wants to know is the role Colonel Race plays in the complicated mystery and intrigue going on in the book: her question will be conclusively answered when she can assign him a unique role in the plot she is in the process of unraveling.

In the following example, the relevant classification is in terms of haves and have-nots: (P. G. Wodehouse, *Cocktail Time*)

— Who is this girl he's marrying?
— I told you at lunch. Belinda Farringdon, commonly known as Bunny.
— No, I mean who *is* she? What does she do?
— She's a commercial artist.

– Any money?
– I imagine not. Still, what's money? You can't take it with you.
– No, but you can do a lot with it here.

Hintikka ([130], p. 46) points out yet an example of this kind from Anthony Powell's novel *At Lady Molly's*. I quote his own description of it:

Everybody is interested in Lady Molly's new guest, but the narrator to his surprise recognizes him as one of his schoolmates:
"I know him."
"Who is he?"
"He is called Kenneth Widmerpool. I was at school with him in fact. He is in the City."
"I know his name of course. And that he is in the City. But what is he like?"
Powell's narrator also intimates why the second speaker, Mrs. Conyers, does not accept poor Mr. Widmerpool's name and profession as a satisfactory answer to the question "Who is he?". This information is not enough for her to place Widmerpool socially and morally in her world, to find his 'essential properties' for her purposes.

Hintikka's description of the example suggests that Mrs. Conyers would have been satisfied by an answer placing Mr. Widmerpool into one of her social pigeonholes, e.g., by identifying him as 'a well-to-do marriageable gentleman". No matter if Mrs. Conyers knows nothing more of him: it suffices that she will not misplace him socially, e.g., mistake him for a prince or a beggar.

If that is the case, Mrs. Conyers would not be likely to claim yet that she knows who Mr. Widmerpool is as an individual. Her information about him leaves all too much undecided about his life and character. For one thing, she cannot be sure of identifying him among a number of different well-off bachelors.

7. PERSONAL IDENTITY

This brings us to the awkward question, why can the narrator, unlike Mrs. Conyers, say he knows who Mr. Widmerpool (the man) is. One way of rephrasing the question is this. Suppose each were given a number of different descriptions of Mr. Widmerpool, say, sets of sentences where the name "Mr. Widmerpool" occurs prominently. The narrator, who knows Mr. Widmerpool, can be expected to be able to say off hand of many such descriptions that they cannot be true of Mr. Widmerpool, while Mrs. Conyers can exclude just a few.

We can now ask, how well must one clear such identification tests in order to know who Mr. Widmerpool is as an individual person?

Recall our syntactic characterization of an individuating function: it is a function, partially defined in a set of descriptions of alternative states of affairs, which picks out wherever it is defined some description of an individual or other.

The 'real' Mr. Widmerpool is picked out by some such individuating function; in particular, that function will pick out Powell's description of Mr. Widmerpool in the different novels where this character makes an appearance.

On the other hand, the name 'Mr. Widmerpool' is associated with another function from alternative state descriptions to descriptions of individuals: this is the trivial function which picks out whatever description (if any) surrounds the name 'Mr. Widmerpool' in each alternative. Now since the narrator knows who Mr. Widmerpool is, his epistemic alternatives form a subclass of such state descriptions where the two functions coincide in values: where the "real" Mr. Widmerpool matches the "local" description of Mr. Widmerpool.

From this we can derive an answer of sorts to the question raised at the beginning. Of course, the narrator does not have to be able to recognize Mr. Widmerpool from any and every description – he does not have to know everything there is to know about him. Why, it is a long time since he last saw his old schoolmate; for all that he knows, the man might have been abroad, got married, or started a business. There may be many descriptions of Mr. Widmerpool of which he cannot say outright whether they are true or not: any of them might be embedded into an epistemic alternative of his without inconsistency.

But one condition stands: whenever the narrator fails to exclude a description that is actually false of Mr. Widmerpool, that is only because he cannot rule out some alternative to the actual course of events where that description would not be out of character for Mr. Widmerpool to satisfy. Say the narrator does not know if Mr. Widmerpool is married; then it cannot be out of the question that Mr. Widmerpool, being the man he is, could have got married had things turned out in a certain way that, as far as the narrator knows, they may have turned out.

In other words, for any description which the narrator thinks just might be true of Mr. Widmerpool, he must allow some factual explanation compatible with his knowledge and with Mr. Widmerpool's personality.

This explication is of course perfectly circular, an explication of meaning

as it is. It does not amount to a real definition of individual essence, which
would be too much to expect here anyway.

Are there cases where a *who*-question does actually amount to an inquiry
into personal identity? The following denouement from a detective story is
as good an example as I have been able to find (Pennington, of course, is
'whodunit' here):

— But there is a whole lot more to explain. Who is this Pennington, anyway, and how
does he come to be mixed up in all this?
— That's a very good question, Jane, Henry said, because it goes right to the heart
of the matter. Once you understand who Albert Pennington is, it becomes very much
easier to understand why he did what he did.
— Well, who is he?
— He's the son of the late Sir Humphrey Pennington, a larger-than-life, hard-drinking,
heavy-gambling character from the fifties, who ran through most of his considerable
inheritance — largely thanks to his string of thoroughbred horses. Albert inherited what
was left of the money — still enough to leave him a rich man by most standards —
together with tendencies to compulsive gambling, transvestism, homosexuality, violence,
and — above all — slumming. He couldn't compete in the really wealthy world of horse-
racing, so he turned his attention to the humbler dog track. For some years now he has
been amusing himself by assuming two personalities. On the one hand, the mustachioed,
upper-class Mr. Pennington, crony of Major Watherby, acquaintance of Sir Arthur
Bratt-Cunningham and his charming daughter, and behind-the-scenes Mr. Big of the
Red Dicky Marsh dogtrack mob. On the other, and always in drag, a formidable, foul-
mouthed female — the mysterious unnamed boss of the Larry Lawson gang. With his
warped sense of humor, he must have a lot of giggles, turning one gang against the
other and watching the fun from his elegant Chelsea house. (Patricia Moyes, *The Curious
Affair of the Third Dog*, p. 208)

We can see that giving an anywhere near adequate understanding of a person's
individual identity may require quite involved explanations of his background
and personality. What is particularly gratifying about the above example, it
vindicates Hintikka's condition of adequacy for knowing who sentences: in
order to know who Mr. Pennington is, one has to be clear which characters of
the plot he can be identified with.

Fortunately, it is seldom necessary to go into full detail about anybody's
personal identity. As Lord Ickenham puts it in Wodehouse's *Cocktail Time*
to Barbara Crowe:

— God bless you, Frederick Ickenham. And who is Albert Peasemarch?
— An intimate friend of mine. To tell you all about him — his career, his adventures
by flood and field, his favourite breakfast food and so on — would take too long. What
will probably interest you most is the fact that he will very shortly be marrying Phoebe.

Here, the last-mentioned fact is conclusive, for it is all that is needed to remove the last obstacle from another successful plot of Lord Ickenham's of spreading sweetness and light into his fellow beings' lives.

8. DESCRIPTIVE VS. DEMONSTRATIVE CRITERIA

In one respect, the situation described in the Powell example is a typical one for asking individual identity questions. In it, Widmerpool is at hand in person for the interlocutors to point at (or if that is a social taboo, otherwise identify demonstratively). In Hintikka's terms, there is a *demonstratively identified individual* spanning the questioner's as well as the answerer's perceptual alternatives (alternative states of affairs that match the speakers' perceptual field).[10]

In our syntactic terms, we can think of such alternatives as alternative verbal descriptions of the speaker's view, placing different objects in them in such relations to each other as they might have as seen from his point of view, and assigning them any properties they might have as far as he can see. Across such alternatives, the viewer will demonstratively identify objects that occupy the same position with respect to his own standing point (i.e., any objects are identified which would appear the same to him from where he is).

What a questioner of a demonstrative search question like Mrs. Conyers'

(68)   Who is he?

wants to accomplish is to align the perceptual world line of 'he' or 'that man there' with a descriptive individuating function that spans her epistemic alternatives: as far as she knows, 'that man' could be anyone. If she cannot do any better by looking more closely (so as to eliminate further perceptual alternatives), someone has to help her exclude the excess of her epistemic alternatives until there remain only such alternatives in which the demonstrative world line associated with 'that man' coincides with, say, the descriptive world line of Mr. Widmerpool.

This duality of cross-identification methods is a common source of questions of individual identity. Demonstrative cross-identification may be what is sought too: for instance someone overhearing the conversation in the above example might feel like asking the question

(69)   Who is Kenneth Widmerpool here?

expecting no more than a demonstrative answer (e.g., 'that man there' accompanied by a gesture).

The positional nature of demonstrative methods of cross-identification can be used as a clue to recognize their presence: (69) is meant as a demonstrative question if it can be paraphrased by a where-question:

(70)   Where is Kenneth Widmerpool here?

9. RELATIVE IDENTIFICATION

The range of a question quantifier is often restricted to some given set of alternatives. When this is the case, the question word to use in English is *which*. *Which* resembles the definite article *the*, in that it carries a presupposition of contextual uniqueness. For instance, in the dialogue

(71)   – Which man won?
        – The best man won.

the question quantifier is likely to be restricted to some contextually available class in which it expects to find just one true answer. It is answered as expected by an equally context-dependent definite description.

In particular, the range of *which* may be specified in the question itself:

(72)   Which one of A, B, and C won?

As a result, the notion of a complete answer can also be relativized to the class of antecedently given alternatives. In order for a putative answer, say,

(73)   The best one

to be conclusive, it is enough for the questioner to be able to keep the 'world lines' of 'A', 'B' and 'C' apart and have just one of them coincide with that of *the best one* – no matter if none of A, B, C, is actually well-defined to the questioner as an individual. It seems that this sort of relative identification is often all a questioner is after. Then the range of the question quantifier is restricted to the 'individual concepts' determined by the answer alternatives. An indication of this is that on this assumption (72) is equivalent to the disjunctive question

(74)   Did A win or B win or C win?

which (72) clearly often is. For another example, one may ask

(75)   Which is heavier, an electron or a proton?

without implying any deeper interest in knowing what an electron or a proton is; the question can be restated without loss of meaning by

(76)   Is an electron heavier or lighter than a proton?

This concludes our discussion of the semantics of questions. We are now in a position for an informed discussion of how questions and their answers are put to use in dialogue.

CHAPTER 4

DIALOGUE GAME RULES

1. SIMPLEST THEORY OF DIALOGUE

The simplest theory of dialogue would have just one rule: *any player may put forward any sentence in any order*. Such a rule should not fall all too short of being observationally adequate: there are few absolute restrictions as to what sequences of sentences might by hook or crook be construed as possible dialogues. One can do a lot by judicious choice of background assumptions and interpolation of suppressed steps of reasoning.

So let us accept the simplest theory as our starting point and see what can be done with it. The first rule of dialogue will be

(D.say)   Any player may put forward any sentence.

An obvious restriction on (D.say) is that dialogue games are *linear* and *discrete*: players move in turns, so that each play of a dialogue game is a finite sequence of linearly ordered moves. Whatever the ultimate explanation of this restriction in terms of, say, limitations of human information processing capacity, this restriction gives rise to "turn-taking conventions" as described by Sacks, et al. [215] . The following is a condensed version of their rules:

(1)   The player at turn may indicate the next player to move.
Else the turn goes to the first player to move.

What (1) does is simply ensure a more or less orderly sequence of moves by (D.say).

I believe that (1), to the extent that it represents a valid generalization at all, can be explained by reference to the linearity requirement and general considerations of dialogue strategy. Therefore, I shall not include (1) or any other explicit turn-taking convention into the theory of dialogue.

The minimal theory of dialogue consisting of (D.say) together with the linearity requirement accords with certain observations made by Sacks, et al. [215] about free conversation. They contrast conversation to e.g., rituals by noting that in conversation, *what parties say is not specified in advance* (by the rules of dialogue):

(. . .)
the turn-taking organization for conversation makes no provision for the content of
any turn, nor does it constrain what is (to be) done in any turn. (. . .)
   But this is not to say that there are no constraints on what may be done in any turn.
(. . .)
   We note only that in conversation, such constraints are organized by systems external
to the turn-taking system. One aspect of conversational flexibility is a direct and important consequence of this feature of its turn-taking organization: its turn-taking
organization (and thus conversational activity per se) operates independently of various
characterizations of what occupies its turns, the 'topic(s)' in them. (p. 710)

I take this to be a convoluted way of saying that there are next to no fixed,
content-independent rules to structure a dialogue over and above (D.say) and
linearity of dialogue. Any further structure dialogues have can be inferred
from the *aims* of dialogue participants and the expressive *means* (language)
at their disposal by essentially game-theoretical (strategic) reasoning. In
other words, the only further pressure a dialogue exerts on its players is the
strategic maxim: *be relevant.*

2. RELEVANCE

The concept of relevance thus becomes a central concept of the theory of
dialogue. The crucial consideration in the well-formedness of a dialogue
will be whether its individual moves have bearing on the topic or subject
matter of the dialogue, or whether they are irrelevant, idle, or beside the
point.

   The dialogue game framework seems potentially well suited for the explication of the elusive concept of relevance. For, it seems to me, the essential logic
of relevance is best visible in a number of its goal-directed near synonyms:
important, useful, helpful.

   Two important points emerge from these paraphrases. First, *relevant*
is a relational word: a move may be relevant (useful) for one purpose but
irrelevant (useless) for another. Second, relevance is relative to is the *aims*
of a discussion — or the aims of individual discussants if their aims diverge.

   Hence to determine whether a given move in a given dialogue is relevant,
one has to determine whether it furthers the aims of one or more participants
of that dialogue. This is the core intuition which particular examples and
explanations should go back to. For instance, an answer is relevant to a
question if anything is. Why? Because the aim of the questioner is to create
a consensus about the (or an) answer to his question, and answering is the
best way to further that aim.

Relevance judgments may vary depending on the presence of a further
maxim of dialogue we have kept in low profile, viz. the *maxim of brevity*:

(2)   Prefer a short dialogue over a longer one.

In a serious information-seeking discussion, the aim may be to share the
available information with the least possible speech effort. In such a discussion, long-winding answers are likely to be dismissed as irrelevant. In social
conversation, where one aim is passing the time pleasantly, the same mean-
derings may be quite welcome and not at all "irrelevant".

In brief, the dialogue game explication of the notion of relevance is
in essence "utility relative to the dialogue aims of the participants of the
dialogue". A full game-theoretical formalization of the concept of relevance
would hence involve *solving* a dialogue game for each player, i.e., finding the
optimal strategies of each player. In practice, we shall be content with local
qualitative comparisons of relative relevance.

The present definition of relevance creates a link between the concepts of
relevance and rationality. A rational player is by definition one who follows
his optimal strategy (or strategies) − i.e., those which (according to the
theory) most effectively further his aims. This means that a rational dialogue
player makes only relevant moves. This implies that the Gricean *maxim of
relevance* becomes a corollary of the game-theoretical reconstruction of
dialogue. In the dialogue game context, 'Be relevant!' says nothing more than
'Be rational!'.

3. MEANING CONVENTIONS

The players are free to put forward any sentences for the other players to
access according to the rules of the game. But what use is this freedom to
them? In order to render this liberty useful, a bridge must be provided from
saying sentences to *accepting* them. I call such bridges *meaning conventions*,
as they spell out what players *mean* by what they say.

The basic and most common principle of this character is what I shall call
the earnestness (or seriousness) convention. This convention can be spelled
out as a rule of dialogue games.

(D.earnest) Put forward a sentence only if you accept it.

At first blush, (D.earnest) sounds like another maxim of conversation:
actually, a close relative to it is listed as one half of Grice's maxim of quality.[1]
The way we have sliced up matters, meaning conventions are linguistic

conventions. What meaning conventions like (D.earnest) accomplish is a link from the sentences one says to positions one accepts: they thus fix salient means for making one's acceptations known. What makes them — including the earnestness convention — conventional is the fact that they have alternatives which serve this same purpose equally well. To pick the most obvious alternative, consider what might be called the *irony* (or sarcasm, or rhetoric) convention:

(D.irony)   Put forward a sentence only if you accept its contrary.

(A contrary is often stronger than a mere contradictory of a sentence; for instance, the contrary of 'That's great!' is not just 'That's not great!' but rather 'That's awful!'.)[2]

As is well known from familiar Smullyan-type puzzles, a speaker consistently following the irony convention is quite as informative as one who consistently says what he means. This is what makes (D.earnest) conventional.[3] Naturally, in some intuitive sense, the earnestness convention is fundamental. (It is also simplest to state.) It is the principle followed in uncomplicated, unsophisticated matter-of-fact information exchanges. The irony convention and other more complicated alternatives can serve subordinate purposes, e.g., those of being offensive, colorful, modest, or funny. They accomplish these subsidiary purposes just because the earnestness convention is the first one that comes to mind.

Of course, the usefulness of obeying a meaning convention at all is predicated on the acceptance of the goal of information-sharing in the first place. If other aims of language exchange override the aim of information sharing, there is no need to follow any rule linking what is being said to what is being accepted: whatever is funny, offensive, colorful, or whatnot, will do.

Another tempting but misleading way of reading (D.earnest) is to see in it a moral principle, an injunction against lying, in the spirit of 'thou shalt not bear false witness'. This temptation is in evidence in Searle's terminology.[4] Searle, in his analysis of speech acts, singles out for each kind of speech act a peculiar felicity condition called the *sincerity condition*. For assertions, the sincerity condition says that the author of an assertion believes the proposition he puts forward — apparently a restatement of (D.earnest). Actually, making the identification would be misrepresenting Searle. Like Grice, Searle does not recognize alternatives to the earnestness convention as real alternatives. His "normal input and output conditions" for speech acts rule out "parasitic forms of communication such as telling jokes"; presumably, being sarcastic is excluded too.[5]

In our approach, considering the earnestness convention a condition for sincerity would be a mistake. One does not have to say what one believes in order to be sincere: one can well be sincere while being sarcastic and saying the opposite of what one believes. In our terms, *being insincere equals cheating in whatever game one is playing*. Cheating, in turn, is violating the rules of the game intending the violation to go unnoticed. In particular, lying is playing the game of cooperative information sharing with the private aim of creating a disagreement of opinions known only to oneself. For this definition of lying, it is immaterial what one says in order to induce the misunderstanding: thus one can lie while speaking the truth (if one is misinformed oneself), even while saying what one believes (if one lets the other think one is being sarcastic).[6] From this, it is clear that it is only under the "normal input and output conditions", i.e., under (D.earnest), that saying what one does not believe amounts to being insincere.

More obviously, (D.earnest) is distinct from the eighth commandment, rephrased as

(3)   Do not put forward falsehoods.

In our terms, (3) represents an amalgam of the earnestness convention with the maxim of truth. The maxim of truth can, if so is wished, be construed as an ethical principle. However, (3) is a far more exacting principle than 'do not lie'. As we noted, one can lie while speaking the truth; conversely, it is possible to say falsehoods with the sincerest of intentions.

4. SUGGESTIONS

It is often useful for players to put forward sentences that they do not actually hold, but do not reject either. This is also information about their epistemic attitudes, and being able to express it may trigger off arguments that would otherwise pass unnoticed. For instance, one may want to *suggest* an explanation, or make a *guess* at an answer to a question, in the hope that others may judge whether they are acceptable.

Questions may represent guesses too: thus a suggested explanation for a search question in terms of a sentential instance is nothing else than a guess:

(4)   Who is it? Is it Jack?

The interpretation of an unadorned sentence as a suggestion is provided for by another meaning convention:

(D.guess)   Put forward a sentence only if you admit it.

As a marked option, (D.guess) is in need of disambiguating context, lest one's contribution be taken in earnest. Such disambiguation can be offered by an explicit request (Guess!) or by the use of appropriate intonation and gesturing.

There are ways to make guesses without relinquishing (D.earnest), too. Suggestions and guesses can be explicitly marked as such by any of a number of modality adverbs: *perhaps* and *maybe* being the most common ones.

The ability of *perhaps* to defuse (D.earnest) can be captured by the following rule of interpretation:

(D.perhaps)   A player P accepts a sentence of form
$$X - \text{perhaps} - Y$$
if and only if P admits
$$X - Y.$$

Thus, whenever a player entertains a sentence S, he can accept the sentence *perhaps S*, and hence is allowed to put it forward in full accordance with (D.earnest).

Note an interesting feature of the above rule of meaning for 'perhaps'. It does not have the form of a Tarskian truth condition 'S is true if and only if p': it is not a condition for truth but a condition for acceptance. In other words, the meaning of a word like 'perhaps' is not a matter of semantics (truth conditions) but pragmatics (conditions of use).

This can be seen as a vindication of Wittgenstein's special concern for the meaning of the word 'perhaps': it does constitute a problem for the extension of the picture theory of meaning which the Tarskian theory of truth has been taken to represent.[7] Note that I am not saying that model theoretic methods could not be used to explicate such pragmatic rules of meaning — that is just what I am doing! What 'perhaps' shows is that the theory of truth for English does not exhaust the theory of meaning for it.

5. SUPPOSITIONS

As was indicated earlier, we want to go even further and all allow players at times to put forward sentences which they need not even admit. It is often a good strategy to assume something just for the sake of the argument, to see if it is a viable position.

The main point to realize is that conducting an argument from doubtful premises is not different from arguing from accepted ones. The only difference is that the set of assumptions being developed does not reflect anyone's doxastic alternatives via some meaning convention or other.

Let us think what actually happens when one conducts a counterfactual argument. Intuitively, one *supposes* something, i.e., lays down one or several hypotheses as the starting-point of the argument, and follows through the consequences of the hypotheses. The steps and methods of argument which one uses to extend the original set of hypotheses are the very same ones of deductive inference and inductive decision one uses to extend one's epistemic alternatives.

Thus the problem of counterfactual conditionals: what would happen if such-and-such were the case, is no simpler than the general problem of theory construction. In each case, one is faced with the task of finding the best complete explanation of a number of evidential facts. What is more, the counterfactual problem is seriously underdetermined as compared with the factual problem.

In the factual case, where one's hypotheses do not decide a question, one can go out and find out more facts. But what can one do in the imaginary situation: where does one find imaginary facts? What we actually do is make a conservative assumption: where the hypotheses of the counterfactual supposition do not decide one way or another, assume the counterfactual situation is like the actual situation.

This strategy has some interesting limitations. It may leave many counterfactual questions undecided, if the actual situation has nothing to say of them. Or there may be a number of competing ways of extending the counterfactual situation, about equally plausible. This indeterminacy creates such familiar paradoxes as

(5)   White to Black: If I were you, I would give up.
          Black to White: If you were me, you would not.

White imagines the players simply switching sides, while Black points out that if White had Black's personality he would be equally obstinate.

With its limitations, this seems to be a fair description of how people in actual fact create epistemic alternatives. They start out as counterfactual imagination; if they turn out to be inconsistent or false to fact, they are rejected; if they pass the muster of deductive examination and inductive evaluation, they become part of a player's system of belief.

To illustrate the uses of counterfactual argumentation, let us consider some examples.

(6)   A person who hurts no one who hurts him hurts himself.

It may not be apparent that (6) is self-contradictory. But it can be shown so by a counterfactual argument:[8]

(7)   For suppose some person A hurt no one who hurt him. Then A would hurt A. On the other hand, A would hurt no one who hurt him. So A would not hurt A.

The counterfactual alternative violates (C.cons) and has to be rejected.

A more everyday use of counterfactual argument is to show a supposition false to fact. The counterfactual alternative is internally consistent here, but it is in conflict with the player's earlier acceptations:

(8)   It wasn't one of your regulars. For if it had been one of your regulars, you would have recognized him. But you did not recognize him.

There are two importantly different ways to handle such conflicts. A conservative (and quite instinctive) way is to treat all and any earlier acceptations as unquestioned evidence: one develops counterfactual alternatives as so many extensions of the intersection of one's epistemic alternatives, rejecting any inconsistent or improbable ones. A more rational approach is not to accord a privileged status to received opinion, but to weigh each counterfactual alternative for its own merits, using as evidence for the decision only such assumptions as are not questioned in the situation at hand. (These may include independent observations and other evidence whose acceptance does not depend on the solution to the problem at hand.)

Thirdly, counterfactual argument is used in developing theories and plans in a noncommittal fashion:

(9)   If I left now, I would avoid the rush and there would be time to stop and shop.

Quite likely, the plan in (9) will actually be put into use, which serves to show that being counterfactual need not mean being averse to the argument.

Now a common indicator of counterfactual argument in English is the subjunctive mood. But what exactly is its contribution to such argument? We may first note that it is not an indispensable index: counterfactual arguments are also conducted in the indicative. It seems to me that whatever counterfactual force is associated to a conditional like (7)–(9) above remains when the sentences are rephrased in the indicative. Briefly, I submit that as to logical force, a past subjunctive sentence is equivalent to its indicative counterpart.[9]

This assumption is confirmed by the observation that a subjunctive conditional licenses detaching an indicative consequent given an indicative antecedent:

(10)   A: If it were raining, I would be in trouble.
         B: It is raining.
         A: Then I am in trouble.

An apparently serious objection comes from sentences like

(11)   I would not try that.

which does not seem to imply

(12)   I will not try that.

However, it seems that the reason why (11) does not imply (12) is that (11) is actually elliptic for

(13)   I would not try that if I were you.

It is a general fact that elliptic sentences cannot be taken at face value, whatever their mood: for instance one who answers the question

(14)   What will you do if he comes?

by

(15)   I will leave.

cannot be said to have promised to leave come what may. If it is clear that all the implicit conditions are present, the inference from subjunctive to indicative seems warranted:

(16)   "You've moved the table."
         "Certainly." . . . "We were told things could be moved."
         "Yeah, the inspector would, with members in the high brackets.
         If it had been a dump he'd have kept it sealed for a moth."

The first speaker's subjunctive *would* seems to imply acceptance of the second speaker's indicative *were*.

Yet clearly, the past subjunctive is not wholly without effect. The way I construe it, it serves an important dialogue function. I shall try to spell it out by the following rule and definition:

(D. subjunctive) Put forward a sentence in past subjunctive only if you suppose it.

(17)   A player *P* *supposes* a sentence *S* iff *S* is a member of a hypothetical alternative for *P*.

By a hypothetical alternative I shall understand a list of assumptions a player may construct by the usual methods of model set construction without (yet) deciding whether or not to include it among his epistemic alternatives. We shall allow players to hold any number of hypothetical alternatives alongside their *bona fide* epistemic alternatives at any stage of the game. Such alternatives represent the players' suppositions, thoughts or plans during the conversation.

In other words, what the subjunctive mood indicates is the relevance of a sentence to a discussion: by using the subjunctive, the speaker not only makes known an assumption of his, but also indicates where it is to be put to use in the dialogue, viz. in some counterfactual argument or other he is constructing.

Such counterfactual arguments are where one is to look for the missing suppositions of elliptical sentences like (11). This force of the subjunctive to suggest unexpressed provisos is what explains its use in cautious or polite statements and questions:

(18)   This would seem to confirm his statement.
(19)   Could you open the window?

In (18), there is a suggestion of some qualification: "unless I am badly mistaken" or the like; in (19) the subjunctive helps construing the question as part of a plan to get the window opened: could you do the job if I asked you to? [10]

6. EXAMPLES OF DIALOGUE STRATEGIES

So the only primitive dialogue game rule we have is (D.say). Of course, this minimum of rules is possible because all of the interesting structure lies elsewhere: in the description of possible game situations (model systems), in the epistemic explication of the question-answer relation, in the statement of the aims of the game (utility functions based on conversational maxims), the linearity requirement, and meaning conventions.

To see how this substructure works to create structure to a dialogue, let us derive a typical question-answer dialogue from it. Let the dialogue be the following:

(20)   A: Who are you?
        B: I am Beth.
        A: So you are Beth.
        B: Yes, I am Beth.

What happened? Simple: A put forward the topical question — one she is interested in for whatever ulterior reasons — by the rule (D.say). B can infer, by (D.earnest), than A accepts the question, i.e., wants an answer for it. Being cooperative, B is ready to join the game and accept the question herself. Having accepted it, she also wants an answer for it. Not surprisingly, she has little difficulty in finding one among her assumptions. Faithful to the maxims of conversation, she also wants to share it with A. This she does by putting forward her answer by (D.say). Hearing it, A can use (D.earnest) to infer that B accepts what she says. This is good evidence for the answer being true, so A is justified in accepting it too. Following the maxim of agreement, she prefers letting B know this, which she does by repeating the answer. Applying (D.earnest) again, B now knows that A accepts the answer too. B may still complete the hermeneutic circle of common understanding by acknowledging A's acceptance. Both players now know who B is and know the other knows it too. The discussion on the topic of B's identity has thereby reached its aim and the players can go on to further topics.[11]

Interesting confirmation of the above account comes from a statistical study of typical topic-closing moves in conversation (Weiner and Goodenough, [180]). Recall the function of the two final repetitive moves in (16): they do not introduce new information on the subject of the discussion, but serve to create a consensus on the information already obtained. As soon as the consensus is reached, the dialogue has attained its aim and the topic can be dropped. This prediction is nicely confirmed by Weiner and Goodenough's data. They make the following observations about the function of the sort of "passing" moves we are discussing:

Typically, no substantive moves occur on the same topic after a passing move pair. However, additional housekeeping moves on the same topic may follow. For example, either speaker may summarize the topic of discussion or assess the progress of the conversation at that point before advancing to the next topic. These additional housekeeping moves appear to be optional, however, since one of the speakers often introduced a new topic directly after the passing move pair:

Example 2: (Doctor-patient study)

Doctor: – and you say, as far as you know, you don't have any other illnesses?
Patient: No, not to my knowledge.
Doctor: High blood, or diabetes.
Patient: No.
Doctor: OK.
Patient: Mmhmm.
Doctor: And you desire to lose weight. (p. 219)

In the last line of the above example, the Doctor, satisfied that the aim of the inquiry about the medical history of the patient has been reached, opens another topic. Notice that this satisfaction is guaranteed by a pair of acknowledging moves.

The above example also exemplifies another important type of dialogue move. That is the Doctor's move of instantiation from 'any other illnesses' into the individual diseases 'high blood or diabetes'. The step here is one of logical inference. Its function may be that of gathering further confirmation for the patient's claim. The doctor may feel, with justification, that the patient's answers are more reliable when they concern the individual illnesses. Again, we have a dialogue step whose rationale is given by our statement of the aims of information-sharing dialogue.

7. RULES VS. STRATEGIES

In games, there is sometimes a certain give and take between the concepts of *rule* and *strategy*. I illustrate this with a (somewhat fictional) example from chess. In chess, the game *rules* specify the admissible moves at each stage of the game and the winning positions, with the understanding that the players of the game aim to win. A chess *strategy* is a particular scheme or plan of moves designed to further the aim of the scheming player. A particular strategy is deemed good or bad depending on whether it serves the aims of its maker.

Rules, in contrast, are given at the outset. They can be considered good or bad only from an external point of view, whether they serve the purposes of the users of the game. For instance, chess is often played from quite cooperative motives: each players wants to entertain and to be entertained. Yet White does his best to defeat Black and vice versa: this is even essential for the game to be entertaining. That is, the choice of the rules of the game (say, chess rather than checkers) can be described as a more inclusive game whose moves include alternative games complete with their rules. Then a particular choice for a rule of chess can be a good or a bad strategy in the game of game choice.

Consider from this point the option of resigning the game when defeat is obvious. It is customary among proficient chess players to admit defeat as soon as it is obvious for both parties that one of the players has a winning strategy in the rest of the game. By now, resignation is an option duly registered in the rules of chess. At an earlier point, it might have been better described as a convention of opting out from a game at a point when it has lost its excitement: when playing the game no more served the ulterior aim of entertainment. By incorporating this external strategical option into the internal rules of the game it is ensured that the game is better apt to serve its ulterior purpose.

This fictitious history of chess could be pushed further. In chess as it is, all other pieces except the king can be captured (replaced by an enemy piece and removed from the board). The original purpose of the game may have been to capture the enemy king. However, by current rules the game is already ended when a king can no more avoid imminent capture. Of course, to actually capture a king once it has no place to go would be futile, and to expose one's king to imminent capture would be suicidal. Such obviously unexciting moves are actually ruled out in modern chess. Again, there is a gain for the interest of the game, as the amended rules prevent certain obviously uninteresting game possibilities. Here, then, may be another case where obvious strategic considerations have become part and parcel of the rules of the game. These rules are not at all unmotivated: actually, they reflect aspects of the optimal strategies in the unamended game.

Analogous situations seem to arise in the theory of dialogue. Sometimes, the question arises whether some feature of communicative behavior should be considered a conventional rule of language games, or as a likely (because effective) choice of communication strategy. For instance, is it a rule of language, or just a good strategy of information exchange, to answer a question if one can? Or, is it a linguistic convention or just common sense that one does not ask what one already knows?

The natural inclination of course is to leave as much as possible to be systematically explained by strategic considerations rather than enumerated by arbitrary rule. For instance, surely it is no grammatical mistake to ask what one already knows. It is just a foolish thing to do if one wants to learn something new. In other contexts, it may be quite rational, for instance, in a quiz or in court.

Ideally, rules ought to state only *conventional* facts: they ought to register what cannot be explained by more general considerations. Rules state what is arbitrary in a game: when a choice is imposed by the rules of a language on its users.

But as the chess example shows, the arbitrariness criterion works on several levels. A good communicative strategy may, by force of convention, get relegated into a rule of language. For instance, a particular form of question may get stabilized as a conventional expression of request. Again, there is a gain in the shortcut. Given the convention, the complicated route from literal meaning to illocutionary force via conversational implication is saved and correct understanding expedited.

Yet again, the resulting rule of meaning is not totally arbitrary. The conversational implication is still there, explaining why this choice of expresion is a natural one. Nonetheless, it has become a convention. Another language may prefer another roundabout construction for indirect request, equally well-motivated conversationally but equally conventional. Each preference is arbitrary in the face of the alternatives.[12]

We can expect similar situations to arise when we start formulating rules for dialogue games. Some communicative strategies, though well motivated by general strategic considerations, may have become the rule by force of convention. Such 'theorems of dialogue' will be considered in the remainder of this chapter.

8. DERIVED RULES

The simple theory of dialogue developed above has the advantage of having a minimum number of primitive concepts. As is familiar from the study of formal systems in logic, this is an advantage when one is out to prove metatheorems, i.e., to describe the system rather than to use it. In exchange, a simple system may be complicated to use: proofs in it get long and tedious in the lack of auxiliary lemmas and derived rules of inference.

This alone is a motivation for enriching the system of dialogue rules beyond the absolute minimum. In addition comes the conventionality argument from the preceding section. As in chess, so in dialogue, some particularly common strategies may have become conventional enough to deserve individual attention, and proper names. The very existence in English of terms such as *question, answer, reply, objection*, and the like is proof of this.

For these reasons, I shall go on to define a number of derived dialogue rules. Their effect is to induce a hierarchical functional structure to a dialogue over and above the linear sequence of its moves. In addition to following each other in a temporal sequence, the moves of a dialogue will thus be functionally related to each other in ways not determined by temporal sequence alone. It is such functional dependencies that the derived dialogue game rules will register. By their means, we will be able to capture explicitly the fact that one and the same sentence (or sequence of sentences) may serve many quite different functions in dialogue, as its intended relations to other utterances in the dialogue vary.

The set of dialogue game rules to be defined in the following sections thus form the basic material for spelling out the functional structure of a dialogue, or the way how the flow of information is organized in a conversation.

Approaching the problem from an abstract angle, we may expect to find moves divided into several general types. First, there is likely to be some rule or rules for *starting* a conversation: for instance, some formulas of greeting have this function.

In opposition to such *initial moves* there will be what I shall call *counter-moves*: moves related to earlier (explicit or implicit) moves as responses or replies to them.

In addition to *countermoves*, we shall consider a set of what will be called *continuation moves*. They are moves that look back to (are defined with reference to) other dialogue moves, but have the additional restriction that they are made *by the same player* as the moves they respond to. Such moves therefore are called dialogue moves by courtesy only, as they will be as much at home in a monologue, a soliloquy conducted by a lone player.

9. GAME RULES FOR QUESTIONS

We start out by writing quite abstract general dialogue rules for asking questions and answering them. The rules will refer to definitions of answer and presupposition for each type of question, which we shall give below in the form of logical game rules for questions and answers.

There will be one initiating rule for asking questions, which at the same time serves as an initial rule of dialogue games:

(D.ask)   Any player may ask any player a sentential (polarity) question.

As the rule makes no reference to preceding discourse, a move by (D.ask) is at hand only when none is being made, either: to make a move by (D.ask) is to start a dialogue, to open a new topic of discussion.

The point of making the initial rule of dialogue games a rule for asking questions should be clear: in our view, dialogues are topic-centered, and topics are introduced by questions which describe the questioner's informational interests. The special property of sentential questions that makes them particularly suitable for the purpose of opening a discussion is that they are *safe*: their presuppositions are tautological. Thus before opening a discussion around some more informative inquiry players can first establish whatever presuppositions such more informative questions are predicated on by putting them into question by (D.ask).

Following the intention of Hintikka's paraphrase of direct questions, the rule for asking further questions will run as follows:

(D.question) When a player has put forward the presupposition of a question, any player may ask him the question.

Observe that (D.question) is formulated as a countermove rule. It requires as a precondition for raising a question that the presupposition of the question has put in an appearance in the dialogue. (We shall see later that this does not imply it has been said out loud or even accepted implicitly.)

Note that the presupposition of a question is construed as an *addressee*'s move rather than the questioner's. A motivation for this is seen in the contrast between the following two dialogues:

(21) A: You said something.
      B: I did not say anything!
      A: What did you say?
(22) A: You said nothing.
      B: I did say something!
      A: What did you say?

It seems to me that (22) is much more natural and fluent than (21). In (22), the questioner denies the presupposition of the question he is asking, but the addressee accepts it. In (21), the opposite is true: the questioner accepts the presupposition but his addressee denies it.

In (21), one gets the feeling that the questioner is not paying any attention to his interlocutor: he does not realize that a precondition of his question is not fulfilled. In (22), A is listening to B. Quite possibly, he may actually believe B, and be asking his question seriously (accept it as admitting of an answer).

There is another alternative, too. A may not actually accept B's claim, so she is not asking the question in earnest. She is almost sure she is not going to get an acceptable answer. Then A is not asking the question seriously under (D.earnest), but noncommittally or even ironically. She might have used the subjective mood to show her doubt:

(23)   What would you have said?

Finnish would use a particle which nicely captures this nuance of the question: it is *muka* 'allegedly', related to the postposition *mukaan* 'according to'. The Finnish translation of the doubtful question (23) would read 'What did you say, according to you?', nicely attributing the question, and its presupposition, to the answerer. A good example of such an incredulous question is the girl's query in

I said gently, "What do you do with yourself down here?" She shrugged her shoulders, "What is there to do?"
    "Haven't you any hobbies? Don't you play games? Haven't you got friends around about?"
    "I'm stupid at games. There aren't many girls around here, and the ones there are I don't like. They think I'm awful." (Agatha Christie, *The Moving Finger*, p. 20.)

The shrug of shoulders eloquently conveys the noncommittal character of the girl's question. Note that the first speaker correctly reads the intention of her question, for he puts his suggestions in the negative form of the expected answers. The girl confirms his guess by demolishing all the alternatives in turn.

In most 'normal' cases of questioning, of course, the questioner himself accepts the presupposition of his question. It is easy to show, using rules of inference given in later chapters, that acceptance of a question implies the acceptance of its presupposition (it would be dialogically inconsistent to accept a question and deny its presupposition). Hence whoever asks a question in earnest (accepts it) must also accept its presupposition.

10. ANSWERING

Rules for asking questions would have little use without a complementary rule for answering them. As Stenius [35] points out, the *point* or *meaning* of a direct question is actually incorporated in the game rule for the answerer.

The dialogue game rule for answering will also refer to an independent explication of the semantics and pragmatics of the answerhood relation:

(D.answer)   When a player has put forward a question, an addressee may put forward an answer to it.

The dialogue game rules for asking and answering are exceedingly simple. This is because the complicated aspect about questions is their semantics, and that aspect has been relegated to the semantic game rules. The only thing that is left for the *dialogue* game rules for asking and answering to explicate is the meaning of the 'optative operator' in Hintikka's analysis, or the meaning of the interrogative *mood*.

As we noted earlier, the dialogue game construction as a whole and the dialogue game rules for asking and answering in particular provide an explanation how it comes about that a questioner manages, by putting forward a direct question to an interlocutor, to put him under a commitment to provide an answer to the question. The crux of that explanation is the assumption that the questioner and the addressee agree to play a dialogue game following the rules of the game and accepting the aims it assigns to them.

The rest, i.e., the inference of the players' beliefs and intentions is simple game theoretical reasoning.

Note that this language game explication of the meaning of the interrogative mood confirms Wittgenstein's insight about the difference in meaning between questions and assertions. A question is *not* a disguised assertion. It is not just accepted or denied, but answered or not. Although it often conveys a questioner's desire for knowledge (and hence, his lack of it), it does not *assert* that desire or ignorance. They can only be *inferred* from the assumption that the questioner is playing the game of asking and answering according to the rules of the game and following a rational strategy choice relative to appropriate background assumptions.

To appreciate this point, note that none of our rules make reference to the desideratum of a question. They are quite neutral about the intention of a question, whether it is a simple request for information, an examination question, or perhaps a rhetorical one. We shall see that all of these question types represent rational discussion strategies under different appropriate background assumptions.

11. LOGICAL MOVES

The moves we shall consider next are *inferential* and *explanatory* steps of reasoning in a dialogue. An example of each sort may be in order:

(24)   Everybody is kungfu fighting.
         Then the President is kungfu fighting.

(25)   Not everybody is kungfu fighting.
        The President is not kungfu fighting.

Inferential moves are often marked as such by various markers of inferential tie (e.g., *then, so, therefore, hence*). At the surface of a real-life dialogue, the inference need not be formally valid (logically binding). Even with enthymematic premises made explicit, the argument may be just a probable one (an inductive inference).

Explanatory moves are reciprocal to inferential ones. An explanandum is related to its explanantia in much the same way as an inference is related to its premises. Thus an explanation need not be a complete one on the surface of a dialogue, and it may remain probabilistic even when fully spelled out.

I propose the following dialogue game rules for inferential and explanatory moves:

(D.infer)   When a player has put forward a sentence, he may infer another sentence from it.

(D.explain)   When a player has put forward a sentence, he may put forward an explanation for it.

The way I have defined (D.infer) and (D.explain), inferential and explanatory moves are *continuation moves*, i.e., moves by the same player as the moves they act as responses to. This seems intuitively right, as a putative second speaker of the dialogues (24)–(25) seems to implicitly accept his interlocutor's claim by his inferential and explanatory moves. His moves will be analyzed as continuation moves to his own implicit intervening moves of acceptance.

Surely, a player may *suggest* to his interlocutor inferences and explanations for assumptions he does not himself subscribe to. But note that in that case, his tone of voice is different: in making a suggestion he is actually prompting his *interlocutor* to draw the inference or adopt the explanation. Intuitively, in such cases, it is correct to append to his move a question mark to convey this questioning tone of voice. Such usage thus rather supports than speaks against our formulation of (D.infer).

12. ARGUMENTS

When an interlocutor refuses to accept an answer, what one may do is *argue* for it by producing evidence for it. Such relevant evidence are of course sentences that confirm the answer.

Hence argumentation is relative to some explication of the relation of confirmation. We shall employ the probabilistic notion of confirmation presupposed in the chapter on inductive acceptance: a sentence is evidence for another sentence if it adds to the probability of the latter. More formally, a sentence *e confirms* a hypothesis *h* if $p(h/e) > p(h)$; if $p(h/e) < p(h)$, then *e disconfirms h* and confirms the denial of *p*, else *e* is independent of *h* and (inductively) irrelevant to it.

This characterization of the confirmation relation is symmetrical as is evident from the definition of conditional probability $p(h/e)$:

$$(26) \quad p(h/e) = \frac{p(h \& e)}{p(e)}.$$

For *e* is relevant to *h* if and only if

$$(27) \quad \frac{p(h \& e)}{p(h)p(e)} \neq 1$$

and then *e* and *h* obviously are relevant to each other (if not always to the same extent). For instance, any sentence is conclusive evidence for its own logical consequences, and hence conversely is confirmed by them to various degrees.

Evidence will be allowed to enter a dialogue game by the following game rule:

(D.argue) When a player has put forward a sentence, he may argue for it by a sentence that is evidence for it.

As a limiting case, of course, any sentence is conclusive evidence for itself, so (D.argue) provides for the (common if somewhat silly) argument by the simple repetition of a claim.[13]

(D.argue) also provides another motive for putting forward logical consequences of one's claims.

The way (D.argue) is formulated, it allows players to defend their own claims only. Of course, one can argue against others, too: i.e., attack another player's claim by producing disconfirming evidence for it. However, such counterevidence will be construed here as evidence for the denial of the claim (or as denial of evidence for the claim).

As an afterthought, an explanation can be recognized as a limiting case of inductive argument.

13. REPLIES

One more type of game rule needs to be introduced: they are rules for declarative countermoves to declarative sentences. The most straightforward reaction to an interlocutor's assertion is to *assent* to it or to *dissent* from it:

(28)   A: He won.
         B: (Yes,) he won.
         C: (No,) he did not win.

Assent and dissent take a definite stand with respect to the assertion: assent is a sign of acceptance, while dissent implies denial, or rejection, of the claim. But sometimes a claim may prompt a more indirect reaction:

(29)   A: I like tea.
         B: Most people like tea.

Note that B does not take a definite stand for or against A's assertion: his reply does not imply it nor rule it out. What B seems to be doing is rather to brush A's comment aside as being of little importance or interest: A is not wrong but he is irrelevant.

This intuition is explained if it is assumed that B construes A as attempting an answer to a more general question than the form of his assertion suggests: perhaps it is the question

(30)   Who likes tea?

What B does is suggest an alternative answer to the same question which has higher information value than the one A was able to come up with. B does not deny A's answer; he just passes it because its epistemic utility is low.

These considerations lead me to propose the following game rule for replying to a declarative sentence:

(D.reply)   When a player has put forward an answer to a question, any player may reply to him by putting forward his answer to the same question.

The important feature about (D.reply) is that anyone who replies to a claim has to decide first what the *issue* is: what question he takes the claim as an answer to. This feature seems to me to capture a central insight about assertion-reply dialogues: people in a conversation do not just exchange assumptions, but are led by their perceptions of what the conversation is aiming at, i.e., what questions are on their mind, what they think the topic of the discussion might be.

What is nice about (D.reply), it includes as a special case assent and dissent to a previous assertion on its own right. For the simplest question which any assertion answers is the question whether it is true or not. To that question, there are two direct answers: yes and no. Thus the dialogue (28) above can actually be understood as a series of answers to the simple question

(31)   Did he win (or not)?

CHAPTER 5

STRUCTURE OF DIALOGUE

1. STRUCTURE OF DIALOGUE

As even casual observation of actual conversations shows, no simple theory of the structure of dialogues can be right. In particular, one can at once dismiss a simplistic view of a dialogue as a linear sequence or Markovian chain of moves where each move is related to, or depends on, only the preceding move in the linear order of utterance. Such dialogues of course occur: for instance, a dialogue may start with a question, which is answered, the answer rejected, the rejection argued for, and so on.

However, that is only a very special case. More generally, one has to allow for *topic change* in real life dialogues: the current topic may be dropped and another picked up in mid dialogue; challenges may be ignored, and whole new topics introduced. In general, the assumption that a move in a dialogue can always be construed either as an initial move or a countermove or continuation move to an immediately preceding move is all too restrictive. The move-countermove structure of a dialogue does not have to coincide with the linear order of moves: these are two independent orders of structure.

In fact, it appears to be an overly restricting assumption to assume that any dialogue move must even have a *unique* premise at all — i.e., that each dialogue move is a response to at most one antecedent move. To take a trivial example, a teacher may put forward a sentence as a correction to a whole number of alternative guesses by his students. Inferences, too, often depend on multiple premises.

More interestingly, recall the format of the game rule (D.reply): according to it, a reply represents an alternative answer to a previously expressed or understood topical question — thus it serves two purposes at the same time, being a correction or confirmation of the answer it surpasses and an answer to the topical question. In fact, it seems that the phenomenon of multiple antecedency is quite common. Another example is the following dialogue. Speaker A accepts the following sentences:

(1)   If anyone won, it was Jack or Bob. Someone won. Who was it?

The following dialogue ensues between A and another player B:

(2) A: Did Jack win?   1
     B: No.   2
     A: So Bob won.   3
     B: No.   4
     A: But then no one won!   5

Move 3 represents at the same time an inference from move 2 and an answer to the questioner's implicit question in (1). Similarly, line 5 is simultaneously an inference from 2 and 4 and an argument against accepting these premises in the face of (1) (as signaled by *but*).

The example illustrates at the same time a third, all-important source of surface complexity in a real life dialogue. It is obvious that dialogue moves often are not addressed to *any* of the *actually expressed* preceding moves in a dialogue, but to some related *implicit assumptions* held by some participant or other, or inferred from their assumptions.

Very often the intermediate steps of reasoning in a dialogue may be quite complicated, and this can lead to difficulty of 'seeing the point' of someone's contribution. Yet a dialogue serves its purpose, and is by all means well-formed, as long as the gaps can be filled out in an appropriate way. Hence there is not likely to be any concept of well-formedness of a sequence of explicit moves in a dialogue in abstraction of the whole description of the implicit game situation as we have been in the process of constructing it. There may be textual principles which are sensitive to the difference between explicit moves and merely implied or tacitly understood ones.[1] The fact remains that a good many such rules and principles must be formulated so as to pay equal attention to explicit and merely understood moves.

A fourth complicating factor is the phenomenon which I would describe as the use of *subdialogues* to do the work of individual moves. For instance, when one invites one's interlocutor to guess at an answer to his question instead of giving a straightforward answer, one is making a guessing subdialogue do duty for a simple application of (D.answer).

These are some of the structural complications that any theory of conversational discourse has to come to grips with.[2]

2. PARAMETERS OF A MOVE

These considerations already indicate some of the parameters which describe a move in a dialogue game.

The first one that comes to mind is of course the *sentence*, or more generally, the expression the move actually consists of.

Next, the type of a move and its place in dialogue is indicated by specifying the *dialogue(s)* it belongs to, the *rule(s)* which justify it, and the moves which motivate it (its topical precedents or *premises*).

Third comes an important triple of indices, which might be called the signature of the move: it consists of a specification of the *author*, the *addressee(s)*, and the *audience* of a move. 'Author' is a noncommittal name for the speaker, utterer, writer, or whoever puts a sentence forward and is responsible for it. The author of a sentence is the referent of the first-person pronoun *I*. The addressees of a sentence are the referents of the second-person pronoun *you*: these are the players who are invited to answer a question, take stand to a claim, comply to a request, and so on. They are also the bearers of vocative noun phrases. The audience, finally, includes all those players who are within earshot of the move, to whom the dialogue move is accessible. I summarize the seven indices of a move in the following list (in the order I shall be indicating them).

(i)   The *author* of the move
(ii)   The *addressee(s)* of the move
(iii)   The *audience* of the move
(iv)   The *sentence* of the move
(v)   The *game rule(s)* which justify the move
(vi)   The *premises* of the move
(vii)   The *dialogue(s)* the move is in.

Instead of further formalization, I shall again use English as its own metalanguage and describe a typical dialogue move by an English sentence, say:

(3)   A says to B in the presence of C that S as an answer to S' in
         (i)   (ii)   (iii)   (iv)   (v)   (vi)

         the dialogue d.
              (vii)

There are a number of questions to ask about the possible combinations of the indices in the signature. Is the author always in his own audience? Can one address oneself? Can Nature put forward moves? What would that mean?

To answer these questions, I shall simply postulate certain constraints and principles of interpretation. First, I decree that *Nature can put forward moves* (she is an admissible author), but *she cannot address anyone else nor can she be addressed by other players*. There is a temptation to let players put questions to Nature, interpreting them as experiments, and interpreting the results of experiments as Nature's answers to the questions. However, I prefer to assume that Nature does not cooperate: one can find out what Nature's assumptions are, but she does not volunteer the answers, they have to be pried out of her. The investigator puts questions to himself and tries to answer them by forcing out Nature's secrets willy-nilly. The investigator does not ask Nature, but searches her as it were.

As a recompensation, *Nature is in the audience of every move*. "God sees and hears everything." *She can herself have other players in her audience.* Such moves by Nature will represent sundry *observations* accessible to other players: facts they see, hear, feel, or observe any other way. Observations may be privileged: Nature may reveal her secrets only to players that face a certain way, do the right experiments, or whatnot.

Remember that we have characterized Nature as the ideal player who is right about everything. Hence 'Nature says that' equals 'it is true that'. Any 'free-standing' truth about Nature can therefore be dressed as an admissible dialogue move by setting its author, addressee, and audience equal to Nature. Conversely, any player in Nature's audience is justified to accept what she says as a *bona fide* observation, for he is assured that it will be to his advantage (in accordance with dialogue maxims).

A player is in his own audience if and only if he is conscious of what he is putting forward. A player who makes an inadvertent slip is not in his own audience: he does not realize what he is actually saying. The same would hold of one who speaks in his sleep or deliriously. Naturally, the unmarked assumption is that one is in one's own audience, and accordingly, I shall not always be explicit about making that assumption. However, I shall not rule out the marked possibility in principle.

Self-addressed moves occur, too. It is not at all odd for a player to ask himself a question (that is called in English *wondering* about a question; the French is actually *se demander* 'ask oneself'), or to address oneself with a declarative clause. (There is a choice between pronouns *I* and *you* in these cases.)

(*Dialogically*) *silent* moves are moves whose audience is restricted to a minimum (oneself and Nature, if the move is conscious; else Nature alone.) It matters little whether the move is said aloud with nobody within earshot, or said silently to oneself: the main thing is one is alone in the audience.

3. INTERNAL DIALOGUES

Our approach to epistemic logic and the solution to the problem of logical omniscience is built on the idea that each person is himself responsible for his own epistemic alternatives. How a player's epistemic alternatives will look at each game situation is up to him.

This means that a player will be allowed, and supposed, to construct, modify, and delete his own epistemic alternatives to his best ability so as to conform with his preferences.

How will a player go about constructing and rejecting epistemic alternatives? An exceedingly simple and natural answer is already available to us: by using operations given to him by the dialogue game rules — by raising questions for himself by (D.ask) and (D.question), deriving further questions from them by (D.explain) and (D.infer), answering his own questions by (D.answer), reasoning further by (D.infer), (D.explain) and (D.argue) — in short, *by playing the dialogue games with himself.*

Now let us ask: what is a player doing when he is occupied with such private activities? My answer has been already anticipated by Plato in his middle dialogues: he is *thinking.* Working on one's assumptions and suppositions is very much like conducting an internal dialogue with oneself; asking questions of oneself, suggesting answers for them as hypotheses, following their consequences so as to explain them or refute them. Let me quote Plato's own words:

So. — . . . Do you accept my description of the process of thinking?
Th. — How do you describe it?
So. — As a discourse that the mind carries on with itself about any subject it is considering. You must take this description as coming from an ignoramus: but I have
a notion that, when the mind is thinking, it is simply talking to itself, asking
questions and answering them, and saying Yes or No. When it reaches a decision — which may come slowly or in a sudden rush — when doubt is over and
the two voices affirm the same thing, then we call that its 'judgment'. So I
should describe thinking as discourse, and judgment as a statement pronounced, not aloud to someone else, but silently to oneself.
                                        (Plato, *Theaetetus* 189e; cf. *Sophist* 263d.)

Let us stop and think what it would mean to take Plato dead seriously here. What it would imply is again reinterpreting our epistemic alternatives or epistemically possible worlds, this time construing them not as unordered sets of sentences, but as such sets structured as so many dialogues (or monologues), or perhaps as sets of small dialogues. Given this reconstruction, it would be immediately clear how such sets are to be extended given the rules of dialogue games.

So let us do that, why not! From now on, our epistemic alternatives are no more just sets of sentences, but structured sets of dialogue moves, each move annotated by the indices (i)–(vii) listed earlier. Exactly the same rules and principles which govern the well-formedness of explicit dialogues are now extended to apply in the internal dialogues.

This innovation requires a refinement of the principles of application of dialogue rules, in particular how internal dialogues influence the flow of actual dialogues. An actual dialogue, or a *dialogue sequence* (as distinguished from a complete dialogue game) is represented by a sequence of explicit dialogue moves in Nature's epistemic alternative, e.g.,

(4)   A asks B: Who are you?
         B answers A: I am Beth.
         A replies to B: So you are Beth.
         B replies to A: I am Beth.

Embedded in the dialogue game, each player has their internal representation of the game in progress, as well as their conjectures for their partners' conceptions of the dialogue. These internal representations of course are what guide the players' choices of strategy in the actual dialogue. Now the internal representations may typically go beyond what is actually said in the actual dialogue sequence: they may describe extensions of the dialogue which no one will ever put into so many words.

It naturally follows that players may address their actual dialogue moves to such merely virtual moves: they may answer questions just hanging in the air, or forestall criticisms which have not been spoken out. It is this further license which accounts for the often strikingly fragmentary character of everyday conversations.

4. PLAYING FOR OTHERS

Each epistemic alternative of a player is of course characterized in the first place by the sentences it includes. On the other hand, each epistemic alternative is a member of the model system constituting a game situation: hence it assumes some particular position in the field of the alternativeness relations for different players.

Assume for instance player A is considering an alternative where the following sentences are true:

(5)   B accepts that A won or B won.
(6)   B accepts that B did not win.

Is A justified to infer that

(7)   B accepts that A won?

In order to figure that out, A must put himself into B's shoes: try to second-guess what is going on in B's mind. In virtue of the truth-definition of acceptance, A infers that the sentences

(8)   A won or B won
(9)   B did not win

are included in the intersection of B's epistemic alternatives. Now if B is careful to follow through the consequences of his acceptations — i.e., goes through the trouble of trying to find a consistent explanation for his position — he will reject any alternative including (9) along with the right disjunct of (8). A can therefore conclude that the left disjunct of (8) will appear in every remaining epistemic alternative of B's, so the inference goes through.

But note one thing here. In drawing the epistemic inference, A must gauge very carefully B's intellectual powers: for the inference is justified *only if B actually draws it.* It is no good for A to see that (7) follows, if B does not see it. At best, A can then argue the conclusion for B, i.e., make him see the consequences of his acceptations. The only thing that A can infer for sure is that *if* B is rational, he will accept (7) if he accepts (5)–(6). And this is exactly the idealization that is involved in the rules and principles of epistemic logic.

The upshot of these considerations is that each player must not only keep order in his own epistemic alternatives, but he must watch all the alternatives for each player to his alternatives, trying to keep them in accordance with his estimates of his fellow players' mental processes. Ideally, this iterates arbitrarily far: a perfectly rational player would have to consider also what his fellow players would be willing to attribute to him and others, and so on. Of course, in practice, model systems can be expected to stay quite limited as far as such iteration of second-guessing is concerned: most real-life conversationalists spend precious little effort in trying to see things from their interlocutors' points of view.

5. DIALOGUE GAMES

The extreme conceptual complexity of a fully specified dialogue game may not have become clear from the necessarily piecemeal process of construction we have been involved in. We started out by describing abstractly an assumption list as the set of sentences accepted by a player at a certain stage of a game. This description was elaborated by allowing a player to entertain several possible alternative lists simultaneously, which lead to replacing the notion of an assumption list by the notion of epistemic alternative.

A result was the description of a momentary *game situation* as a model system, a set of epistemic alternatives ordered by an accessibility relation for each player.

Most recently, we imposed a further order of structure within each epistemic alternative, by reinterpreting these unordered assumption lists as so many collections of *dialogue sequences*, i.e., sequences of dialogue moves related to each other by dialogue game rules. This innovation induces a second order of structure among the moves of a dialogue game situation.

A *dialogue game* (in extensive form) is an object of yet a higher order of complexity, as it in turn consists of dialogue game situations ordered into a tree of possible plays.

The recursive structure of a fully specified dialogue game is easiest to illustrate by taking as a starting point the last move in some dialogue sequence in some designated epistemic alternative. This move may bear two sorts of relationships to other moves in the game: in terms of playtime, it follows the earlier moves in the same sequence; in terms of functional dependency, it may constitute a countermove or continuation move to one or several earlier moves in the same sequence or in its epistemic alternatives.

Looking back in the game tree from the alternative we started from, we find a decreasing sequence of initial segments of the dialogue sequence, representing earlier stages of the same actual dialogue, each embedded in a predecessor of the epistemic alternative we started from. This gives us the game history of the play we are considering. Looking down in the game tree, we can discern an indefinite number of possible continuations of the dialogue, spelling out what might happen at the next move.

Looking sideways, we see even more complexity. For each player in the game, we find a number of epistemic alternatives to the dialogue situation we started from, representing their individual views of the move at hand and its relations to earlier moves. Once we step over to one of these alternative

views, the whole story can be started again from the beginning, from a move
to its neighbors in the same alternative, from the alternative to its historical
predecessors and successors, and to its epistemic alternatives for each player.
Fortunately, thanks to the limitations of human imagination, epistemic
alternatives are likely to get progressively less elaborate as we move farther
away from Nature's own alternative, drying up completely rather quickly.

To get an idea of the structural complexity of even the simplest two-move
dialogue, consider the following simplified diagram:

(10)

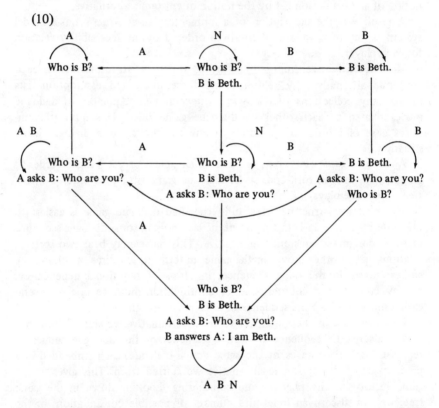

The middle column of the diagram describes three successive steps of the
actual dialogue in Nature's epistemic alternative. Nature knows all the way
the answer to A's question about B's identity (though she does not tell).
The left column describes A's view of the game at each stage of the game:
following the vertical arrows, we can figure out what A believes, remembers

or conjectures) about earlier and later stages as well. Analogously for B. As the diagram indicates, at the end of the exchange, the players have come to a common understanding: A, B, and Nature share just one epistemic alternative.

6. TURN-TAKING AND TOPIC HIERARCHY

Let us take a closer look at the turn-taking convention proposed by the ethnomethodologists (Sacks, et al., [215]). The convention has two essential subrules:

(i)   If the turn so far is so constructed as to involve the use of a 'current speaker selects next' technique, then the party so selected has the right and is obliged to take next turn to speak; no others have such rights or obligations, and transfer occurs at that place.

(ii)   If the turn so far is so constructed as not to involve the use of a 'current speaker selects next' technique, then self-selection for next speakership may, but need not, be instituted; first starter acquires rights to a turn, and transfer occurs at that place. (p. 704)

In simple-minded language, whoever speaks first speaks next, unless someone has been particularly given the floor by the previous speaker.

If I have understood correctly, the crucial technique for speaker selection intended in (i) is *addressing* someone by name or gesture; this technique works most effectively when the move addressed is a 'first pair-part' in an 'adjacency pair', e.g., a question, an invitation, or a greeting. The expected countermove, of course, will be the corresponding 'second pair-part', i.e., an answer, an acceptance, or return of a greeting.

These rules would seem to work as a first approximation. However, they miss an important systematic source of counterexamples because they ignore the deeper functional motivation of the sequence of moves in conversation. We have argued that an answer is a likely response to a question because, and just when, it is the best way to further the aims of a conversation. Accordingly, we may expect otherwise whenever there are more urgent matters to tend than answering the question asked. In particular, turns may be jumped quite naturally when the intervening move addresses a superordinate topic which constitutes a necessary condition for the preceding move. Consider the following examples:

(11)   A to B: Are you with him?
         C to A: What did you ask?
         A to C: I asked if he was with you.
(12)   A to B: Did you take my pen?
         C to A: I took it.
(13)   A to B: Do you want this?
         B to A: Do you want it?

In none of (11)–(13), does the player addressed by a question immediately answer it. In (11)–(12), another player makes the next move. Yet all of (11)–(13) are fully natural and fluent dialogues. (11) is a kind of counterexample that Sacks, et al., recognize under the name of 'repair question' (p. 709, 720). Note that C's question to A addresses a higher topic, viz, what was A's choice of topic.

This feature is shared by the second counterexample. A has lost his pen: the topic he is interested in is

(14)   Who took my pen?

Instead of asking (14) directly, A does some detective work. He sees that B is wielding a pen exactly like his, so the question arises if B has taken A's pen. C, who is watching the situation, can guess that the source of A's question in (12) is the more general question (14) and answers it directly. This satisfies A's interest, so the dialogue is satisfactory although B never got around to answering A's question. The structure of (12) is described in fuller detail in [3]

(15)   A to A: Who took my pen?

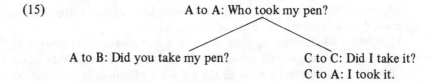

A to B: Did you take my pen?   C to C: Did I take it?
                                          C to A: I took it.

Example (13) is somewhat different. The situation is familiar: there is just one cocktail sandwich left, and two hungry but polite players. Their politeness consists in that each wants the bread if and only if the other does not. Neither can answer the question whether he wants it before the other has answered the analogous question. Here, the two topics are not hierarchically ordered but interdependent. The only solution to the vicious circle is for one of the players to yield either to temptation or to the other player. However, the fact remains that it is a rational strategy for B in (13) to reply by another question: hence the apparent violation of adjacency is actually no violation at all. The exceptions to turn-taking conventions, as well as the conforming instances, turn out to be consequences of more fundamental considerations of rational dialogue strategy.[4]

CHAPTER 6

LOGICAL GAME RULES

1. LOGICAL GAME RULES

The dialogue rules (D.infer) and (D.explain) can be used to spell out a sense in which the semantic games of verification of Hintikka's game theoretical semantics can be viewed as special cases of dialogue games. Looking away from its genuinely semantic aspects and concentrating on its syntax, a semantical game can be looked upon as a game of debate whose moves are restricted to applications of (D.infer) and (D.explain). Any move of the proponent of a sentence put forward in a semantical game replaces the original sentence by one which logically implies the original sentence: thus it is a special sort of an explanatory move. Any move by the opponent invites the proponent to defend a logical consequence of the original sentence: it thus involves a move by (D.infer) forced on the proponent by the opponent. The game rule of negation switches the players' roles as opponent and proponent.

What I propose to do is to put this idea to use in the following way. We shall turn a number of the rules of the semantical games into as many rules of dialogue games. They will essentially be natural language equivalents for the model set conditions that were discussed in Chapter 2. We then define inference and explanation in terms of these model set construction principles. Any complicated chains of reasoning will be ultimately reduced to iterated applications of the model set proof procedure and the inductive decision procedure described earlier. (As will be seen, the former can naturally be looked upon as a special case of the latter.)

The following are a list of such natural language natural deduction principles:

(C.and)   From a sentence of the form
$$X - Y \text{ and } Z - W$$
infer either of the sentences
$$X - Y - W$$
$$X - Z - W.$$

(C.or)   Explain a sentence of the form
$$X - Y \text{ or } Z - W$$

by either of the sentences
$$X - Y - W$$
$$X - Z - W.$$

(C.if)   Explain a sentence of the form
               X if Y
            by X or by the denial of Y.

(C.an)   Explain a sentence of the form
               $X - [a(n) \ Y \ \text{Comp} \ V - t - W] - Z$
            by a sentence of the form
               A be a(n) Y, $V - P - W$, and $Y - P - Z$.

'P' stands for a pronoun whose antecedent is A. (The cash value of this antecedency is the truth of the identity P be A.)

The game rule for *some* is an exact copy of (C.an). The following rule will do for the definite article.

(C.the)   Explain a sentence of form
               $X - $ the $Y - Z$
            by a sentence of form
               A be (a(n)) Y, any Y be A, and $X - P - Z$

Here (and elsewhere) I let the infinitive *be* do duty for whatever inflected form of the copula is appropriate in each context.

For *be*, we have the rule

(C.be)   Infer from sentences of the form
               A be B, $X - A - Y$
            the sentence
               $X - B - Y$.

The meaning of the locution *the same Y as B* is captured by rewriting it as *the Y that B be*.

Universal quantifiers obey the rule

(C.every)   Infer from a sentence of the form
               $X - $ every $Y - Z$
            any sentence of form
               if A be (a(n)) Y,
               $X - P - Z$

The game rules for *any* and *each* will be copies of (C.every).

(C.no)   Infer from a sentence of the form
$$X - \text{no } Y - W$$
the denial of any sentence of the form
$$A \text{ be } (a(n)) \ Y \text{ and } X - P - W$$

(These rules are just special cases of more general and detailed rules that no one has seen so far. But they once more suffice to illustrate a principle.)

It remains to give a game rule for negation. The effect of a negation is to reverse the direction of explanation and inference in the following sense:

(C.neg)   Infer from the denial of a sentence X
the denial of any explanation for X.

The concepts 'inference' and 'explanation' are interchangeable in the rule (C.neg) in virtue of their reciprocity:

(1)   A sentence X is an explanation for a sentence Y
if and only if Y is a consequence of X.

That is, it follows from (C.neg) and (1) that the denial of a sentence can be explained by the denial of any one of its consequences.

The above rules make reference to the *denial* of a sentence. By that should be understood the most immediate expression of the contradictory of a sentence. For a positive singular sentence with no quantifier words, the negation transformation of Chomsky (1957) will work. Conversely, if the uppermost semantical operator in a sentence is *not*, the denial is obtained by simply leaving *not* out. I shall not try to define 'denial' more closely. In case of doubt, the cop-out prefix 'it is not the case that' will do.

Note that there is nothing in the above rules that prevent them from applying to questions so as to produce further questions from them. In fact, it will be assumed all through that all of the above rules apply to questions equally well as they do to declarative sentences.

In applying the rules of inference and explanation, one has to be careful to apply them in the right order, as specified by a set of ordering principles familiar from the semantical games of verification. The following are rough versions of the general constraints that guide the order of application of the rules:

(C.comm)   A rule which applies in a main clause has precedence over a rule which applies in a subordinate clause.
(O.LR)   A rule which applies to an earlier phrase has precedence over a rule which applies to a later phrase.

Particular, lexically governed ordering principles specify exceptions to these general ordering principles in terms of individual game rules. For instance, (C.some) goes before negation against (O.LR) while (C.every) yields to it; (C.any) goes before (C.if) in violation of (O.comm).

Specific constructions may import further exceptions. One is Hintikka's ([130]:127) finding that unmoved question phrases take precedence over the preposed interrogative pronoun in multiple search questions. Thus the likely direct answers to (2)–(3) are different:

(2)   Where did Mary buy what?
(3)   What did Mary buy where?

In each case, the answer is likely to start by specifying values for the unmoved question word first: (2) goes with (4) and (3) with (5).

(4)   The hat, Mary bought at Filene's, and the gloves, at Bonwit Teller's.
(5)   At Filene's, Mary bought the hat, and at Bonwit Teller's, the gloves.

The mechanism of these answer preferences will be discussed in Part II (Ch. 3.6).

To do justice to quantified modal logic, care must be taken in choosing the substituends 'A' and 'B' in the quantifier rules and in the rule (C.be). For one thing, 'A' and 'B' are meant to act as singular terms (proper names, definite descriptions) with respect to the criteria of identity assumed in the quantifier phrases they replace. This does not always imply that they need be syntactically definite; for instance, quantification may be over kinds of things rather than individual objects:

(6)   There is something I hate, and that is a wise guy.

Here the indefinite (or generic) phrase 'a wise guy' serves to instantiate the quantifier 'something' in an intensional context: the quantification is over kinds of things, and *a wise guy* does make definite reference to a particular kind of person.

Secondly, a quantifier phrase which quantifies into an intensional context must be replaced by a term which designates one and the same individual throughout that context. In English, personal pronouns may be the best approximation for such 'logically proper names', so we use them for free bindable variables.

Third, we want to restrict (C.be) to apply only in extensional contexts, in analogy with the rule (C.=) of Appendix II.

2. LOGICAL GAME RULES FOR QUESTIONS

We shall now try to encapsulate some of Hintikka's insights into the semantics and pragmatics of questions in the form of logical rules of dialogue games. We do this by devising another set of rules of explanation and inference, dissecting complicated questions into simpler ones until a trivial characterization of answerhood is applicable.

The majority of writers on questions assume that simple questions like

(7)   Did A win?

are not semantically that simple: semantically, they have the underlying form of a disjunctive yes-no question. Thus (7) is actually short for

(8)   Did A win or (did A) not (win)?

I will take a slightly different approach. In my analysis, *positive* simple questions like (7) are actually semantically ambivalent. As Hintikka and others observe, (7) does do duty as an abbreviation of (8). However, it also has a meaning on its own right, as a semantically *elementary question*. Simple negative questions like

(9)   Did A not win?

will always be elementary questions in my approach.

What makes an elementary question elementary is its semantic simplicity: an elementary question requires no further anlaysis to be answered appropriately.[1]

For semantically elementary questions, an exceedingly simple rule of answering suffices:

(C.answer) Answer an elementary question by its declarative form.

The declarative form of a simple question is, of course, the transformational source of that question, or its inverse transform under the rule of subject-auxiliary inversion. Thus the elementary question (7) has as its only direct answer(s) the corresponding declarative sentence(s)

(10)   A won (A did win),

and the negative elementary question (9) is only answered by

(11)   A did not win.

The idea of an elementary question may seem at first self-defeating: who would need to ask a question which has but one answer. I shall argue later that we all often do. Even that aside, the concept is far from useless: with the help of rules (C.or) and (C.answer), it yields just the intuitively correct explication of answerhood to sentential questions. For according to (C.or), the inquiry (8) must be explained by either of the elementary questions (7), (9), which in turn are answered by one of (10)–(11). By inference, to answer (8), one must put forward either one of the answers (10), (11).

More generally, a question of the form

(12) $X - Y_1$ or Y_2 or ... or $Y_n - Z$

is explained by any of the elementary questions

(13) $X - Y_i - Z$

and hence is answered by answering any one of them.

One may observe that the semantic ambiguity of (7) can lead to an infinite regress, if (7) is repeatedly expanded to (8) and reduced back to (7) by (C.or). There is, actually, a precedent in sentences of the form

(14)   A is a man.

Sentences like (14) are also ambiguous. On the other hand, they represent semantically elementary predicate attributions (meaning, roughly, that A is a member of mankind); but they also double as existential identity sentences, as is predicted by the fact that (C.an) is applicable in them to produce something like

(15)   A is B, and B is a man.

To stop a regress, the second conjunct of (15) had better be understood as an elementary attributive sentence.

In the same vein, whenever a simple question emerges as the outcome of (C.or) from a disjunctive question, it is best construed as an elementary question requiring no further semantic analysis.

3. GAME RULES FOR SEARCH QUESTIONS

To capture the meaning of simple and multiple search questions, two further dialogue rules of explanation and inference will be proposed. First, a rule for explicating existentially understood questions.

(C.wh-e)   Explain a search question of the form
$$X - [V - \text{wh-word } W] - Y - t - Z$$
where t marks the source of the bracketed question phrase, by any sentence
   (i) $i(X - Y - V - A - Z)$,
   (ii)   be A (a(n)) W, and
   (iii)   wh-phrase be $T - A - U$
where 'A' is a dialogue definite phrase of the same category as 'wh-word W' and (ii) is omitted if W is empty.

A number of auxiliary syntactic concepts in (C.wh-e) need explanation. (C.wh-e) is formulated so as to apply to preposed wh-phrases as well as to unmoved ones. In the former case, X is empty, in the latter, Y. We call 'A' the substituend of 'wh-word W'.

$i(S)$ is the *interrogative form* of the sentence S, defined to be the sentence itself if it is a direct question, and the result of applying appropriate question transformations to produce a direct question if it is not (i.e., wh-movement and subject-auxiliary inversion).

Let us look at the motivation of the clauses (i)–(iii) one by one. (i)–(ii) represent the actual explication of the original question: the questioner considers the original question satisfactorily answered if he obtains an answer to (i)–(ii) provided he also has an answer to (iii). (iii) expresses the conclusiveness condition, i.e., the condition that the questioner knows the substituend in the sense of the identity criteria of his original question. The conclusiveness clause (iii) is formulated quite loosely so as to allow a player to spell out the identity criteria of his question more explicitly in the process of applying (C. wh-e). For instance, in a sports context, the question

(16)   Who won?

can be explicated by (C.wh-e) as

(17)   Did Vainio win, and what is the name and nationality of Vainio?

In the simplest case, 'wh-phrase' in (iii) equals 'wh-word W' and T, U are null: then (iii) yields an unadorned identity question, in the above example, the question

(18)   Who is Vainio?

Assuming the simplest explication of the conclusiveness condition, (C.wh-e) produces from the examples

(19)   Who won?
(20)   Who did A play with? With who did A play?
(21)   What did A win?
(22)   Where did A play?
(23)   What game did A play?
(24)   Which one of A and B won?
(25)   Who played who?
(26)   Who played who in what game?

the respective explications

(27)   Did A win, and who is A?
(28)   Did A play with B, and who is B?
(29)   Did A win a medal, and what is a medal?
(30)   Did A play inside, and where is inside?
(31)   Did A play tennis, is tennis a game, and what game is tennis?
(32)   Did A win, is A one of A and B, and which one of A and B is A?
(33)   Who played B and who is B?
(34)   Who played who in tennis, is tennis a game, and what game is tennis?

The universal interpretation of search questions is captured by a companion rule of inference to (C.wh-e):

(C.wh-u)   Infer from a search question of the form
$$X - [V - \text{wh-word } W] - Y - t - Z$$
any sentence
$$i(X - Y - V - A - Z) \text{ and wh-phrase be } T - A - U,$$
if A be (a(n)) W and $p(X - Y - V - A - Z)$
subject to the same constraints as in (C.wh-e).

One new syntactic definition is needed: the *presupposition* $p(S)$ of a question S is defined as follows.[2]

(35)   The presupposition of a choice question is the declarative form of the question.

The (existential) presupposition of a search question is the
result of replacing every (direct) interrogative pronoun in it by
a corresponding indefinite (existential) pronoun.

The definition of presupposition leads to ambiguous results in syntactically
simple sentential questions depending on whether the definition is applied
before or after the question is first completed to a disjunctive form. This
ambiguity will be put to use later in explaining the functional differences of
positive and negative simple questions.

For example, (C.wh-u) generates the following sequence of inferences
from (36):

(36)   Who played who in what game?
(37)   Who played who in tennis, and what game is tennis, if tennis
        is a game and someone played someone in tennis?
(38)   Who played B in tennis, and who is B, if someone played B in
        tennis?
(39)   Did A play B in tennis, and who is A, if A played B in tennis?

4. *WHICH*-QUESTIONS

To do justice to the peculiarities of *which*, the following addition to (C.wh-e)
is indicated.

(C.which)   (An appendix to (C.wh-e):) If the wh-word mentioned in the
            rule is *which*, infer from (i)—(iii) any sentence of form
            (iv) Be B A if B is (a(n)) W and $p(X - Y - V - B - Z)$.

Let us see if this addition suffices to capture the salient facts about *which*.
The first one that meets the eye is that simple *which* questions imply uniqueness of answer: it would be quite unexpected to get (41) as an answer to
(40).

(40)   Which player won?
(41)   A won and B won and C won.

This expectation of uniqueness is independent of grammatical number. If
several teams of players are competing,

(42)   Which players played well together?

may equally expect that just one team did; it would be odd to have an answer like

(43)   The Germans did and the Dutch did and the Italians did.

This assumption of uniqueness is spelled out in so many words in (C.which). The questioner of a *which* question cannot be satisfied with an answer to his question before he has made sure that any alternative answer is either unacceptable or identical with the answer first offered. Thus (C.which) forces the questioner of (40) to raise the further questions (44)–(45) on hearing (41):

(44)   Is A B if B won and B is a player?
(45)   Is A C if C won and C is a player?

A negative answer to these identity questions would constitute a violation of the speaker's presuppositions given that A is an acceptable answer to (40).

(C.which) predicts among other things that *which* questions cannot be asking for examples: (46) and (47) do not share this interpretation.

(46)   What would you like to drink, whisky, or gin, or vodka?
(47)   Which would you like to drink, whisky, or gin, or vodka?

(47), unlike (46), expects a unique choice of poison among those offered.

A second characteristic of *which* we observed earlier is its context-dependence. I am not referring to the fact that a free-standing *which* such as in (47) always harks back to some head noun explicit or implicit in the context; this fact can be captured syntactically by stipulating that *which* is a determiner whose head may be omitted when it is obvious from context. What is more intriguing is the fact that even when a head noun is supplied, a *which* question makes no definite sense until its field of search, or the domain of discourse it ranges over, is made clear. Thus, e.g., (49), if asked just out of the blue, is quite puzzling:

(49)   Which color is the sky?

(49) makes sense only if some well-defined spectrum of choices is supplied from the context, e.g., a list of samples.

As we observed earlier, a similar context dependence characterizes the definite article:

(50)   Close the window!

makes definite sense only if a unique choice of window is obvious from the context – including the sentence introducing the article. Thus in (50) the window meant can be the only window in sight that is open, as it is the only choice that makes the command rational.

In each case, I submit, this context dependency is a simple matter of logic. All quantification is sensitive to the choice of universe, but unique quantification is exceptionally so. While existential quantification is preserved uner extensions of the model and universal quantification under submodels, uniquely quantified sentences satisfy no simple preservation theorem.[3] In order to make sense of a unique quantification, one has to carefully define the field of search. Thus in order for (49) to have a definite answer, the spectrum of colors has to be narrowed down so that there is only one way to describe the sky in terms of it. *What*, in contrast, might admit any number of correct answers.

Having disposed of the two main peculiarities of simple occurrences of *which*, let us proceed to multiple *which* sentences. To begin with, note that we have no modifications to (C.wh-u) in respect of *which*. Consequently, we can expect multiple *which* questions to be open to a quite straightforward universal interpretation. This expectation seems fulfilled in examples like

(51)   The timetable tells which local train has a connection with which express train.

It seems clear to me that (51) need make no assumptions about the uniqueness of connections. For instances, (51) is perfectly in order even if

(52)   Every local train has a connection with every express train.

Karttunen ([243], p. 22) agrees, with an interesting reservation. Commenting on his example

(53)   Which boy likes which girl?

Karttunen says, "if there is any uniqueness implicature at all, it perhaps has to do with each girl being paired with at most one boy, and vice versa, but I am not sure about this." Hirschbühler [241] seems inclined to agree with Karttunen's intuitions.[4]

It is therefore interesting to observe that precisely the intuitions reported by Karttunen are predicted if one of the two *which* phrases in (53) is first handled by (C.wh-u) and the remaining one by (C.wh-e) as modified by (C.which).

A couple of minor points remain. First, Karttunen's [243] treatment of the uniqueness implicature of *which* predicts that (53) expects one and only one pair of boy and girl in a liking relationship. Our treatment does not have this effect. Even if both occurrences of *which* in (53) are played off using (C.wh-e) and (C.which), there remain differences in the uniqueness implications depending on the manner of application of the rules. If the rules apply linearly, the uniqueness entailments are accordingly asymmetric. If they apply left to right, (53) implies

(54)   Only one boy is someone who likes only one girl

any if they apply right to left, we obtain

(55)   Only one girl is someone who is liked by only one boy.

However, these readings seem inferior to a "third reading" to (53) which does allow one and only one pair in a liking relationship. Now a similar third reading is available to

(56)   Only one boy likes only one girl.

as well. In another paper, I suggest that such "third readings" arise from parallel (simultaneous) applications of game rules to several quantifier phrases.[5] I shall bypass this complication in the present context.

Second, nothing in our rules eliminates the possibility of universally quantified occurrences of simple *which* questions. They are certainly pretty hard to find, but I think that they do exist. Thus I find it admissible to paraphrase (57) by the conjunction of simple *which* questions in (58):

(57)   Some of the babies here are boys and some are girls. Doctor
         Spock here can tell you which baby is which.
(58)   Some of the babies here are boys and some are girls. Doctor
         Spock here can tell you which baby is a boy and which baby is
         a girl.

5. CONCLUSIVENESS

A quick inspection shows that the rule (C.wh-e) is recursively applicable to its own output. As the clause (iii) in it indicates, a search question is not conclusively answered until a question about the identity of the fresh substituend is conclusively answered.

In order to stop a regress, we have to assume some independent characterization for conclusive answerhood to identity questions of the sort (iii). I cannot do better than restate the informal characterization of Chapter 3.4: an identity question of the form (59):

(59)   (Wh-word X) be A t?

is *self-answering*, i.e., conclusively answered by

(60)   A be A

in a given set of epistemic alternatives, if the "world line" associated with 'A', i.e., the function that picks out from each of the given set of alternatives the description of A in that alternative, describes a *bona fide* individual in the sense of the identity criteria associated with the question phrase in (59).[6]

A minimum requirement for the above informal condition to hold has already been mentioned: two well-defined individuals should not get confused with each other. For instance, if the police know who committed one murder and they know who committed another one, they ought to know whether both murders were committed by the same individual or not. If they cannot answer that question, it seems dubious that they really know who the culprit is in each case.

This requirement of well-definedness is easy enough to spell out as a further game rule of inference.

(C.wh-id)   Infer from the questions
                  (wh-word X) be A t?
                  (wh-word X) be B t?
              where both questions have the same criteria of identity associated
              to them, the question
                  Be A the same X as B or not?
              with the same criteria of identity associated to *the same X*.[7]

Let us take an example. In a prize quiz, a contestant is asked the following two questions.

(61)   Who is the author of the book *The Sex Life of the Savages*?
(62)   Who won gold in steeplechase in the Moscow Olympics 1980?

The contestant gives both questions the same answer:

(63)   Bronislaw Malinowski.

Surprisingly, the answer is correct each time. However, the quiz master wants to test whether the contestant actually knows who he is talking about: he asks the further question

(64)   Is the author of the book the *same* Bronislaw Malinowski as the gold medalist?

The contestant does not know that; indignantly, he argues that he is not supposed to know who Bronislaw Malinowski is. All he is asked is to supply the name of the person in each case, i.e., the conclusiveness clause of the quiz is obtained by replacing "who" by "what is the name of the person who" in each question. And the *name* Bronislaw Malinowski is Bronislaw Malinowski, whoever the man be in each case. Although he does not know conclusively who the person is in each case, he knows the name full well: he can even spell it right.

The rule (C.wh-id) is a useful test for solutions of detective story whodunits. For instance, in the adventures entitled *A Case of Identity* and *The Man with a Twisted Lip*, Sherlock Holmes cracks the case by testing out such identity hypotheses. In the former, the mysterious Hosmer Angel is actually no one else than the greedy father-in-law Mr. Windibank; in the latter, the suspect Boone character — the man with the twisted lip — turns out to be the missing Mr. St. Clair cleverly disguised.

CHAPTER 7

LOGIC OF DIALOGUE

1. CONSISTENCY

In this chapter, I want to show how players can use the dialogue rules to keep order within their epistemic alternatives. Let us first consider how one may check for the consistency of one's assumptions. Let the topic of interest be the question

(1)   Who won?

about which the subject already holds the assumptions

(2)   A is a player, B is a player, A is not B, and A won.

Then someone comes and suggests to him

(3)   B is the player who won.

The player wants to see if he can accept (3) along with his other assumptions. In order to know, he has to explain what (3) actually means. Applying (C.the), he tries the explanation

(4)   A is a player who won, any player who won is A and B is A.

But a simple application of (C.and) forces him to infer 'B is A', contradicting his earlier assumptions. So that explanation will not work. The only alternative explanation is

(5)   B is a player who won, any player who won is B, and B is B.

This time there is a problem with the second conjunct, for (C.any) allows the inference

(6)   If A is a player who won, A is B.

(6) in turn must be explained by (7) or the denial of (8).

(7)   A is B
(8)   A is a player who won.

(7) contradicts (2). Denying (8) in turn would imply denying all of its instances, including

(9)   A is A and A is a player and A won.

derived from (8) by (C.an). The denial of (9) again must be explained by one of

(10)   A is not A
(11)   A is not a player
(12)   A did not win.

(10) is a self-contradiction, and (11)–(12) contradict (2). Finding no way of making consistent sense of (2)–(3) together, the player cannot add (3) to his assumptions if he wants to keep (2). If he accepts (2), he has to reject (3) and vice versa.

Let us make the intuitive procedure followed in the example more precise. It is a simple modification of the model set disproof procedure discussed earlier. First, we need to spell out the elementary conditions of non-contradiction which were appealed to in the example. These principles can be registered as two further analogues of model set conditions:

(C.cons)   Do not admit a sentence together with its direct denial.
(C.self)   Do not admit any sentence of form *A be not A*.

(C.cons) of course does not forbid admitting contradictories into separate alternatives: it just rules out self-contradictory alternatives.

What gave the player the right to reject an extension of (1)–(2) by (3) was the fact that there was no way of explaining that list of assumptions without violating (C.cons) or (C.self). To make this more precise, we have to spell out what we mean by a *complete explanation* of a list of assumptions (the dialogue game analogue of a model set). Intuitively, it is clear that a player cannot trust a list of assumptions before he has explained everything that is in need of explanation in it. On the other hand, to be satisfied about the consistency of an explanation the player needs to consider all of its consequences.

Let us call a sentence that can be explained by some explanatory game rule *directly explainable*. Similarly, a sentence is *directly inferrable* from a given set of assumptions if it is the result of an application of a rule of inference to lexical material already present in the list of assumptions. (Both sentences and noun phrases mentioned in the structural description of the rule must be found among assumptions already in the list.) Using the auxiliary notions, we may write the definition

(13)   A list of assumptions is *completely explained* if
        (i) every directly explainable sentence in it has an explanation in it
        (ii) every sentence directly inferrable from it is included in it.

Then, in virtue of Hintikka's results, we may state

(14)   A list of assumptions is consistent if it can be completely explained without violating (C.cons) and (C.self).

(14) presents the players with a method (not always effective, but often so) which helps them conform to the maxim of consistency. Although the players may not be able to recognize consistency on the face of an assumption list, they can test for it by recursive application of the dialogue game rules. This lets the players themselves take care of the consistency of their assumptions: A player who is negligent with his logical game rules may conform to the principles (C.cons) and (C.self) on the surface of his epistemic alternatives but still entertain hidden inconsistencies.

2. INDIRECT INFERENCE

The above described method of eliminating inconsistent epistemic alternatives can be turned into an indirect method of establishing arbitrarily complicated conclusions. What the player has to do is to generate a family of exhaustive and exclusive epistemic alternatives and eliminate any inconsistent ones among them. The remaining alternatives represent a gain in information obtained by purely deductive means.

To have an example, let us turn the argument from the previous section into a deductive inference. The player accepts the sentence

(15)   A won, A is a player, and B is not A.

The other player's suggestion

(16)   B is the player who won

naturally raises the question whether it is true, i.e., the question

(17)   Is B the player who won or not?

There are two exhaustive and exclusive alternative answers, (16) and (18):

(18)   B is not the player who won.

The player forms two epistemic alternatives, one including (15) and (16), the other (15) and (18). Following the steps described in the previous section, he finds out that the former alternative is inconsistent, so in virtue of the maxim of consistency, it has to be rejected. As a result, (18) is now true in one and all of the player's remaining epistemic alternatives, so he has ended up accepting (18).

3. INDUCTIVE DECISION

But the player could have reacted to the interlocutor's suggestion in a different way. Instead of questioning it using his own answer as evidence to resolve the question, he might have asked a less biased question:

(19)   Did A or B win?

Again, the question has two exhaustive and exclusive alternative answers, the player's own

(20)   A won

and the interlocutor's suggestion

(21)   B won.

Since the present problem setting (19) puts (20) into question, it is only fair that it is not treated as evidence. The player ends up with the following two epistemic alternatives this time:

(22)   A won, B did not win, A is a player, B is a player, and A is not B.
(23)   B won, A did not win, A is a player, B is a player, and A is not B.

Both alternatives are internally consistent, so nothing is gained by purely deductive methods. But there is indirect evidence for each alternative, namely the fact that the player himself accepts (22) while his interlocutor accepts (23). If the player has enough confidence in his own knowledge, or if he values his interlocutor's opinion highly enough, he may be able to exclude one of (22)–(23) by an inductive procedure of the sort described in Chapter 2. If he rejects one of the exclusive alternatives, he ends up accepting the other. The procedure of inductive decision making followed here is closely similar to the above deductive decision method. In fact, the deductive method can be viewed as a special case of the inductive one, as the epistemic utility of an inconsistent alternative is always smaller than that of a consistent one. The most striking difference, therefore, between the two approaches to opinion formation just described, is not in the certainty of the inference (whether deductive or inductive), but in the treatment of earlier acceptations. In the deductive example, the player treated his accepted beliefs as *evidence* (or *premises*) against which he tested his interlocutor's conflicting claim. In the present case, the player reconsidered any of his own conflicting claims together with the new suggestion against whatever independent evidence he had at his disposal.

4. ANSWERHOOD

So far, we have only defined answerhood for an artificially simple class of questions (the so-called elementary questions). But a hint was already given as to how the definition of answerhood is to be extended to more complicated questions.

The extension will employ an analogue to the notion of complete explanation introduced above. We shall call an assumption list *completely answered* if it is completely explained and closed under (C.answer), or more explicitly,

(24)   A list of assumptions is *completely answered* if it is completely explained and every elementary question in it has an answer in it.

This is not yet a definition for the notion of a complete answer to a given individual question. As we observed earlier, the concept of a complete answer cannot be defined in the abstract, without reference to the context of asking a question, but it is a function of what the questioner already accepts. Roughly, anything counts as a complete answer to question whose acceptance implies the satisfaction of the question, i.e., the truth of its desideratum. Thus the notion of complete answerhood involves some notion of consequence among questions and their answers: acceptance of a complete answer should imply satisfaction of the question.

We approach the problem of defining the appropriate relation of entailment again indirectly, by the way of the dual concept of inconsistency of rejecting a question while accepting an answer to it. To do so, we first have to clarify what we mean by acceptance and rejection of questions.

Our earlier definition of acceptance is not specific as to the mood of an accepted sentence: according to it, a player accepts a question if that question belongs to the intersection of his epistemic alternatives. Now I want to explain what the acceptance – or rejection – of a question *means*.

The idea is simple enough, given all that has been said of questions and the aims of the players. To accept a question is to prefer for its desideratum to become true: a player who accepts a question wants to find an answer to it. That is what acceptance of a question should intuitively mean, and that is what it will be understood to mean in this essay.

Conversely, then, rejecting a question should mean being indifferent or averse to looking for an answer to the question. A question may be rejected for different reasons. It may be that the question has no answer because its presupposition is not true; clearly, a player is justified to reject a question if he rejects its presupposition. A question may be rejected for other reasons too, which are outside the scope of the very rationalistic considerations of this essay. A player may consider a question intrusive, out of place, or just uninteresting, all according to some ulterior motives or preferences he holds. However, our task is not to devise rational rules of choosing topics of discussion, but just to look at rules for rational conduct in a discussion given some choices of topic. Therefore, we shall assume that the players are free to choose topics for discussion as long as their choices are consistent.

To spell out what it means to ask questions consistently, we need to be able to represent the *rejection* of a question in our syntactic terms. An appropriate representation is not difficult to find when one follows closely the analogy of declarative sentences. A player rejects a declarative sentence if he accepts its denial. What we have to look for is an erotetic analogue for the denial of a declarative sentence. Now the way to reject, e.g.,

(25)   Someone won

is not accepting its syntactic negation

(26)   Someone did not win

but (for instance)

(27)   It is not true that someone won.

Analogously, to reject

(28)   Who won?

one does not ask

(29)   Who did not win?

but says something to the effect of

(30)   It is not interesting (important) who won.

Or, to choose a simpler phrase:

(31)   Never mind who won.

Now it is intuitively right to call a player inconsistent if he accepts (31) and yet accepts (is willing to ask) (28), just as it would be inconsistent to accept (27) alongside (25). Accordingly, we shall define the *denial* of a question as follows:

(32)   The (or a) denial of a direct question is the result of prefixing *never mind* to the corresponding indirect question.

To form the corresponding indirect question out of a direct question, it suffices to take its declarative form (inverse transform under subject-auxiliary inversion) and, if the question is sentential, to prefix it by *if* or *whether*. For example, the denials of (33)–(35) are (36)–(38), respectively:

(33)   Did A win?
(34)   Who won?
(35)   Who played who?

(36)   Never mind if A won.
(37)   Never mind who won.
(38)   Never mind who played who.

In order to extend our model set methods of inference to entailment among questions and answers, it suffices to add a simple condition of consistency for a player's interests and his information. As we argued earlier, to be disinterested in a question means being indifferent to its answers: it would be inconsistent for a player to deny an interest in a question he prefers to hold an answer to. This intuition is spelled out in the following principle of consistency:

(C.consq) Do not accept an answer to a question you deny.

For instance, someone may quite well accept

(39)   The number of planets is even or odd

and yet deny any interest in which is the case, i.e., he may also accept

(40)   Never mind whether the number of planets is even or odd.

What he cannot accept, still holding on to (40), is either of

(41)   The number of planets is even
(42)   The number of planets is odd

though of course he may admit both as conceivable alternatives. What he cannot do is adopt either into the intersection of his epistemic alternatives.

The notion of a completely answered list of assumptions and the rule (C.consq) allow us to characterize the notion of *complete answer* to a given question relative to some assumed set of background knowledge. For instance, why is it that

(43)   B lost

counts as a complete answer to the question

(44)   Did B win or not?

A necessary piece of background information is the zero-sum assumption that

(45)   If B lost, B did not win.

If a player accepts (45) and adopts (43), he cannot feign a lack of interest in (44), i.e., (43), (45) are inconsistent with the denial of (44) in the sense of (C.consq). For from the denial of (44)

(46)   Never mind whether B won or not.

one can infer

(47)   Never mind if B did not win;

but on the other hand, given (43), the only consistent explanation of (45) is

(48)   B did not win

and accepting (47) and (48) together would violate (C.consq).

On the other hand, given the very same background assumptions,

(49)   B did not lose

does not constitute a complete answer to (44). For (49) leaves open the possibility of a draw: B did not lose nor win. (49) is a complete answer only if the converse or (45) is true, viz.

(50)   If B did not lose, he won.

To take a more complicated example, why is

(51)   Who played who?

completely answered by

(52)   Everyone played everyone

assuming that the identity question

(53)   Who is everyone?

is already completely answered? Now (54), as the denial of (53) understood as a universal (exhaustive list) question

(54)   Never mind who played who

must be ultimately explained by some sentence of form

(55)   Never mind if A played B.

On the other hand, whatever the choices of A and B, (52) together with (55) implies

(56)   A played B

— a contradiction of (C.consq). On the other hand,

(57)   Everyone played someone

is not a complete answer to (51) given the same background assumptions, for independent explanations may exist for (54) and (57), say (55) for (54) and

(58)   everyone played C.

for (57).

The insight that emerges from these examples can be summarized in the following definition of a complete answer to a direct question:

(59)   Sentence S constitutes a complete answer to question Q (relative to a list of assumptions A) if S entails Q (given A).

5. IMPLIED QUESTIONS

The present method of indirect inference is equally applicable to inferring questions from other questions. Perhaps it is good first to explain what should be meant by a question being a logical consequence of another one. According to Hintikka's explication, a question is the expression of a request for an addressee to make the desideratum of the question true. The desideratum of the question is a declarative sentence which entails other declarative sentences. Among its entailments may be in particular desiderata for certain further questions. No it is a reasonable assumption that an ideally rational player's preferences are consistent (satisfiable and closed under logical consequence), so that a player who prefers (perhaps, under some conditions) for a sentence to be true also prefers for its entailments to be true on the same conditions — i.e., a rational agent should consider all the consequences of his actions when he weighs their value to him. Therefore a player who prefers for some desideratum to be brought about should prefer that any entailed desiderata be brought about as well. Such implied requests can then be expressed as further direct questions.

Let us look at an example of an inference of a question from another question. Imagine the famous private detective Sherlock Holmes is investigating a murder, i.e., trying to solve a particular question

(60)   Who is the murderer?

Applying his usual methods, Holmes is able to deduce that

(61)   The murderer wears square-toed boots.

Naturally enough, the next question he poses, to the surprise of everyone present, is

(62)   Who wears square-toed boots?

To see how (62) follows from (60) and the partial answer (61), we try to deny (62) while accepting (60)–(61). (60) is first explained in virtue of (C.wh-e) by some pair of sentences

(63)   Is the murdered N.N.?
(64)   Who is N.N.?

(63) can only be answered by

(64)′   The murderer is N.N.

From (64)′ and (61) it follows in virtue of (C.be) that

(65)   N.N. wears square-toed boots.

On the other hand, (62) cannot be denied without denying one of

(66)   Does N.N. wear square-toed boots?
(67)   Who is N.N.?

Either way, a violation of (C.consq) is countenanced, for we already have accepted (65) and (64)'.

6. DIALOGICAL ENTAILMENT

The function of a sentence as a move in a dialogue permits certain inferences from it which would not be valid were the sentence considered by itself out of context. Actually, it would be more correct to say that it is not the sentence itself that permits such *dialogical inference*, but the fact that the sentence functions as a move in a dialogue. However, it is a convenient – and, if the basis of the inference is kept clear, innocuous – simplification to speak of the sentence as dialogically implying certain other sentences.

What makes an inference a dialogical inference? The answer is: an inference is essentially dialogical if its reconstruction as a logically binding inference essentially involves describing a dialogue game: if some of the steps of the argument involve application of dialogue game rules, or if the argument is binding only in the condition that players in a dialogue game are following their optimal strategies.

One particular type of dialogue entailment is exemplified by the feel of self-contradiction in the Moore type sentences like

(68)   The cat is on the mat but I don't believe it.[1]

In dialogue terms, the contradictoriness of (68) has a most straightforward explanation. (68) is put forward by the referent of 'I' as a dialogue move. His audience is then justified to assume that the author of the move is obeying a meaning convention, say (D.earnest).

(D.earnest), applied to (68), permits the inference that

(69)   I believe that (the cat is on the mat but I don't believe it).

where 'I' still refers to the author of (68). (69), in virtue of the logic of belief, given a minimum of logical acumen to 'me', entails

(70)   I believe that the cat is on the mat.

(68), on the other hand, already implies the contradictory of (70),

(71)   I don't believe it.

Hence an attempt to construe (68) as a serious move in a dialogue game leads to attributing to its author of a pair of contradictory sentences.

That it is not what the sentence (68) says, but its use in dialogue that leads to contradiction, is seen from the fact that the feeling of contradictoriness disappears when the sentence is turned into third person:

(72)   The cat is on the mat but he does not believe it.

An application to (D.earnest) to (72) would only assign incompatible beliefs to two different subjects, the author of (72) and whoever is referred to by 'he'. Therefore (72) need not describe a confused mind, but just a disagreement between two minds.

7. CONVERSATIONAL IMPLICATURE

In our framework, the so-called *conversational implications* of Grice [10] come out as dialogue entailments. These are inferences that are valid only in the context of a dialogue with suitable background assumptions about the participants' aims and epistemic attitudes, together with the crucial assumption that the players play the game rationally, i.e., follow strategies that are optimal with respect to their aims.

To say that conversational implications arise from violations of conversational maxims would be quite misleading. At best, one could say that they play a prominent role only when they are brought in to account for *apparent* violations of the maxims. A conversational implication is an assumption that has to be made about a player's aims or assumptions in order to construe his choice of strategy as a rational one. Often, the logical step is not even deductive at all, but inductive, a guess at an explanation.[2]

A conversational implication can convey new information to a player who needs to add it to his own assumptions in order to recognize the well-formedness of a dialogue. What is more, a conversational implicature can be intentionally invited by a player. A player may know that some move of his will appear irrational to his partners because they are not correctly informed about his aims and attitudes. However, he may proceed to make the move anyway expecting his audience to be able to fill in whatever premises are necessary to construe his move as a rational choice of strategy. In this manner, he may succeed to convey some of his acceptations without ever putting them into words.

The point of the whole exercise is that despite appearances, there will be no violation of the rules of the game: the author of the move does accept the necessary premises, and expects his audience to be able to figure them out too.

Actual violations of the rules of dialogue games and irrational choices of strategy do happen. However, then conversational implications go awry too. A scheming player may make an irrational move intentionally, knowing that his partners will assume him to play rationally; the result is deception by conversational implication. An accidental slip of tongue is apt to shake out unwanted implicatures.

The way we have defined utility functions in a dialogue, the different maxims of conversation never clash, there is always a definite tradeoff. To explain why Grice's example

(73)   A: Where does C live?
        B: Somewhere in the South of France.

implicates that B knows no better, it suffices to assume that the move B is putting forward is epistemically optimal given his evidence, i.e., B is playing rationally.

There are other examples too whose treatment in our account differs from Grice's. By treating irony as a meaning convention on a par with serious conversation, we have moved irony from the field of conversational implicature into linguistic convention. Some varieties of exaggeration and understatement can be correlated with manipulation of the index of caution: a cautious person is apt to understate, while an audacious one says more than he has evidence for.

8. SELF-TRANSPARENCY

Given the idea of dialogical implication, it is easy to see why the principle of transitivity of belief (or acceptance)

(74)   If anyone accepts that p, he accepts that he accepts that p

should have certain intuitive appeal as an axiom of the logic of rational belief (acceptance).

Intuitively, what (74) says is that people's beliefs should be evident to them: no one in his right mind should be able to sincerely deny accepting something he in fact accepts.

In terms of the dialogue game setup, it is easy to see why (74) is so appealing. Its strongest intuitive appeal comes from *inspecting one's own beliefs*.[3]

As Hintikka puts it in *Knowledge and Belief*, explaining the argument from introspection,

It may seem that a mind cannot help being aware of its own states, among which there are the states of knowledge and belief. At the very least, it seems impossible to doubt that a mind can always become aware of its own states. If I actively believe something, it might be said, surely I must be able to recognize that I do. What could there be preventing me from knowing my own mind? (p. 53)

To illustrate this, assume someone is actually able to verify an instance of the antecedent of (74),

(75)   I accept that *p*.

According to the dialogue truth definition of acceptance, this means that the subject can find out whether *p* holds in all of his own epistemic alternatives. But of course anyone has free access to his own alternatives, hasn't he conjured them up himself!

In order to verify the consequent of (74), he must next pass this 'outside information' about his epistemic alternatives to his various 'alter egos' within those epistemic alternatives. This is a *prima facie* innocuous assumption too, for what could it mean for him to be identical to his alter egos if not that he shares his thoughts with them? Therefore, these alter egos can end up in the privileged epistemic position of knowing everything about their worlds that the actual subject, as their maker, has first hand information of.

When the argument from introspection is spelled out thus crudely, it is obviously not logically binding. The first assumption, that maker's knowledge is somehow privileged, is doubtful; for instance, one who draws a picture with his eyes blindfolded has little idea of how the picture will look like. Too, it is easy to forget what one has once accomplished.

Even more doubtful is the assumption of conservation of information in personal cross-world identification. Surely, a person can gain or lose knowledge while staying the same person. What is even more destructive, consider a subject who has no conception of its own self. For instance, a baby can well have beliefs about its environment without having any notion of its own role in it. It then has no beliefs about itself, as it has not (yet) formed a concept of itself. Then there is no way of even making the cross-identification between the two occurrences of 'he' in (74).

Thus there seems to be reason enough to suspect (74) as a conceptual truth. However, it does have quite a lot of practical interest: as a matter of fact, we often are able to inspect our own epistemic states so as to be able to make true statements about them.

As it happens, this possibility is already provided for by our framework. Recall that we allow players to make observations in the course of an actual dialogue. Such observations are represented as so many declarative moves by Nature, who may or may not allow a designated number of players the privilege of being in her audience. The nicest property of Nature's moves was their reliability: Nature could be relied upon not to tell jokes, lies, or falsehoods. As a result, players can safely transfer any moves by Nature they happen to catch upon over to their epistemic alternatives.

Moving over to an arbitrary epistemic alternative, any sentences accepted there will be also represented as so many moves by Nature: they are sentences true in that epistemic alternative. A player who takes the trouble to consider what his alter ego in that alternative can observe will be in a position to move his observations another step deeper in the dialogue, into the epistemic alternatives of his epistemic counterpart in that alternative — provided that the counterpart is in the audience of that internal observation! And that depends on how good an internal observer one considers oneself. If one is inclined to doubt one's own capacity to introspection, one may well allow room for mismatches between one's internal and external powers of observation. It is quite possible (and even likely, what with all this modern stuff about subliminal observation, levels of consciousness and whatnot) that not all assumptions registered in one's epistemic alternatives get transferred to one's epistemic alternatives to those alternatives: one may believe a thing without ever becoming aware of believing it, or be mistaken about one's own acceptations. It may require an active effort of introspection, often helped by interview and experimentation, to make valid observations about one's propositional attitudes.

Summing up, the applicability of the transitivity axiom (74) is a contingent fact. It is up to players of a dialogue game to assess their powers of introspection. Thus we can construe (74) as another principle true of an ideally equipped player, an all-observant introspectionist.[4]

CHAPTER 8

QUESTION-ANSWER DIALOGUES

1. LANGUAGE-GAMES VS. SPEECH ACTS

My dialogue game approach to the use of language in general and the meaning of grammatical moods in particular shares many assumptions with Searle's theory of speech acts. We both "hypothesize that speaking a language is engaging in a rule-governed form of behavior", using familiar parlor games as objects of comparison, and subscribe to the view that a theory of (the use of) language is well considered a part of a theory of action.[1] It is therefore of interest to see where the most conspicuous differences seem to lie between the speech act approach and the language game approach.

The crucial difference is in evidence in the respective names of the approaches. It is a difference in the basic unit in the description of the use of language. Searle's hypothesis is that the *speech act* is the basic unit of communication:[2]

The basic form that this hypothesis will take is that speaking a language is performing speech acts, acts such as making statements, giving commands, asking questions, making promises, and so on . . . p. 16.

Therefore, the typical question Searle asks is, "What are the different kinds of speech acts speakers perform when they utter expressions?"[3] Accordingly, his primary research aim is "to formulate sets of constitutive rules for the performances of certain kinds of speech acts".[4]

In contrast, the basic unit of description in the present approach is a complete *language game*. Speech acts, if they need be singled out in our approach, are represented by the several possible moves of language games considered in the context of one particular language game or other.

What possible gains might accrue from our approach over Searle's? Without claiming that there are any irreducible differences between our global approach and Searle's more atomistic starting-point, I wish to suggest that the language game framework offers certain heuristic advantages. Let me mention three.

(i) The language game framework forces one to study individual speech acts in the wider context of a whole conversation. This helps avoiding too categorical descriptions of the felicity conditions of different dialogue moves, and naturally extends the study of individual speech acts into the study of speech act sequences.[5]

(ii) The game parameters suggest a natural basis of classification of different speech acts. It enables one to derive certain repetitious felicity conditions of individual speech acts from the more general boundary conditions on rational action involved in the game theoretical concept of solution (optimal strategy) of a game.

(iii) The game framework forces a clear separation of the *aims* of the players of a language game from the *strategies* (means of expression) available to them, explaining the wide variability of uses of expressions. By this means, the language game approach seems to avoid a somewhat embarrassing question raised by Coulthard [6] , p. 17:

How many different functions of performatives does one have to recognize? Austin suggests that the number of functions is equivalent to the number of performative verbs, which he estimates at between one and ten thousand.

There are two questions to be asked at this stage: the first, posed by Searle (1965) is whether there are 'some basic illocutionary acts to which all or most others are reducible' . . . The second question is whether it is wise to rely on natural language as a means of categorization . . .

In our approach, it is not necessary to assume that each move in a dialogue has any one well defined aim or function, which may be described by a suitable performative verb. Some moves may have several independent aims or functions, and the precise force of some moves may be quite hard to put into words. I think it is symptomatic that in attempts to develop the performative analysis into a systematic theory, it has been found necessary not to take performative verbs (or individual speech acts) as primitives, but rather to try and define the meaning of performative verbs by a systematic description of their proper conditions of use. This seems to me to suggest that the interesting structure does not lie so much in individual performative verbs as in the contexts of use which define their meaning. Instead of describing use of language in terms of performative verbs, one ought to describe the meaning of performative verbs in terms of an independent description of language games.[6]

To illustrate these points, let us compare Searle's treatment of the interrogative mood to ours. Searle's research strategy is the following.

In order to give an analysis of the illocutionary act of [asking a question], I shall ask what conditions are necessary and sufficient for the act of [asking a question] to have been successfully and non-defectively performed in the utterance of a given sentence. I shall attempt to answer this question by stating these conditions as a set of propositions such that the conjunction of the members of the set entails the proposition that speaker [asked] a successful and non-defective [question], and the proposition that the speaker made such a [question] entails this conjunction.

If we get such a set of conditions we can extract from them a set of rules for the use of the illocutionary force indicating device.[7]

The felicity conditions for questions include, as a *preparatory condition*, that the author of the question does not know 'the answer' to the question, and as a *sincerity condition* that the author wants this information. The *essential condition* is that the question counts as an attempt to elicit this information from the addressee. If any of these conditions fail, the act of asking the question is defective. These conditions of successful questioning are to go over as so many rules for the use of the relevant illocutionary force indicating device, the interrogative mood. A question, by implication, will be inappropriate (infelicitous or insincere) whenever the above conditions are not satisfied.

My aim in the following sections is to show by example and adjoining argument that this theory of questions is all too narrow. Its main weakness is the incorporation of likely dialogue aims (strategic motivations) of questions as part of the meaning of the interrogative mood. All that is needed to characterize the interrogative mood are the dialogue rules of asking and answering. (A reflection of these can be discerned in Searle's essential condition. Even that condition seems too strong as it stands.)

In contrast, the (likely or unlikely) motivations of asking a question need no separate attention in the rules for the interrogative mood. They can be systematically inferred from the aims common to all moves in information-sharing dialogues and the opportunities the rules for asking and answering provide for realizing those aims.

Searle recognizes one limitation of his statement of the felicity conditions of questions. In a comment appended to his rules, he admits that there are two kinds of questions, 'real questions' and 'exam questions'. In exam questions, the sincerity condition of real questions is replaced by the condition that the author of the question wants to know if the addressee knows the answer to the question.

In the following sections, we shall see that there are a lot more uses for questions than even these two. The best generalization one can make is this: use questions whenever they are relevant to the dialogue. In other words, ask a question when asking it can be calculated by the rules of the game to further the aim of the game. This aim has been described in the games of cooperative information sharing as that of creating a common understanding (consensus) about the topics of a dialogue (the questions asked in it) as well as about the answers accepted to the topical questions.[8]

2. PLEADING IGNORANCE

Our rules for question-answer dialogues appear to have a conspicuous gap. They do not seem to provide for one of the most common responses to inquiries, the plea of ignorance, as in

(1)   A: Did you make it?
         C: I don't know.

This gap, however, is no accidental oversight. I have been saving my account for it until the discussion of iterated acceptance in Chapter 7 Section 8 above. To expose the correct logic of dialogue (1), I submit, we need to interpolate in it an implicit step of inference. C, in (1), is actually *not* answering A's literal query directly, but is putting forward a direct answer to another question, quite immediately suggested by A's actual question. That question is of course nothing else than

(2)   A: Do you know whether you made it?

To justify this analysis of dialogue (1), we have to show that question (2) is actually entailed in some sense by A's original question in (1). To see this, assume the contrary: A is asking her question in (1) while she denies (2), i.e., accepts

(3)   Never mind whether you know whether you made it.

We want to show that A cannot accept (3) and still expect C to answer her original question in (1) without violating (C.consq).
     It is very easy to see why. Assume C were able to answer A's question in (1) directly, say by

(4)   C: I did make it.

In order to understand what C means by (4), A cannot help drawing some definite consequence about C's epistemic attitude. Assuming C is being serious, A must infer by (D.earnest),

(5)   C accepts that she did make it.

But (5) already constitutes a positive answer to (2), making it impossible for A to deny interest in (2).

In brief, if A expects B to be able to answer her original question, she expects a positive answer to the implicit question (2). It is this implicit presupposition which B's answer denies in (1) by answering the implied question (2).

Note an extremely interesting feature of the above line of inference. The entailment here is not logical, but rather *dia-logical*. It is not the question in (1) in the abstract that entails the question in (2). That is, A might be able to obtain an answer to her original question in (1) without being informed about (2), if she doesn't ask C directly but makes more roundabout inquiries. Rather, it is the *asking of the question of C* in (1) that makes it impossible for A to deny an interest in (2). This is an example of a genuinely dialogical inference.

3. REJECTION OF QUESTIONS

Similar explanations apply to another common class of apparent responses to questions, exemplified in the dialogues

(6)   A: What did you say?
           B: I did not say anything!
(7)   A: What did you say?
           B: Never mind what I said.

These dialogues represent rejections of proposed topics of discussion. In (6), a question is in effect rejected through a rejection of its presupposition. In it, B is not actually addressing A's question directly, but his reply is directed one step higher up in the dialogue:

(8)   A: Did you say anything or not?

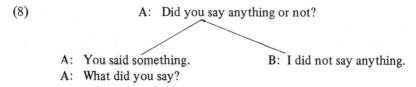

A: You said something.   B: I did not say anything.
A: What did you say?

This reconstruction of presupposition-denial construes the denial as a move by (D.reply) in the preparatory dialogue whose topic is the presupposition.

Dialogue (7) represents a more radical rejection of a topic for discussion.

From the point of view of the dialogue initiated by A's question, B is not even playing: he is not obeying the maxim of agreement. In order to reconcile (7) with conversational maxims, a higher-order dialogue must be interpolated around the topic of choosing an appropriate topic:

(9)   A: Shall we mind what you said?

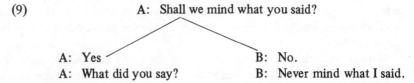

A: Yes   B: No.
A: What did you say?   B: Never mind what I said.

In the higher order game, possible answers are possible choices of topic (possible first-order dialogues). Thus, B's rejection of A's answer for the higher order topic amounts to opting out from the dialogue A wants to initiate. B is still being cooperative, albeit only one level up from A.

4. ELICITING QUESTIONS

The most generally recognized "exceptional" context for asking questions which one knows the right answers to is an examination situation. There, the questioner knows the answer to his question; what he wants to know is whether the addressee does too.

In our terms, this in no way an exceptional situation, nor does it require any addition to the rules and principles we have already laid down. For recall the statement of the aims of players in an information sharing situation: the players aim to arrive at a *common understanding* on the topic of the dialogue. They do not only want to each adopt an epistemically optimal answer to the topic at hand, but they want to agree about the answer, and *know* that they do; all this is implied by the concept of common understanding as defined. For this reason, players want to know what the others think of the question at hand whether or not they have set opionions about them on their own.

This statement of aims embraces the aims and attitudes of an examining teacher, intent upon securing that the students have assimilated the answers that have been offered them, as well as those of an ironical Socrates, who knows that his interlocutors do not know the right answers to his questions any more than himself but wants to make them realize their ignorance and share it with him.

Thanks to the rules of asking and answering and the meaning conventions, questions are an excellent way of eliciting opinions, whether for acceptance or rejection. What is less generally observed, questions are also used to elicit further *questions*. Questions are commonly used to create an agreement about *topics*: to arouse other people's interest in what the questioner is interested in — and quite possibly knows the answers to.

For instance, one may hide something behind one's back and ask:

(12)   What do I have here?

not to test the addressee nor to expose his ignorance — that is being assumed all along! — but to make him share an interest in the question, and preferably to get him to ask it himself:

(11)   Well, what do you have there?

Such eliciting can be accomplished in a more roundabout way, too, by asking a question which is dialogically implied by the real topic of interest:

(12)   Do you know what I have here?

In order to catch the drift of (12), the addressee must find an explanation to the questioner's interest in (12); finding the obvious one (10), he can join the game and ask (11). This sort of ploy is very common in starting conversations where the first task is to create a consensus on the topic of interest.

An eliciting question can have a function even when the players already have a consensus about the answer to it. As a response to another question, such an eliciting question may serve to suggest an answer to the first question. Our earlier Sherlock Holmes example might well have this interpretation:

(13)   W: Who is the murderer?
          H: Who wore square-toed boots?

We may assume Watson already knows who wore the boots, and knows Holmes does, and both know the other knows it, and so forth: in short there is a common understanding about that matter. Why, then, should Holmes ask that obvious question? Some intervening step of inference must be interpolated. The shortest interpolation sentence is of course

(14)   The murderer wore square-toed boots.

Given (14), one particular answer to Holmes' question automatically answers Watson's mystery; if there was just one pair of square-toed boots around, Watson can conclude from (14) and his answer to Holmes' question the identity of the murderer. Thus the necessity (given Holmes' reputation as a close and cogent reasoner) of finding a logical connection between Watson's question and Holmes' counterquestion lets Watson guess at Holmes' hidden premise (14). Holmes' apparently superfluous question turns out to give away the key to the mystery.

A more colloquial example of the same dialogue strategy is the following:

(15)   A: Who won?
        B: Who do you think?

B's question entails (and explains) A's query given the interpolation sentence

(16)   Who you think won won.

(Of course, there are other possible interpretations of (15): B might be sincerely interested in, and ignorant of, A's opinion. In that case, the connection between A's and B's moves is dialogical rather than logical: if A's question is accepted as the topic, the players derivatively accept an interest in each other's assumptions concerning it, in accordance with the aims of cooperative information exchanges. Hence B's interest in A's guess.)

A further interesting case of eliciting question is the sarcastic interchange in (17):[9]

(17)   A: Is Reagan republican?
        B: Is the Pope catholic?

Here, B retorts to A's question by (what he thinks is) another question with an obvious answer: by analogy, A is to figure out that the correct answer to his question is equally obviously positive. What is the mechanism which leads A to actually draw the analogy?

It is, I suggest, the need, and search, for a *common topic* to the two questions. Why should B reply by asking A another question? I mean, what is the logical connection between the question? Asking himself this question, A is expected to try to construe both questions as entailed, as subordinate queries, by some common topic. In (17), the intended topic is of course something like

(18)   What is obvious?

In other words: to grasp the analogy, A has to find what the two questions in (17) have in common; what they have in common is expressible as a common topic they both address. And the search for the common topic is ensured by A's need to see the relevance of B's counterquestion to his own query.

Note that the conversational ploy employed in (17) is quite versatile, the essential point in it being the suggestion of a common topic. One may indicate that a question is inappropriate:

(19)   A: Are you Jewish?
        B: Are you gay?

One may apply the same methods to assertions:

(20)   A: Reagan will solve the economic crisis.
        B: Yeah, and all good children will go to heaven.

Here, the topic B is rhetorically eliciting could be either of

(21)   What else is new?
(22)   How gullible can one get?

depending on B's convictions.

5. A THREE-PERSON DIALOGUE

Recall the game situation with the three cheerleader applicants.[10] As we noted, each girl was desperate to know how she had fared in the exam. However, they just cannot bring themselves to ask the others directly about their own fates. It would be just too cruel to hear a negative verdict from a more fortunate competitor! Therefore A, who is a resourceful girl, decides to go about it in a more roundabout way. She asks C:

(23)   Did you make it?

(of course A already *knows* that C made it, and she also knows that C does *not* know that. Yet the question has a point!) Predictably, C answers,

(24)   I don't know.

Allowing time for the answer to sink in, A then turns to B and asks her the same question, and B answers in the same way. Triumphantly, A embraces her companions and cries:

(25)   So we all made it!

The task now is to reconstruct this somewhat surprising dialogue.

Let us go over the background once more. What each girl knows as background information about the test is the following:

(26)   Every girl knows that every girl knows of every other girl whether
        she passed or not.
(27)   Every girl knows that every girl knows that some girl passed.

What A could tell in particular was that

(28)   B passed and C passed.

She also knows that every girl is interested in the question

(29)   Who passed?

Applying (C.wh-u), she derives from (29) three conditional questions:

(30)   Did C pass if C passed?
(31)   Did B pass if B passed?
(32)   Did A pass if A passed?

The only question which is still open is the last one. Now A can explain it,
in virtue of (C.if), in either of two ways, by assuming a positive answer to
the main clause

(33)   Did A pass?

or by assuming the denial of the conditional clause, i.e.,

(34)   A did not pass.

She decides first to try out the latter possibility. What she tries to figure out
is what B will know in that case. Instantiating (26), she can infer that

(35)   B knows that C passed
(36)   B knows that A did not pass
(37)   B knows that C knows that A did not pass
(38)   B knows that C knows whether B passed or not.

So she thinks it is worth taking a look at what is going on in B's pretty head.
Applying the possible worlds definition of acceptance, she finds the following
in the intersection of B's epistemic alternatives:

(39)   C passed
(40)   A did not pass
(41)   C knows that A did not pass
(42)   C knows whether B passed or not.

Furthermore, B can be assumed to ask herself the question (31), and to follow its consequences. Again, there are two alternatives for B, to answer the main clause of (31) in the affirmative, or to consider the contrary hypothesis,

(43)   B did not pass.

But if (43) is the case, (42) reduces to

(44)   C knows that B did not pass.

So B would do well to look what C might be able to infer in that case.

The intersection of C's epistemic alternatives to the alternative A is assuming B to consider here contains the following sentences:

(45)   A did not pass
(46)   B did not pass

and the question C is asking herself is

(30)   Did C pass if C passed?

Now C knows as well as the others (recall (27)!) that

(47)   Some girl passed
(48)   Every girl is A or B or C.

These hypotheses already exclude the denial of the conditional of (30), namely

(49)   C did not pass.

Hence, if this alternative were correct, C could already conclude that she passed, being able to eliminate the other two candidates. What A aims to do in asking C (23) is test out this alternative she is conjecturing B to entertain. Of course, *she* (A) knows the correct answer and she also knows what C's reply is going to be, but she specifically wants B to be in the audience of the exchange. For when B hears that C, contrary to the expectation of the current hypothesis, does not know her own position, B can chuck that line of thought if she ever entertained it. At this stage, things get exciting for A. For she knows there are now two alternatives left: either A failed, and then B can already infer from C's indecisiveness that she (B) passed; or no one failed, in which case B cannot yet be sure of passing either. So A now asks B a million dollar question: did she (B) pass?

Thank God, B pleads ignorance, so the only remaining alternative which covers the facts is the one which answers A's question (33) in the affirmative.

Combining the results in (28) and the newly gained piece of information, A is in a position to announce (25).

What is most instructive about this example of indirect questioning, it shows that no all too narrow statement of the felicity conditions of asking questions can be right. We have just witnessed a case where it has been fully rational for a person to address a question, which she already knows the answer to, to a person who she knows *not* to be able to answer the question. One must not forget one's audience: often enough, questions are asked for the benefit of an audience rather than the main characters. Once the general point is appreciated, it is not hard to think of more every-day examples of it, say from courts of law.[11]

6. QUESTIONS IMPLYING IGNORANCE

Once the dialogue logic of iterated acceptance is appreciated, it is not difficult to explicate the use of questions as responses to questions to indicate ignorance. The following example is a case in point:

(50)   A: What will Jack say?
         B: Who knows?

B's question seems rhetorical, in the sense that B is not likely to expect or even want an answer from A. Rather, B seems to be conveying a message about his own ability to answer A's question. Note that B need not believe that *no* one could answer her question — for instance, there is no reason for B to exclude the possibility that Jack, for one, might know. B's point seems to be a weaker one. She is only implying that she cannot point to anyone who could answer A. Since in particular, if B knew the answer to A's question, B would be the first person to know that, B's asking her question suggests that B does not know the answer to A's question. And this is the main thrust of B's message: she might have said "Don't ask me!" instead.

We see that the reasoning behind B's counter-question is quite similar to that in Section 2 above. A's asking B in (50) implies an interest by A in the question

(51)   Do you know what Jack will say?

But (51) in turn logically implies its existential generalization, the (existentially understood) search question

(52)   Who knows what Jack will say?

which is precisely the question B puts forward in an elliptic form in (50).

How does B succeed to express his ignorance by asking A (52)? The reasoning is not difficult to appreciate if the epistemic context of (50) is understood. The natural context for (50) is one where A does not have an answer to her question, where she assumes that B will have one, and where B assumes A to hold these assumptions. Then, if B is playing rationally (obeying an optimal strategy dictated by the maxims of cooperative information exchange), it is easy to show that he cannot have an answer to A's question in (50).

For assume B did indeed have an answer to A's question, say

(53)   Jack will say no.

If B assumed (53), she could have simply put forward (53) as a direct answer to (50). So why did she not do so? Moreover, B could infer from (53) by (D.earnest)

(54)   I know that Jack will say no.

But (54) immediately implies

(55)   I know what Jack will say,

so B would also agree with A about one answer to (52). Why should she then ask (52)? There is no reason at all. To the contrary, the very fact that B still finds (52) a live topic shows that she cannot agree with A about (55).

One puzzle still remains to be solved. Why is B's question rhetorical – how come it is clear that B is not likely to expect or even want an answer to her question? The reasoning here is close. Recall that B was led to accept her counter-question by the force of A's willingness to ask B her own question. Now as we saw, B's counter-question shows A that she will gain nothing from asking her question of B – she should go and ask others. A's loss of interest in asking B therefore removes the reason for B to go on wondering about the counter-question. As soon as A realizes that she should not have asked B in the first place, both players can safely relinquish interest in B's counter-question. The question becomes void on the very asking of it – it turns out to be a mere rhetorical device, a self-defeating question.

7. BIASED QUESTIONS

It is well known that questions often import a bias as to what the questioner thinks is the correct answer to them and what answer he is expecting to get from his addressee. The very notion of *questioning* some proposition carries a negative implication, suggesting that the questioner is not convinced of that proposition, that he doubts it or downright disbelieves it. *Questionable* actually becomes a synonym of *doubtful* or *suspect*.

I shall try to construe this property of questions as a special case of a more general phenomenon. That is the general tendency of any expressions of doubt or indecision to suggest disbelief or disinclination. To question something almost means to doubt something, and to doubt something almost amounts to assuming the opposite. It often seens as if Christ's famous law of excluded middle in questions of faith were valid: who is not with me is against me.

Given such a law of excluded middle, the scopes of verbs of propositional attitudes and negation become interchangeable, so that (56) comes to mean the same as (57):

(56)   I don't suppose he is right.
(57)   I suppose he is not right.

The tendency of (56) to mean (57) is so strong that it has led some linguists to propose a grammatical process of negative transportation, actually moving the negation sign from the inside of certain propositional attitude verbs to the outside of them; for instance, (57) would be related to (56) by a meaning-preserving transformation. This transformation would have to be lexically governed, as not all verbs of propositional attitude are susceptible to it to an equal degree: (58) is not equivalent to (59), for instance.

(58)   I don't presuppose he is right.
(59)   I presuppose he is not right.

The lexical selectivity of the negative transportation phenomenon does suggest that whatever process creates it has become a conventional rule in the clear cases. However, what interests me more than the exact nature of that rule is the possibility of a dialogue theoretical rationale for the existence of such a rule.

I think there is an obvious one, on the following general lines. In the case of a difference of opinions between dialogue participants, it is more *guarded*, and more *polite*, to express the disagreement in the milder form of doubt (uncertainty).

To develop this idea, consider the following example.

(60)   A: This is good.
        B: Well, I don't know.

Notice that the relevant attitude verb *know* is not one of the negative transportation verbs: (61)–(62) are not equivalent.

(61)   I don't know that this is good
(62)   I know that this is not good.

Rather, the right expansion of B's speech in (60) would be

(63)   I don't know if this is good

i.e., a plea of ignorance.

Why is there a feeling that B's professed ignorance, or suspension of judgment, carries with it an implication that B has reason to disagree with A — he actually has some evidence against A's thesis? Actually, the inference is immediate from our treatment of rational epistemic decision making.

We may assume that both speakers are addressing the topic

(64)   Is this good or not?

Furthermore, we assume that both players are serious and that they respect each other's judgment: each player's professed opinion on a question is confirming evidence for that opinion. Assuming all this, if B had no evidence for or against either answer to (64), he should be inclined to accept A's opinion, unless he has special reason to proceed with extreme caution.

Therefore the fact that B chooses to remain undecided in the face of A's protestations suggests that B's prior probabilities actually speak against A's thesis. A's testimony is sufficient to make B suspend judgment; it does not suffice to tip the scales in A's favor.

Actually, B may still prefer his original position to A's thesis, and would stick to that if he had to choose between them. However, he takes the more cautious option of suspending judgment. Indeed, A's opposite opinion may have had the precise effect of increasing B's index of caution concerning (64). B might have held the opposite view until A's diverging opinion made him realize that the question is open to debate. Even if A's testimony did not essentially change B's preference for his own thesis over A's, it may scare him to raise his index of caution. (B may be afraid of getting involved in a dispute about a thesis he is none too sanguine about anyway.) Still, on his less guarded moments, B will continue to prefer his original opinion — hence the bias.

We said that politeness was a likely motive for passing a claim rather than challenging it. The maxim of politeness involved is essentially *be agreeable*: i.e., do what your beneficiary wants.[12] In a game of information seeking, this may amount to acting as if the interlocutor knew better. Such an attitude is all too polite where it actually overrules the epistemic maxims, occasioning epistemically suboptimal moves. The maximally polite thing for B to do would have been simply to agree with A even against his own better judgment; and he might well have done so if the matter was of small importance. However, assuming B finds it essential not to put forward straight falsities for reasons of politeness, there is the option of increased degree of caution. This serves to show that he feels he has to treat his interlocutor's evidence with great respect. At the same time, it makes the interlocutor aware of a divergence of evidential base without disputing his claim; moreover, it blames the divergence of opinion on B's lack of conclusive evidence.

A thus can infer from B's guardedness that B has reason to doubt A's thesis; knowing B to be a polite person, A can also suspect that the evidence B has against A's claim is quite strong: politeness aside, B actually disbelieves A's thesis. The negative bias is explained.

To connect this explanation of the negative bias to questions another rationality argument has to be introduced. That is that in a matter of fact dialogue, a player will not make a move which he need not make: in more game theoretical terms, a player will ask a question only if it is in an optimal strategy of his for attaining the goal of shared information.

Consider how this straightforward corollary is applied in the following example.

(65)   A: He is all right.
         B: *Is* he all right or not?

In (65), A has just told B that someone is OK: B replies by questioning what he has been just told. Clearly, if A's thesis were sufficiently confirmed, B would not need to question it, for he knows that A assumes it, and it would suffice for him to assent to it for there to be a common understanding of the matter. Hence assuming that B is convinced in (65) would entail that he is speaking idly, following a suboptimal discourse strategy.

But, one wants to ask, is it any more rational for B to ask a question A has in effect just answered? It is, if B (as we have already argued) is suspending judgment because he has increased his level of caution, and knows that A can infer that is the case. Although B knows what A is inclined to accept at the level of caution A was initially operating with, he will not know if A will still accept the same answer as optimal if A also raises his level of caution. Hence, it is rational for B to repeat the question, as the conditions of answerhood are going to be readjusted by the very repetition. The result is that B is in effect *checking* A's answer against a higher index of caution in (65): he wants to know how strong A's conviction in his answer is. Thus we have been able to explain the intuition that B in (65) is *checking* A's claim and therefore maybe politely *challenging* it.

This line of argument is supported by the fact that checking questions typically exhibit intensifying adverbs:

(66)   Is he really? Indeed?

Presumably, the intensified sentence requires a higher degree of confidence to be accepted than the unadorned sentence. Eliciting the intensified sentence thus equals asking for a repetition of the original sentence against an increased index of caution.

Note also that a checking question can be paraphrased by an explicit inquiry about the reliability of the claim or its evidential base:

(67)   Are you absolutely sure? How do you know?

8. ELEMENTARY QUESTIONS

So far, we have shown that the very act of questioning a fact carries with it an element of doubt. What remains is to connect the direction of the bias to the syntactic form of simple questions. Consider

(68)   A: It is all right.
        B: Is it all right?
(69)   B: It is not all right.
        A: Is it not all right?

Intuitively, B's question in (68) suggests B has doubts about A's claim, and is inclined towards its denial in (69). Conversely, A's question in (69) indicates A is doubtful (perhaps even surprised) about B's claim and is himself inclined to assume the opposite claim in (68).[13] An amusing illustration of this regularity is the following dialogue from Ross Macdonald's novel *The Doomsters* (Ch. 5):

"What do you intend to do about this alleged car theft? You want to see Hallman punished, naturally."

"Do I?"

"Don't you?"

"No."

The direction of bias in simple questions can be explained with reference to the notion of elementary question. Here is how the explanation goes.

An elementary question is elementary in the following way: it only has one answer, viz. the declarative form of the question itself, and that answer is its presupposition as well. So when one asks an elementary question, one naturally enough expects to obtain the only answer it admits of. This is why the natural form of checking question in (68)–(69) is just the corresponding elementary question, the interrogative form of the preceding presupposition. This is what links each form of simple question to the expected answer. The qustioner's *own* presumption (also called presupposition in much of the nontechnical literature on the subject) is the opposite of the expected answer, for reasons presented in the preceding section.

An essential link in the above argument is the assumption that *simple questions are not always alternative questions.* A syntactically simple question may represent a semantically elementary question: a question that has no other direct answer than its own declarative form. Earlier, we recognized the possibility of doubt as to the utility of such one-alternative questions: why ask a question which has only one answer? True, such a question would be rather useless to wonder about: one who accepts an elementary question and asks it under (D.earnest) needs no help in answering it. However, as we have already seen, there are a host of other reasons for asking questions.

Bolinger (1978) has independently arrived at the somewhat surprising thesis I emphasize above. He also has an admirable list of no less than twelve uses of sentential questions where the simple form of the question is not replaceable by a disjunctive (yes or no) form. My interpretation for most if not all of these uses agrees with his: these questions represent semantically elementary questions. Some of them are *loaded* questions: questions which do actually expect just one answer, viz. precisely the declarative form of the question; some represent likely *guesses* derived from a superordinate search question. To the first batch belong Bolinger's classes

(i)   Invitations: *Do you want some?* – It is polite to expect a positive answer of the addressee, as an encouragement.

(ii)   Self-evident facts: *Are you still around*? – There is no room for doubt here. The questioner wants to raise the question rather than hear the answer.

(iii)   One-way questions: *John, are you awake*? – A negative answer is not expected for obvious reasons.

(iv)   Self-answering questions: *Do you realize that today is the tenth*? – The factive presupposition gives away the answer.

(v)   Ritual questions: *OK, is everybody ready*? Asked pro forma before an event, expects silence as a sign of positive answer.

(vi)   Requests: *Will you help me*? – Shows the questioner expects help.

To the second category I put Bolinger's titles

(vii)   Suggested answers to search questions: *What's the matter*? *Are you tired*? – The elementary question represents an explanatory move; its negation is not relevant for it would explain nothing.

(viii) Specification questions: *Is today the seventeenth*? – The implicit main topic is a search question (What day is it?) and the elementary question again represents the questioner's guess; in Bolinger's words, "you are not interested in a possible denial; you want the date".

(ix)   Queried inferences: *Does he always snore*? – Asked on hearing someone snore. Again, the question suggests an explanation. (Bolinger: "You can also pose this as a suggested answer to a wh-question: Why? Does he always snore?")

These examples ought to show impressively the importance of elementary questions in actual usage. It is very useful to have a category of loaded questions at one's disposal; the indirect force of the implied expectations can be much more effective than explicit argument.

Elementary questions can of course be responded to against expectation too. The only point to make about such denials (or affirmations) is that theoretically, they do not constitute direct answers to the relevant elementary questions but represent denials of their presuppositions. The structure of the dialogue is roughly this:

(70)

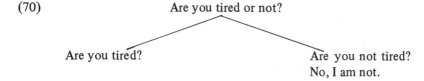

Are you tired or not?

Are you tired?   Are you not tired?
                        No, I am not.

9. RHETORICAL QUESTIONS

An apparent weakness in the above account comes forth in the terminology "expected answer"; for someone who asks a checking question as often as not really expects to hear the denial of the expected answer, i.e., expects the addressee of the question to come round to his point of view.

One can make the point nicely by saying that checking questions are, as often as not, actually a sort of *rhetorical question*:[14] the questioner puts a question feigning interest in it but actually expects the question to be unanswerable. What he expects to hear is not an answer to the question but rather if anything, the denial of the presupposition of the questioner's point of view. Thus one who asks — or exclaims —

(71)   Isn't this delicious?

would be as disappointed to hear the straightforward answer 'No' as one who asks

(72)   Who cares?

would be on hearing the *bona fide* answer

(73)   I do.

This gives us the necessary clue for understanding the logic behind such rhetorical questions. They turn out to be *the erotetic counterpart of sarcastic (or ironic) assertions*.

Let me spell this out more explicitly. What distinguishes the sarcastic or ironic interpretations of assertions like

(74)   That's just great!

(as a comment on an evidently unpleasant observation) from their sincere (or better, serious) counterparts is the choice of convention linking what is said to what is believed (accepted). Instead of the straightforward seriousness convention (D.earnest) they obey the opposite convention, which we termed the *irony convention*:[15]

(75)   Put forward a sentence only if you accept its contrary.

Now what I want to say about rhetorical questions of the sort of (71)–(72) above is that they are *questions produced in accordance with the irony convention*. One who asks a rhetorical question of this sort conveys the message that he actually *does not* accept the question!

Earlier, we have discussed the reasons for a player to deny a given question. First of all, a player may be simply uninterested in a question, whatever his reasons. He need not have any particular beliefs one way or another as to whether the question admits of an answer or not: he simply could not care less.

It seems to me in fact that precisely this interpretation is involved in the idiomatic sense of the rhetorical question (72). Consider the dialogue

(76)   A: What will Jack say?
        B: Who cares?

It is obvious that A for one is concerned in the question he is asking: A does care. Aware of this, B cannot easily be implying that he assumes, for a fact, that no one cares. Rather, what B is implying is that no one *should* care, and that *he* does not care: it is all the same for *him* what Jack will say. How do these implications come out?

According to the present hypothesis, B's rhetoric question is actually equivalent to its serious denial, i.e.,

(77)   Never mind who cares what Jack will say.

If (77) is what B (seriously) means by (72), we can explain why B seems to imply by (72) that

(78)   I for one do not care what Jack will say.

without necessarily implying that he believes A does not care either. For what (77) actually implies are the following denied questions:

(79)   Never mind if A cares what Jack will say if A does care what Jack will say.
(80)   Never mind if I care what Jack will say if I do care what Jack will say.

How can (79)–(80) be explained consistently with what B already knows? We assumed B recognizes that A *does* care what Jack will say – A's question just implied as much. But then the main clause of (79) must be true, i.e.,

(81)   Never mind if A cares what Jack will say

along with an answer to the very question it denies – a contradiction of (C.consq). The obvious way out for B is that he simply *ignores* A's concern – is simply not interested if A or anyone else cares. An analogous argument applies to (80). Either B does not care whether he cares, or he has decided he will not. Since it is likely that B is interested in his own decisions, the latter alternative is the more likely one here. Summa summarum, B's question (72) is most naturally explained by assuming that B does not care what Jack says, and does not care if anyone else does.

More frequently, perhaps, a question is rejected because its presupposition is. It is easy to prove that any question implies its presupposition, so conversely, the denial of the presupposition of any question implies the denial of that question. As a result, often the most straightforward explanation of a rhetorical question is the assumption that the author of that question denies the presupposition of the question. For instance, someone who asks with a rhetorical flourish

(82)   What do I know?

is clearly not asking a serious question: for one thing he is likely to know best what he knows, so why ask others. So we assume he is asking a rhetorical question, i.e., in effect denying (82). Why? Is he just not interested in the question? That is not likely; in fact, it would run counter to the cooperative maxim (the maxim of agreement). So another explanation must be sought for − and is easy to find, for clearly the author of (82) is implying there is no answer to his question, i.e., its presupposition fails. So the most likely explanation for (82), hence its most likely serious paraphrase, is the denial of its presupposition, viz.

(83)   I know nothing.[16]

Now this explanation of rhetorical questions is easy to extend to elementary questions like (71). It is important to realize that a negative question like (71) has two easily distinguishable natural environments, exemplified by (84)–(85):

(84)   Why don't you go out with Jack? Isn't he nice?
(85)   Jack asked me out. Isn't he nice?

The intonation of the question in these contexts is apt to differ significantly. In (84), a rising question intonation is appropriate; in (85) the natural intonation is the falling pattern of a declarative sentence.

Accordingly, we shall argue, (84) represents a serious question under (D.guess) or (D.earnest), while (85) is a rhetorical question.

For evidence, notice that different expectations are connected with (84) and (85). (84) is a serious question expecting an informative answer; according to our rules, the expected (i.e., the only direct) answer to (84) is

(86)   He is not nice.

True, the questioner in (84) may well be biased against the expected answer himself; the mechanism of that bias has already been explained. What should not escape attention that there still is a clear expectation in (84) that the direct answer is what the questioner is going to get. The natural context of (84) is one where the questioner assumes — or has assumed previously — that Jack is nice but suspects that the addressee disagrees.

The situation is quite different in (85). Here, the speaker has no reason to suspect there will be any disagreement about Jack's agreeability. The speaker puts forward here a question which she thinks does not have a direct answer at all: its presupposition (86) is simply false. This is precisely what the speaker is trying to convey in (85) intuitively.

What is interesting, the difference of (84)–(85) actually has a syntactic reflex in at least one language, namely Finnish. Finnish does not recognize rising question intonation, so the contrast between (84)–(85) cannot be expressed by means of melody. Instead, Finnish uses the two particles *-kin* ('too') and *-kaan* ('either'). The negative item *-kaan* marks a negative question as a serious one expecting a negative answer, while the positive item *-kin* marks it as a rhetorical one, with positive expectations. Thus the respective translations of (84)–(85) in Finnish would be

(87)	Eikö	hän	olekaan	miellyttävä?
	not-whether	he	is-either	nice

(88)	Eikö	hän	olekin	miellyttävä?
	not-whether	he	is-too	nice

If my analysis of the contrast between (84)–(85) is right, the rhetorical question is not actually in need of an answer: no question has really been asked. This prediction is nicely confirmed by the following example from literature:

"It was an illiterate sort of letter", I said thoughtfully, "written by somebody practically illiterate, I should say."
"Was it?" said Owen and went away. Thinking it over afterward, I found that "Was it?" rather disturbing. (Agatha Christie, *The Moving Finger*, p. 15)

The narrator obviously finds the question disturbing because he cannot miss its irony: the question is so much out of the question that the doctor does not even stay to hear out the reply.

There is one more loose end to be tied. Intuition tells that positive simple questions are less leading than negative ones:

(89)   Do you like it?

is much more likely to be a neutral question than

(90)   Don't you like it?

which is anxious or coaxing. This asymmetry is explained by the option of expanding a positive simple question like (89) into a full disjunctive question

(91)   Do you like it or not?

before applying the definitions and rules. As a result, (90) can serve as a topic-opening move by (D.ask) while (90) can only be a checking move by (D.question).

10. TAG QUESTIONS

In the preceding section, we found that elementary questions come in two varieties, rhetorical ones (which expect the denial of their direct answer) and serious ones (which expect their direct answer). This duality is also in evidence in the peculiarly English device of tag question formation.

I should confess right away that I do not think there is a need for a specific syntactic rule of tag formation in sentence grammar. In my view, tag questions are a conventional use of certain elliptic questions, formed by quite everyday methods of question formation, anaphora, and ellipsis, and predictably related to their premises by the textual devices of thematicity and bias.

Be that as it may, it is the pragmatic question of bias that is my concern here. Consider the following logically possible combinations of polarity:

(92)   Writers will accept suggestions, won't they?
(93)   Writers won't accept suggestions, will they?
(94)   Writers will accept suggestions, will they?
(95)   Writers won't accept suggestions, won't they?

There is a distinct difference in feeling between the two first and the two last examples. The switch in polarity in (92)–(93) is so much the commoner case that it is often made out to be the unexceptional rule. Given our considerations of bias, this is not surprising. Reasonably enough, one who seriously puts forward an assertion questions its denial rather than his own point of view.

If the tag question is serious, the author of (92)–(93) may have some reason to suspect that his interlocutor possesses conflicting evidence; the tag then serves to elicit any possible objections. Quite as often, the tag is a mere rhetorical device for prompting a noise of agreement. The inflection of the tag will differ accordingly.

That this account of the polarity switch is correct is confirmed by comparing other ways of putting the checking question:

(96)   Writers won't accept suggestions, isn't that so?

What stays invariant here is that the proponent of a claim doubts that he is wrong, however he may phrase the question. Compare also

(97)   I don't suppose they will, will they?

where the tag questions what the premise doubts.

What remains to be clarified is the status of the matching-polarity sentences (94)–(95). The few transformational sources which recognize their occurrence at all grudgingly concede that they are possible, if associated with "incredulous or sarcastic overtones".[17]

What these writers seem to have overlooked is that matching-polarity tags are used quite colloquially to check likely guesses. There is no incredulity or sarcasm in the following examples from Patricia Moyes' novel *Black Widower*:

(98)   "You knew Sir Edward well, did you?" Henry gestured to encompass the elder Barringtons. "That's to say – your families were friendly on Tampica?"

(99)   " . . . That's why Sam will leave most of the talking at the Conference to Eddie."
          "Oh, there's a Conference scheduled, is there?"
          "Certainly there is. Didn't you know? Next week."

(100)   "You know Tampica well, do you, Mr. Schipmaker?" Emmy asked, quite innocently. Henry had not repeated to her the conversation at the Barrington home. There was a little pause. Then Otis cleared his throat and said, "I've been there before, yes. Some years ago."

(101)   "So you and your husband are staying with Miss Pontefract-
Deacon, are you, Mrs. Barrington?"
"Yes, just for a few days. We always come to Lucy when we
manage to get back to Tampica."

Clearly, the tags here are sincere requests for confirmation. The essential
difference to the preceding examples seems to be in the character of the
foregoing declarative move: As is clear from various indications in the above
examples (the inferential *so*, and the surprised *Oh*), the premise of the tag
represents a conjecture rather than well-founded opinion: this conjecture
is immediately followed by a request for a confirmation of the guess. The
expected answer is the repetition of the conjecture here, as predicted by
our rules.

What is the bias of the questioner? In (98)–(101), the questioners seem
inclined to accept the conjecture, if anything. In other cases, which seem
to have had the limelight in earlier discussions, the questioner is indeed
incredulous, even sarcastic:

(101a)   "As soon as Mr. Wolfe finds the murderer everything will be
rosy."
"You don't say. Wolfe's going to find the murderer, is he?
That's damn kind of him." (Rex Stout, *Not Quite Dead Enough*,
p. 58)

A strong element of scorn is felt in (102) as well:

(102)   So writers won't accept suggestions, won't they? Well, then we
won't publish them![18]

Here, the premise of the question is clearly something the writers are responsible for, not the speaker, and therefore it is only natural for him to
question it. Compare again other ways of expressing the doubt:

(103)   So writers won't accept suggestions, is that so?

Some informants tell me that there is a difference between the double
negative construction (95) and the double positive one in (94): unlike the
latter, the former cannot easily represent an unbiased request of information. This difference is probably due to the asymmetry between simple
positive and simple negative questions noted at the end of the previous

section: only positive questions allow an unbiased (presupposition-free) interpretation.[19]

11. ECHO QUESTIONS

One of the novel — and perhaps initially disturbing — features of the present approach is the indiscriminate treatment of interrogative and declarative sentences in our game rules. In our treatment, sentences of both moods can be accepted or rejected, they may entail other sentences and follow from them, they can be equivalent or contradictory. This indiscriminatory treatment pays off in an unexpected way in the unified account it allows for the so-called *echo questions*.[20]

Typical examples of echo questions are B's responses in (104)–(110):

(104)   A: I am hungry.
        B: You are hungry?
        A: Yes, I am hungry.

(105)   A: I am hungry.
        B: You are angry?
        A: No, I am not angry, I am hungry.

(106)   A: Are you hungry?
        B: Am I hungry?
        A: Yes, are you hungry?

(107)   A: Are you hungry?
        B: Am I angry?
        A: No, never mind that, but are you hungry?

(108)   A: I am hungry.
        B: You are what?
        A: I am hungry.

(109)   A: Are you hungry?
        B: Am I what?
        A: Are you hungry?

(110)   A: What did you say?
        B: What did who say?
        A: What did you say?

As the examples show, echo questions provide a device for players to check what moves have been just put forward: here, the premise of an echo question is some preceding move, which is repeated as the correct answer to the echo question.

The examples also indicate the severe limitations that hold of the syntax and phonology of echo questions. Sentential (polarity) echo questions such as in (104)–(107) differ from their presuppositions at most in their intonational contour. It is worth noting that there do not exist genuinely disjunctive (choice) echo questions: for instance, (111) is quite odd. (112) is of course possible, as it construes the echo question as sentential:

(111)   A: Are you hungry?   (112)   A: Are you hungry?
        B: Am I hungry or angry?   B: Am I hungry or angry?
        (cf. Did you say hungry or   A: No, are you hungry?
          angry?)
        A: Are you hungry?
        (cf. I said hungry.)

Search (wh-) echo questions are formed by simply replacing any doubtful constituents of the topic sentence by corresponding interrogative pronouns. The result is distinguishable from 'bona fide' questions when a question word appears to have failed to move left — as in (108) — or the result seems to violate cross-over constraints, as in (110).

As the examples (104)–(110) clearly show, these methods of echo question formation are quite impartial as to the mood of the topical sentences. Also, the whole question-answer-reply routine works heree completely independently of the mood of the original move.   .

The latter observation is directly captured by our mood-independent formulations of the notions of acceptance and rejection of sentences, the mood-independent operation of the logical game rules for questions and the abstractness of our pragmatic rules for asking and answering. All that needs to be said about the semantics of echo questions over and above what has been said of *bona fide* questions concerns the definition of the syntactic notions of *declarative* and *interrogative form* for these questions. For them, these notions are trivial: both the declarative and the interrogative form of an echo question (or a sentence derived from it by the logical game rules) equals that sentence itself.

It is not difficult to see how our definitions of presupposition and (direct) answer apply to echo questions given their simple syntax.

For the declarative sentential echo questions in (104)–(105) the presupposition is simply the sentence itself: thus declarative sentential echo questions are in effect elementary questions. Of course, there still remains the possibility of replying to B's question in the negative: but that amounts in our terms to denying the presupposition of the question rather than to a straightforward answer.

Similarly for interrogative sentential echo questions. The presupposition of B's question in (106) is the *bona fide* question attributed to A (*modulo* personal pronoun changes, of course). What B is questioning here is A's acceptance of that question: is A really interested in (prepared to ask or asking) *this* question?

As for search echo questions, nothing new worth of mention springs up in the declarative case (108). As for interrogative echo questions in (109)–(110), their presuppositions can be computed to be (113)–(114), respectively.

(113) Are you something?
(114) What did someone say?

And it is not difficult to prove, using the rules we have already described, that A's respective questions in (109)–(110) do imply these presuppositions.

The main formal differences between echo questions and *bona fide* ones turn out to be these: echo questions can be formed out of interrogative sentences as well as out of declarative ones, and they have particularly simple definitions for the syntactic notions of declarative and interrogative forms.

What about their function? We must first observe that the functional characterization given at the outset was too restricted. As Kuno and Robinson [144] point out, echo questions do not have to repeat an actual earlier utterance. They are also quite popular in a quiz or in court:[21]

(115) The Boston Marathon this year was won by who?
(116) You were informed of the fact on what day?

Bolinger [287] goes even further, maintaining that "the end position is quite normal for original questions: it merely presupposes more than does initial position", citing the example

(117) "They're planning to buy a new house."
"And they're going to pay for it with what, love and hope?"[22]

An echo question can be used also to forestall a question, as in the common commercial ploy

(118) You won't want to be without this wonder product. What does it cost? Only $99.99!

No one has asked a question, but the announcer assumes they would.

In the following example, the questioner does not ask for repetition but for a specification:

(119) "We get reports in every day from various places."
"Reports from where?" she asked sharply. "What do they say?"

The questioner would not be happy with 'various places' here: she heard all right, but she thinks she has a right to hear more.

These examples suffice to show that echo questions are not a mere hearing aid. Where they differ from the usual run of questions is where their simple syntax is most helpful: they they serve to indicate the syntactic form of an explicit or implicit premise by copying it word by word. Thus (115)–(116) suggest that an answer of the indicated form is readily available to the quiz master or the examiner; (117) indicates that someone at least ought to have given a thought to the financial problem. Similar pressures are exerted by (118)–(119) on their addressees.

APPENDIX I

This Appendix describes the essentials of the decision theoretic approach to inductive acceptance developed in Levi [46] and Hilpinen [42]. The program divides into two tasks. The first task is to describe the epistemic preferences stated in the maxims of truth and information in the form of a linear utility function. The second task is to define a Bayesian rule of inductive acceptance which maximizes expected epistemic utility in a probabilistically defined decision situation.

1. FROM PREFERENCES TO UTILITIES

For the maxim of truth the utility function is trivial: all hypotheses divide into two classes, the true ones and the false ones, with no intermediate cases. A simple utility function which suffices to characterize the contribution of the maxim of truth is the valuation function which assigns each hypothesis its truth value (1 for truth and 0 for falsity).

It is less obvious how to represent the utility of information. At the very least, a player ought to prefer a hypothesis to any of its watered-down versions (proper consequences) if they have equal chances of being true.

Such considerations constitute logical conditions of adequacy for any function representing the utility of information. Conventionally, we may assume that the function is normalized to take values between 0 and 1. Naturally enough, a logical truth has the least information value and a logical contradiction a maximum one:

(1)   (i) $0 \leqslant \mathrm{cont}(h) \leqslant 1$
         (ii) if h is logically true, $\mathrm{cont}(h) = 0$
         (iii) if h is logically false, $\mathrm{cont}(h) = 1$.

Further, it seems reasonable to assume that information is additive in the following way:

(2)   When p and q are mutually exclusive answers,
         $\mathrm{cont}(p \vee q) = \mathrm{cont}(p) - \mathrm{cont}(\text{-}q)$.

The motivation of (2) is that the loss of information occasioned by adding a disjunct to an answer should equal the information value of denying that disjunct. As a special case, (2) implies that the utility of any answer exceeds that of its entailments. We also get a simple rule for negations:

(3) $\text{cont}(\text{-}h) = 1 - \text{cont}(h)$.

(1)–(2) spell out the relation of informativeness to logical force. How to compare logically independent hypotheses in terms of informativeness is a much trickier question. There are different alternative approaches to defining informativeness with different merits and weaknesses. Two specific approaches my be mentioned.

Levi [46] assumes that the problem setting provides an equal weighting among alternative complete answers. The problem is assumed to be formulated so that all of its complete answers would satisfy the inquirer's informative needs equally well. That is, in Levi

(4)   whenever p and q are complete answers,
         $\text{cont}(p) = \text{cont}(q)$.

As a consequence, in Levi's approach, for any complete answer p,

(5) $$\text{cont}(p) = 1 - \frac{1}{n}$$

where n is the number of alternative complete answers in the problem setting. Note that the information content of a sentence can vary with the context of inquiry (the number of alternatives available).

In Hilpinen [42], the information content of an answer is assumed to be complementary to its a priori (or prior) probability, i.e.,

(6) $\text{cont}(h) = 1 - p(h)$

Thus it is assumed that the alternative answers to the problem come with (possibly unequal) prior probabilities assigned to them: the more likely an answer, the less information is gained by accepting it. It is easy to check that the definition (6) satisfies the logical conditions (1)–(2). The prior probabilities may be thought of as logical probabilities or as determined by some factual background information.

The next step is to define the tradeoff between utilities based on the maxim of truth and those based on the maxim of information. Naturally enough, we should give the maxim of truth the right of way,

(7)   False answers are never preferable to true answers.

Among answers of like truth value, utility should grow with content:

(8)   Among answers of like truth value, a more informative answer is preferred to a less informative answer.

In order to arrive at a linear utility function satisfying the conditions (7)–(8), a rule for comparing differences of epistemic utility is needed. A simple assumption to make is that differences of epistemic utility can be represented as weighted sums of utility differences in terms of the two component desiderata.

The utility of truth can be represented by the simple valuation function which assigns a true sentence 1 and a false one 0. Then the simple rule of addition just mentioned can be represented by

(9) $u(h) - u(k) = (1 - a)(v(h) - v(k)) + a(\text{cont}(h) - \text{cont}(k))$

where the coefficient a $(1 \leqslant a \leqslant 0)$ represents the weight assigned to information. If a is high, information is valued highly; if it is low, truth is more important. However, it follows from (7) that a cannot exceed the value $\frac{1}{2}$ lest false answers be preferred to true ones.

With the help of some convenient normalization measures, we can calculate from (9) formulas representing the epistemic utility of true and false answers:

(10) $u(h) = 1 - q\,\text{cont}(\text{-}h)$ if h is true
        $u(k) = \text{-}q\,\text{cont}(\text{-}h)$ if k is false

(10) is obtained from (9) by setting conventionally

(11) $u(k) = 0$ if k is contradictory

and replacing the coefficient a by an index $q = \dfrac{a}{1 - a}$ taking values between 1 and 0.

The coefficient q intuitively measures the investigator's lack of caution, in the following sense. If $q = 0$, the utility of an answer equals its truth value. The weight of information vanishes completely and the utility function is exclusively based on the maxim of truth.

When $q = 1$, the utility of information is maximized to the extent that the utility of the least informative true answer (the presupposition of the problem) actually equals the utility of the most informative false answer (the denial of the presupposition), both having utility 0. For values of q in excess of 1, informative falsehoods would gain preference over tautologies, violating (7).

Intermediate values of q reflect different inductive attitudes, varying from player to player with personality and for the same player from occasion to occasion.[1]

2. AN INDUCTIVE DECISION RULE

With an epistemic utility function at our disposal, we can turn to the question of the decision maker's knowledge of the state of Nature.

It is obvious that the decision maker is not assumed to know the state of Nature off hand. Else there would be no decision problem, as the player could choose the optimal answer straight away.

The weakest assumption is that the decision maker has no idea what Nature is likely to do; then the situation is called a *decision problem under uncertainty*. Several principles have been suggested as solutions to decision problems under uncertainty, but there is little consensus about them.[2]

In inductive logic, a stronger assumption is usually made. It is assumed that the decision maker has some evidence e at his disposal which lends the different alternative answers (possibly unequal) probabilities, so that

(12) $p(k/e) = 0$ if k contradicts e
        $p(\lnot h/e) = 1 - p(h/e)$
        $p(h \lor k/e) = p(h/e) + p(k/e) - p(h \& k/e)$

It follows that the presupposition of the topical question is its most probable answer. As a rule, the probability of an answer grows as its information content diminishes. Thus the decision problem usually involves finding an acceptable balance between the risk of error and the gain in information implied by each choice of answer.

The acceptance of an answer can lead to one of two possible outcomes, depending on the state of nature: the answer is true or false. In either case, a linear utility value for the outcome is defined by (10).

Given a linear utility function and a probability distribution, the Bayesian decision rule of maximizing expected utility is applicable. The Bayesian principle recommends choosing an answer so as to maximize the expected yield of epistemic utility, measured by the sum of the utilities of the different possible outcomes weighted by their probabilities.

This yields a simple formula for calculating the expected epistemic utility of a given answer h:

(13) $E(h/e) = p(h/e)(1 - q\text{cont}(\text{-}h)) + (1 - p(h/e))(\text{-}q\text{cont}(\text{-}h))$
            $= p(h/e) - q\text{cont}(\text{-}h).$

What is particularly nice about the behavior of the expected epistemic utility function E thus obtained is its additivity. It is not difficult to prove that

(14) $E(h \lor k/e) = E(h/e) + E(k/e) - E(h \& k/e).$

When h and k are incompatible, the expected epistemic utility of their disjunction equals the sum of their individual expectancies. Therefore including a further complete answer as a disjunct to an answer already accepted represents a gain in expected utility only if its own expectancy is positive.

   This observation allows formulating a simple rule for eliminating complete answers from the presupposition of the problem:

(15)   Reject any complete answer k for which $E(k/e) < 0.$

What remains after application of (15) is the epistemically optimal answer.

   Depending on the measure of informativeness adopted, the condition (15) can be rewritten in different ways. For Levi's definition, it assumes the form

(16) $p(k/e) < q/n$, where n is the number of complete answers.

Hilpinen's definition in turn leads to the condition

(17) $p(k/e) < qp(k)$, where $p(k)$ is the a priori (or prior) probability of k.

The differences between Levi's and Hilpinen's solutions are in evidence in (16)–(17). Levi's approach is tantamount to assigning equal a priori probabilities to the alternative complete answers of an inductive decision problem. As a result, the acceptability of a given sentence may vary with the context of inquiry: a sentence may be acceptable as an answer to one question but unacceptable with respect to another, even if the evidence remains the same.

APPENDIX II

The following conditions (a slight modification of Hintikka's formulations) suffice to define a model set for extensional first-order logic with identity:

(C.&)   If '$p \& q$' is in m, then 'p' and 'q' are in m.

(C.∨)   If '$p \vee q$' is in m, then 'p' or 'q' is in m.

(C.⊃)   If '$p \supset q$' is in m, then '$-p$' or 'q' is in m.

(C.E)   If '$(Ex)p(x)$' is in m, then '$y = a$' and '$p(y)$' are in m for some a and y.

(C.U)   If '$(x)p(x)$' and '$y = a$' are in m, then '$p(y)$' is in m.

(C.=)   If '$a = b$' is in m and 'p' is an atomic formula in m, then the result 'q' of replacing one or more occurrences of 'a' by 'b' in 'p' is in m.

(C. – &) If '$-(p \& q)$' is in m, then '$-p$' or '$-q$' is in m.

(C. – ∨) If '$-(p \vee q)$' is in m, then '$-p$' and '$-q$' are in m.

(C. – ⊃) If '$-(p \supset q)$' is in m, then 'p' and '$-q$' are in m.

(C. – E) If '$-(Ex)p(x)$' and '$y = a$' are in m, then '$-p(y)$' is in m.

(C. – U) If '$-(x)p(x)$' is in m, then '$y = a$' and '$-p(y)$' are in m for some a, y.

(C.≠)   No sentence '$a \neq a$' is in m.

(C.–)   If '$-p$' is a sentence in m, then 'p' is not in m.

In these rules, 'x' and 'y' stand for bindable variables, while 'a' and 'b' can be any singular terms (variables or proper names). Sentences are formulas with no free variables. To see whether a set of sentences is consistent or not, try to extend it to a model set by closing it under the above principles. if this cannot be done without violating (C.≠) or (C.–), the set is inconsistent. To prove that 'q' follows from 'p', show that $\{p, -q\}$ cannot be extended to a model set.[1]

To define a model system for quantified epistemic logic, add to the extensional model set principles the following rules for modalities and identity:

(C.K)   If '$K_a p$' is in m and n is an epistemic a-alternative to m, then 'p' is in n.

(C. − K) If ' $-K_a p$' is in m, then '$\cdot p$' is in some epistemic a-alternative n to m.

(C.T)   If '$K_a p$' is in m, then 'p' is in m.

(C.K=)   If '$K_a p(x)$' is in m, then '$K_a (x = b)$' is in m for some b.

(C.x=)   If '$x = y$' is in m and n is an epistemic a-alternative to m, then '$x = y$' is in n.

(C.x≠)   If '$x \neq y$' is in m and n is an epistemic a-alternative to m, then '$x \neq y$' is in n.

The last two identity rules prevent genuine individuals from splitting or merging when one moves from a world to its epistemic alternatives.

These rules ensure that '$Kp(a)$' implies '$(Ex)Kp(x)$' only in the presence of '$(Ex)K(x = a)$', and that '$a = b$' does not suffice to derive '$Kp(a)$', 'p' extensional, from '$Kp(b)$' while '$K(a = b)$' does. Unlike Hintikka's original rules, quantification according to the present rules is over actually existing individuals. "There is someone I do not know who he is" can be simply represented by

(1) $(Ex) - (Ey)K(x = y)$

and "I know who everybody is" by

(2) $(x)(Ey)K(x = y).$

It is not difficult to prove that (1)–(2) are two contingent but contradictory sentences in the present system.[2]

PART II

DISCOURSE GRAMMAR

CHAPTER 1

DISCOURSE GRAMMAR

1. DISCOURSE ANALYSIS AND DISCOURSE GRAMMAR

The first Part of this essay has been concerned with discourse analysis, defined as the study of what makes a sequence of sentences a coherent piece of discourse. My general answer to this main problem of discourse analysis can now be formulated: *a text is coherent (well-formed) if it can be extended into a well-formed dialogue game*.

The theory of dialogues developed in this work is of course primarily a theory of conversational exchanges. It is my belief that such exchanges bring out the essentials of text structure most clearly.

Yet the theory of dialogue applies to the analysis of monologue as well – i.e., to the description of a connected text. The key to such applications is the idea of *textual interpolation*. In order to reveal the implicit structure of a piece of discourse, extend it into a dialogue, by adding implicit dialogue steps which make the connections between the sentences of the text explicit. The function of the sentences of the original text will be spelled out by their role in the reconstructed dialogue, and their connections to one another will be represented by the sequences of moves that connect them in the reconstructed dialogue.[1]

Here is an illustrative example of such textual analysis. The original sentences of a passage from Carroll's *Alice in Wonderland* stand out as italicized.[2]

(1)   1.   *"I want a clean cup"*, *interrupted the Hatter*: *"Let's all move one place on."* (D.say)
         2.   Did they move? Who moved when? (D.question) to 1.
         3.   *He moved on as he spoke, and the Dormouse followed him.* (D.answer) to 2.
         4.   Who got whose place? (D.question) to 3
         5.   The Hatter got a clean cup, while the Dormouse took the Hatter's place. (D.infer) to 1, 3, (D.answer) to 4.
         6.   Who took the Dormouse's place? (D.infer) to 4–5.
         7.   *The March Hare moved into the Dormouse's place*, (D.answer) to 6.

8. And who took the March Hare's place? (D.infer) to 4.7; (D.and) to 6.
9. *And Alice, rather unwillingly, took the place of the March Hare.* (D.answer) to 8, (D.and) to 7.
10. Why was Alice reluctant to move? (D.question) to 9.
11. Did Alice perhaps lose in the change? (D.explain) to 10.
12. Who gained what in the change? (D. explain) to 11.
13. *The Hatter was the only one who got any advantage from the change,* (D.answer) to 12.
14. For the Hatter got a clean cup (D.explain) to 13, (D.infer) to 5.
15. *And Alice was a good deal worse off than before,* (D.answer) to 12, (D.and) to 13.
16. *As the March Hare had just upset the milk-jug into his* plate. (D.explain) to 15, (D.answer) to 10.

This analysis is only illustrative; no claims of ultimate accuracy are implied. In all its simplicity, it does point out some of the obvious properties of the italicized paragraph. The excerpt is a description of a change of seats at the mad tea-party. The subject of the paragraph is given away by the first sentence of the text, which immediately suggests the first sub-topics in 2 and 4. These topics are dealt with in the moves 3—9. Move 9 serves as a point of transition to the final subtopic 12; this it does by inserting, apparently superfluously, a comment on Alice's reaction to the Hatter's suggestion. The insertion indicates that the motives of the characters are relevant for the discussion, thus raising the question 12. The conflict of interests between Alice and the Hatter in 13—15 will contribute to Alice's decision to abandon the party in the sequel, which connects the present paragraph to later developments.

How do we arrive at the interpolations in the example (1)? The present approach does not offer any mechanical way of finding the (or a) correct analysis of a given text. There is no algorithm for generating appropriate dialogue contexts. In effect, we are faced with a problem of content analysis: how to make the best possible sense of an elliptic message. The success of a suggested reconstruction is ultimately gauged by its ability to faithfully reflect the implicit intentions of the author(s) of the discourse.

However, things are not quite hopeless. Certain grammatical clues give definite boundary conditions to a proposed expansion: sentences of certain syntactical shapes will be appropriate in certain dialogue contexts but not in others. This observation can be turned into a sort of transcendental deduction of the discipline of *discourse grammar*. As the findings of Part I of this essay show, a dialogue has an important further order of structure over and above the sequence of its explicit moves. Since this further order of structure is far richer than the linear order, considerable ambiguity is left in the problem of figuring out the structure of a piece of discourse from its explicit sentences. It is therefore not surprising to find in natural languages different grammatical devices whose function is to aid speakers in guessing at the implicit structure of discourse from its explicit moves. The study of such expressive means is the task of discourse grammar.

In this Part of the essay, I shall try to show by means of case studies that the function and distribution of many devices of discourse grammar can be accounted for in simple and natural ways by the conceptual machinery of dialogue games. The success of the dialogue game framework to account for facts of dialogue grammar will thus constitute important supporting evidence for the dialogue game approach.

2. APPROPRIATENESS, COHERENCE, AND COHESION

The choice of a complete dialogue game as the basic unit of text grammar has important consequences to the analysis of individual sentences. The concepts and rules of discourse grammar are not directly concerned with an absolute property of grammaticality (acceptability) of individual sentences. What they characterize in the first place is the relative property of *appropriateness* of sentences as moves in dialogues. From this relative property, absolute properties can be defined, as indicated, by quantification over all well-formed dialogues: a sentence is strictly admissible if it can be embedded in some well-formed dialogue game; it is strictly ill-formed if it cannot be embedded in any dialogue game.

This creates a crucial element of indeterminacy in absolute judgments of naturalness of sentences. When one is asked whether a sentence – or some reading of it – is natural, how one sets about generating a judgment is by trying to imagine that sentence as a fragment of a dialogue; in other words, one tries to embed it in a well-formed dialogue game. It follows that a naturalness judgment is a faithful index about actual functional properties of a sentence only if the subject's judgment is not imparied by irrelevant assumptions about the likelihood, interest, ethical or aesthetic properties of the dialogue contexts to consider. Chances are that a subject deems a sentence unnatural not because it has no place in any well-formed dialogue, but just because the subject does not come to think of, or rejected, certain possible dialogues on the basis on what he assumes people usually are (or should be) interested in, say or believe.[3]

Another interesting consequence has been anticipated by G. Lakoff [579]. Although the notion of well-formedness of a fully specified dialogue is a decidable notion (it suffices to see if its individual moves are well-formed and if all connections between the moves obey the dialogue game rules), the question of the well-formedness of an arbitrary piece of discourse is not, thanks to the extra existential quantifier in our characterization of the notion. To find out if, say, a step of indirect inference is valid, one will have to decide if there is a proof for it from the logical game rules. And this question is known to be undecidable even for the minimum of logical machinery implicit in our logical game rules.

Given a suggested dialogue reconstruction of a text, we can check it for *cohesion* by making sure that the augmented dialogue is well formed: i.e., that each move is properly related to its premises by rules of dialogue grammar.

However, the analysis, to be successful, should also represent a *coherent* dialogue: a dialogue whose participants are following reasonably rational dialogue strategies given our assumptions about their aims and attitudes. We expect a well-formed discourse to make reasonable sense besides hanging together by discourse grammatical criteria. This aspect is what distinguishes a coherent text from the incoherent though fluent speech of a schizophrenic patient.

These considerations suggest a neat distinction between textual *cohesion* and textual *coherence*. Cohesion is a property of a well-formed if not a well-played dialogue game: one whose moves conform to the rules of dialogue grammar. Coherence pertains to considerations of dialogue *strategy*: a coherent dialogue is one whose moves appropriately serve the dialogue purposes of their authors.[4]

3. AUTONOMY OF DISCOURSE GRAMMAR

The main theses of my approach to discourse grammar are these. First, I want to distinguish clearly between *structure* (rules of formation) and *function* (rules of interpretation). Rules of formation define a class of well-formed sentences with no reference to outside information: they are exclusively couched in the primitives of grammatical theory, whether they be stated constructively, as in phrase structure or categorial grammar, analytically by means of rules which filter out grammatical strings from arbitrary strings of formatives, or by mixed means (as in transformational grammar). Rules of formation are thus characterized essentially by their *autonomy*.[5]

Rules of interpretation, in contrast, *relate* grammatical constructions to some further, independently defined structures, be it the actual world (Bloomfield), some specified aspects of it (cognitive psychology), a class of possible worlds or models (model theoretic semantics), another formal language (Montague, or Katz semantics), or games (game-theoretical semantics, dialogue game theory). Functional rules thus are essentially relational.[6]

Of course, the distinction is relative to the choice of primitives of the grammatical theory. Grammatical theory can always be reduced to rules of formation only, if enough of the domain of interpretation is included into the primitives of grammar.[7] (This is what happens in extreme developments of generative semantics.) Such shuffling of grammatical primitives is of course ultimately constrained by considerations of simplicity of the grammar. If the result of the inclusion of further primitives leads to a very heterogeneous and unconstrained class of grammatical rules, chances are that the power of the theory would increase from factorization of types of rules into separate components. This is of course the argument against generative semantics raised by the grammarians of the standard transformational school.

In the modular extreme, it even makes sense to speak of interpreting different orders of (what is traditionally considered) grammatical structure onto another. It is customary to speak of one level of grammatical structure being translated into structures generated by another component. Thus the difference between structural and functional rules concerns the factorization of different rules of grammar into components, or the *modularity* of grammar, to use the fashionable term.[8]

Thus what my insistence on distinguishing rules of formation and rules of interpretation in text grammar really amounts to is a claim for relative autonomy of dialogue grammar. Specifically, I want to separate rules determining well-formed dialogue structure from rules determining well-formed sentence structure. Certain sets of rules will determine constraints on how sentences are put together from words and how they are pronounced.

Another set of rules tells us how sentences can be embedded into dialogue structure. In the process, some further filtering of sentences may occur, if some grammatical sentences find no appropriate contexts of use. Such sentences will be rejected as grammatical but uninterpretable.

A second thesis is the autonomy of different components of dialogue grammar. The pragmatic lexicon, functional syntax, and prosody operate independently of each other. They are coupled only by the fact that they fulfill some of the same functions in relating sentences to dialogue context. Any distributional constraints which emerge represent interaction of independently defined rules. They need not be spelled out directly by grammatical rule.

The components of dialogue grammar can be roughly divided by the traditional categories of lexicon, syntax, and phonology.

To the functional lexicon belong such words as connectives (coordinating conjunctions) *and, or, but*; subordinating ones such as *while, whereas, if, although, unless, because, since*; adjuncts like *yet, however, still, therefore, then, so, also, too, even, only, again, on the other hand*; anaphors including personal pronouns and words like *one, do, so, yes, no*; certain intensional words such as *know, regret, manage, surprise, odd*, and interjections such as *Oh! Aha!*, or *Well!*

Functional syntax features prominently syntactic subordination and linear order, certain specific grammatical constructions (existential sentences, cleft sentences), and ellipsis (deletion). Finally, a central phonological vehicle of text organization is *intonation*, traditionally divided into prominence (stress), phrasing (pauses, duration), and accent (pitch).

In the following case studies, I shall pick out from this wealth of expressive means such as are specifically oriented towards signaling the structure of a dialogue.

This part of the essay is organized faithfully following the assumed modular structure of dialogue grammar. This presentation creates certain expository difficulties, for the obvious reason that it is hard to find examples where the different orders of text structure would not interact in interesting ways. What is more, the most impressive arguments for the autonomous treatment often come from the interaction of the different textual means. In particular, some of the most interesting observations about word order concern its interaction with intonation, which topic will be completely omitted here.[9]

CHAPTER 2

CONNECTIVES

1. *AND*

I start out by considering the use of the two commonest coordinating conjunctions, *and* and *or*. I want to suggest that the elusive constraints on the use of these conjunctions and the frustrating subtlety of intuitions concerning their appropriateness are due to the multiplicity of structural possibilities of dialogue games. Thanks to the structural complexity of dialogue games, the game rules for *and* and *or* can be left quite simple. The full complexity of acceptability judgments can be left to be predicted by systematic variations of dialogue context.

The first observation that one is likely to make about *and* is that not any two sentences can naturally be conjoined with it. Some conjunctions do not seem to make much sense:

(1)   Reagan is smart and a whale is a fish.

Certain further observations should follow close at the heels of this one. First, (1) would be an odd couple even without the *and:*[1]

(2)   Reagan is smart. A whale is a fish.

Second, the same two sentences can make a perfect, though sarcastic, dialogue:

(3)   A: Reagan is smart.
         B: And a whale is a fish.

Third, even (1) ceases to be odd if a good reason for saying it is provided, for instance, the question

(4)   What did you learn at school today?

All of these observations involve instances or violations of the overriding principle already discovered in Part I: *be relevant* (play rationally). A dialogue move sounds inappropriate in a given context if it seems an irrational move to make in that dialogue, given the aims and the attitudes of the participants. By implication, a sentence in isolation sounds odd or unacceptable as long as one is hard put to find any good reason for anyone to say it in any dialogue context. As soon as a suitable context is provided, the feeling of oddity subsides.

The particular trouble with (1) and (2) seems to be this. If one tries to construe the two sentences in (2) as a single dialogue move, one has a difficult time conjuring up an informational interest which that move would satisfy, a common topic to which both halves of the move could be addressed. As expected, the trouble is immediately alleviated when such a topic is found. Sometimes, the topic may itself be a curious one. For instance, (1) could be construed as a sadly misinformed teacher's answer to two of his students at the same time:

(5)   A: Why is Reagan president?
         B: And what is a whale?
         C: Reagan is smart and a whale is a fish.

However, it is not too difficult how the double-barreled question in (5) might have arisen in turn, for instance as two questions that were left unclear in the course of reading an assigned text. The common denominator for them would be the teacher's question

(6)   What is unclear in the text?

Let us return to (3). The workings of the sarcasm in (3) have already been explained in Part I.[2] In brief, B is suggesting that A may subsume both of their contributions under one and the same topic, presumably not very much different from

(7)   What common misconceptions are there?

The interesting question is, why does the insertion of 'and' help B to get this innuendo through here? The explanation lies in the dialogue game rule for *and*:

(D.and)   When a player has put forward a dialogue move, he may continue on the same topic by conjoining a further sentence to it by *and*.

Thus 'and' in (3) indicates to A that B does not intend to change the topic, but has in mind one that will cover both moves.

(D.and) has been formulated as a continuation move. This explains why one who conjoins another sentence to another player's move implicitly accepts the first move:

(8)   A: Who will buy this book?
         B: I will buy it!
         C: And I will buy it!

Here, *and* is in order if there are several copies of the book for sale: B will buy one and C another. It would be odd or inappropriate if there is competition for just one copy, for then C could not accept that B buys the book as well.

The formulation of (D.and) helps narrow down the possible dialogue functions of a sentence begun by *and*. A sentence starting with *and* must address the same topic in the same manner as its premise. Thus it serves to turn a sentence which otherwise could be construed as a reply or an explanation into a simple addition in

(9)   A: Gold is expensive.
         B: And it is scarce.

The conjunction tells that B has in mind a topic that both sentences may address, say, what is gold like.

The formulation of (D.and) is noncommittal as to the mood of the sentences conjoined. What is required is that the sentences conjoined share dialogue function. Therefore, as a rule of thumb, sentences of different moods do not freely conjoin.

(10)   Who are you, and I am Bob.

The first half of (10) is likely to be a move by (D.question), and thus can only be continued by a further question. There would be nothing wrong with

(11)   Who are you, and who is he?

The rule of thumb is not without apparent exceptions. The permutation of (10) in (12) is quite natural:

(12)   I am Bob, and who are you?

I think that (12) is really only an apparent exception. (12) is just yet another case of a dialogue rule applying to a suppressed premise. The structure of the turn in (12) actually involves two dialogue moves. The first constitutes an answer to a dialogically silent question, and the second constitutes a continuation of the suppressed question. The structure of the dialogue might be

(13)   Who is who?
         Who am I? — and — Who are you?
         I am Bob.

This explanation also accounts for the asymmetry between (12) and (10). In the converse case (10), a reconstruction similar to (13) is not available, for there the missing first conjunct, an answer to the first question, has yet to be supplied. Once it is at hand, the continuation is all right:

(14)   B: Who are you?
         C: I am Carol.
         B: And I am Bob.

Another interesting corollary was pointed out to me by Paul Kiparsky. The following dialogue sounds somewhat disjointed:

(15)   A to B: Who are you?
         B: I am Bob.
         A to C: And who are you?
         C: And I am Carol.

Carol, one feels, should not have begun her answer by *and*. This is as expected: although A is continuing his question to B by *and*, C's answer is in no way a continuation of B's answer to the first half of it. By using *and*, Carol as it were ignores the question A is presently addressing to her and looks back to join her answer to B's contribution.

2. *OR*

The dialogue game rule for *or* differs only minimally from that for *and*:

(D.or)   When a player has put forward a dialogue move, he may continue
           it by adjoining a further disjunct to it beginning with *or*.

The dialogue properties of *or* also provide analogous arguments to those supporting (D.and). Wildly disparate disjuncts are odd in the same way as topically incoherent conjuncts.

For instance, it would be quite odd for someone named Smith to blurt out

(16)   Five men fit into a Fiat or my name is Smith.

Again, it is not difficult to imagine contexts where what seems nonsensical at first becomes eminently natural. One particular context is of special interest, as it nicely illustrates the interplay of the logic of *or* with its discourse properties. Assume it is common knowledge that the name of the author of (16) is not Smith. Then (16) becomes a fully idiomatic way of emphatically affirming the first disjunct of (16).

How does this implicature of (16) come about? The explanation ties up (D.or) with insights from deductive and inductive logic.

First note that (D.or) creates an asymmetry between the disjuncts of a disjunction. The first member of a disjunction alone constitutes a *bona fide* dialogue move; for instance, the first disjunct of (16) already constitutes an adequate answer to the question

(17)   How many men fit into a Fiat?

In virtue of (C.or), a dialogue move can optionally be amended by the addition of a further disjunct, designed to take over the burden of the answer in case the first disjunct fails. This is why (16) seemed wrong-headed to start with: what has the speaker's name to do with the seating capacity of a Fiat?

Fortunately, the asymmetry of (D.or) also suggests what the connection is. In virtue of the asymmetry, (16) is recognized as equivalent to a particular *conditional* sentence, namely

(18)   If five men do not fit into a Fiat, my name is Smith.

The riddle about (16) can now be restated as a problem of logical inference: what on earth may establish a relation of consequence as curious as (18)? An answer is ready at hand: it is a familiar fact of logic that from an impossibility, anything follows, any arbitrarily chosen further absurdity included. In other words, given the indisputability of the premise

(19)   My name is not Smith,

both (16) and (18) turn out as logically equivalent to the categorical assertion

(20)   Five men fit into a Fiat.

Good: we have established that granted (19), (16) is only a roundabout paraphrase of (20) – no matter if the second disjunct seems irrelevant to the inquiry at hand.

However, something important remains unexplained – why is (16) a particularly *emphatic* way of putting (20), not, say, a tentative or perhaps just functionally indifferent paraphrase? This is where inductive considerations enter the explanation.

The premises of the explanation are that the author of (16) considers the first disjunct of (16) an adequate move in itself, say as an answer to (17), and that he assumes it to be common knowledge — i.e., an assumption accepted by all with a high degree of confidence — that his name is not Smith.

Given that the first disjunct is already optimal against some reasonable index of caution, the second disjunct seems eminently foolish: why should he weaken his position by an obviously unlikely assumption?

There is one situation where an amendment may be in order: that is if the index of caution the player is operating with is dramatically increased, with a consequent lowering of the rejection threshold for the denial of the first disjunct (and for other equally unlikely suppositions). Examples of disjunctive amendments in the presence of increased caution are common: here are some from Patricia Moyes' novel *Death and the Dutch Uncle*.

(21)   You don't get outsiders here. Or if you do, they don't stay long.

(22)   — What's his name, by the way?
        — Weatherby, sir. Or so he says.

(23)   — Nobody else saw Pereira slip and fall.
        — Ah well, that was just a matter of luck.
        — Was it?
        — Or bad luck, from the poor old — gentleman's point of view.

In each case, the author of the disjunction sees fit to watch his words on second thought, involved as he is in a police investigation. In (23), the increased caution is actually prompted by an incredulous checking question from the interviewer.

As these examples illustrate, the addition of a disjunct to a *prima facie* optimal answer may be rational if an increased index of caution is indicated. How does this connect up with the sense of affirmation in (16)? The argument is simple. By appending the obviously exaggerated proviso to his answer in (16), the author invites his audience to figure out a conversational implicature: what assumption should be made about the speaker to explain the amendment as a rational move. The simplest assumption is that the author is operating with an uncommon high degree of caution, one inversely related to the improbability of the preposterous disjunct. This balance helps the audience gauge the degree of confidence with which the author accepts the first disjunct: it is as high as the degree of caution needed to admit that particular amendment. For anyone operating with a lower index of caution,

(16) therefore amounts to a particularly confident affirmation of the first disjunct.

An extreme case of this dialogue strategy is the use of *or* to introduce counterfactual *reductio ad absurdum* arguments:

(24)   — But it wasn't one of our regulars.
            — Of course not, said Henry. None of your regulars were here,
            were they? Or you'd have recognized them.

Or again equals *else*: the counterfactual alternative is complementary to the first disjunct. The logic of Henry's argument in (24) is clear: Suppose, for the sake of the argument, that it were rational to amend

(25)   None of your regulars were here

with its contradictory

(26)   Some of your regulars were here,

which is the suppressed premise of the subjunctive clause. Given the obvious axiom

(27)   You recognize your regulars,

(26) would indeed imply the subjunctive clause in (24). But, earlier in the dialogue of which (24) is a fragment, it has been already agreed that

(28)   You didn't recognize any of them.

Hence accepting (26) would lead to accepting contradictory sentences in violation of (C.cons). This suffices to eliminate the hypothetical alternative (26) so as to affirm just (25). A full dialogue reconstruction of (24) could look like

(29)   1. H: Was it one of your regulars? (D.ask)
          2. W: It wasn't one of our regulars. (D.answer) to 1.
          3. H: Of course not. (D.reply) to 1—2.
          4. H: None of your regulars were here. (D.explain) to 3.
          5. H: Were they? (D.question) to 4.
          6. H: Or some of your regulars were here. (D.or) to 4.
          7. H: Then you'd have recognized them. (D.infer) to 6, (27).
          8. H: Did you recognize any of them? (D.question) to 7.
          9. W: I didn't recognize any of them. (D.reply) to 7—8.
         10. H: So none of your regulars were here. (D.infer) to 6—9.

Lines 6–9 violate (C.cons), so the counterfactual alternative must be rejected. Notice how the subjunctive mood of the *or* clause gives away the fact that none of it is (ostensibly) accepted (cf. Part I, Ch. IV.5).

Example (24) is a good reminder that the key moves of a dialogue may well remain implicit: the rejected alternative (26), which actually motivates *or*, is never said aloud but has to be inferred from one of its consequences.

One point about *or* that needs attention is the application of meaning conventions to a move and a disjunctive continuation to it. We have to require that (D.earnest) and its alternatives are retrospectively reapplied to the *completed* dialogue move. This is why one who adds a further disjunct to a move need not continue to endorse its premise. Neither does he have to accept the amendment. What he does have to accept is the completed disjunction, whether by accepting one of its disjuncts or by admitting several of them.

Examples of this observation are

(30)   "It could have been Mario, though. He's so slim and pretty. Or Sylvie, or Chantal, – "
         "Or you!" Mario spat out the words.

(31)   "Hell, Henry, don't be this way. Look now. Nobody knew about the leakage of information last night except you and me. This morning Trapp knew about it. The note in the typewriter makes that clear enough. So, by a simple process of deduction, you must have told him."
         "Unless you did, or he found out himself."

By completing the first speaker's move, the second speaker here indicates he accepts it only as amended. Yet he need not consider the amendment any more likely than the other alternatives.

3. INCLUSIVE OR EXCLUSIVE *OR*

Another long-standing puzzle about *or* is its apparent vacillation between inclusive and exclusive senses. As has been pointed out by several writers, it will not do just to say that there are two *or*'s in English, one equivalent to logical inclusive disjunction and the other to logical exclusive disjunction (contravalence, or contradictory of material equivalence).[3]

One reason is that iteration of contravalence is not logically equivalent to a multiple exclusive *or* in English. As McCawley has pointed out, a three-way contravalence is not only true if one and only one of its members is true, but also if all of the members are true. This extraordinary truth condition clearly fails the intention of the exclusive *or* in sentences like

(32)   Either I won or you won or it is a split decision.

(32), if understood as a three-way choice, does not allow all of its members to turn out true at once.[4]

The binary notion of contravalence is best matched by connectives like *else* or *unless*. Iterations of these connectives may be self-correcting:

(33)   I won unless you won, unless it is a split decision.
(34)   I won, else you won, else it is a split decision.

Here, the last alternative may actually cancel the first contravalence, allowing for all of the disjuncts to turn out true.

A syntactic difference between *or* and the binary disjunctions confirms the semantic distinction. We shall note below that *and*, unlike the binary *but*, allows coordination of an arbitrary number of conjuncts into one conjunction, with the option of omitting all but the last occurrence of *and* between the conjuncts. *Or* (whether inclusively or exclusively understood) has a similar syntactic liberty, while *unless* and *else* do not.

The best one can say about the exclusive use of *or* that it goes with a uniqueness presupposition to the effect that precisely one of its disjuncts is true.

But what sort of a requirement is this? Where does it come from, and when is it present? To approach this question, consider (35) which is not only acceptable but a completely ordinary thing to say indicating that precisely one of the disjuncts should be chosen:

(35)   Either I won or you won or we both won.

What is peculiar about (35) is that ordinarily, we would assume the last disjunct to entail both of the earlier ones. But then the three alternatives are not exclusive after all!

In order to construe the three alternatives in (35) as mutually exclusive, they are best considered as three alternative proposals for a complete answer to some underlying question, say

(36)   Who won?

Although logically compatible, the disjuncts in (35) cannot all be complete answers to (36). Thus, it seems to me, the exclusivity of *or* is a matter of dialogue grammar. As far as semantics goes, *or* has the meaning assigned to it by (C.or), i.e., that of an inclusive disjunction. *Or* seems exclusive when a uniqueness presupposition is conferred to it by its role in a dialogue.

In our example (35), it is the function of (35) as a disjunction of alternative complete answers to (36) that is responsible for the uniqueness presupposition.

It is even easier to understand why *or* obtains an exclusive interpretation when (38) is construed as an answer to the *which*-question in (37):

(37)   Which player won?
(38)   A won or B won or C won.

Due to the uniqueness entailment of *which*, any direct answer to (37) is at once a complete answer to it, and as such eliminates any other alternatives.

This line of explanation leads one to expect that *or* ceases to seem exclusive where it combines alternative answers to an existentially understood question. (Recall that an existential question can have any number of equally good and compatible complete answers.)

This expectation is actually confirmed:

(39)   What do old people do for physical exercise?
(40)   They walk or swin or play shuffleboard.

Surely, there is no implication in (40) that the alternative forms of exercise exclude each other.

Our examples so far have come from declarative sentences. I do not think that anything new need be said to capture the behavior of *or* in questions. Consider the following example:

(41)   Did John visit Sweden, Norway, or Denmark?

It is well first to dispose of the possibility that (41) represents a simple sentential question formed out of a disjunctive sentence. On this analysis, (41) admits of only two answers, yes and no. This interpretation is easiest to hear if one appends *or not*.

Two more interpretations remain, corresponding to the topics (42) and (43), respectively.

(42)   Which country did John visit?
(43)   Which countries did John visit?

In the context of (42), (41) expects one and only one choice among the alternatives, while in the context of (43), more than one alternative may

be right, and the questioner wants the whole list. In the face of these observations, it seems to me unnecessary to add anything to the rules and
principles we have for disjunctive questions. (41) represents a unique-alter-
native question if it is offered as an explanation for (42); it obtains a conjunctive interpretation if it represents a series of guesses derived from (43)
as the ultimate topic. There is nothing in the structural description of (41)
which decides for one of the interpretations rather than the other.

4. *BUT*

The English *but* exhibits even more surface divergence in its distribution than
and. This has led dictionaries and earlier linguistic literature to distinguish
several distinct if related senses of this useful word. My intention again is
to try to reduce a diversity of different uses of *but* to just one dialogue rule,
applied in a corresponding multiplicity of dialogue contexts.[5]

For this purpose, it is useful to have something of an overview of the
apparently different uses of *but*. A handy way to distinguish them is to relate
them to appropriate disambiguating adverbials, which help to fix a specific
sense of *but* when appended to the word or substituted for it.[6]

The existence of such disambiguating words in a certain sense justifies
the subdivisions we shall make. Although they do not constitute sufficient
reason to say that *but* itself is ambiguous (it needs but one rule, after all),
they show that the subdivisions at least represent possible senses of adversative conjunctions. The existence of such disambiguating particles in English
and in other languages lends the present study particular interest. If the
dialogue game framework helps predict which particular subdivisions of the
domain of *but* should occur in English and recur in other languages, so as
to yield the makings for a universal typology of adversative conjunctions,
there is good hope for claims of universality for the approach.

With these vistas in mind, let us get to the facts.

Perhaps the most commonly recognized *but* is the *contrary-to-expectation*
but, aptly paraphrased by *yet*:

(44)   My name is Sue, but I am a boy.
(45)   The President is past eighty, but he is still bright as a button.
(46)   She is busy, but she helps us all the same.

Another fluent paraphrase for this sense of *but* is to subordinate the first
sentence to the second by *although* or *despite*. In these examples, the first

sentence constitutes inductive counterevidence for the second sentence, whence the epithet 'contrary-to-expectation'.

However, as more than one author before me has observed, there is no necessity of an inductive dependence between the two sentences conjoined by *but*. There is none in

(47)   I like it, but I cannot afford it.
(48)   Mary is intelligent, but she is ugly.
(49)   He tried, but he failed.

In order to accept (47)–(49), it is not necessary to assume that people as a rule prefer things within their means, that smart people are beautiful, or that most trials are followed by success. This sense of *but* can be paraphrased by *however* or *on the other hand*. *Although* and *yet* would not be appropriate here.

Intuitively, the point about (47)–(49) is that they weight the evidence for and against some unspoken supposition: the author of (47) may be deliberating about a purchase, (48) may discuss Mary's chances of success in male society, (49) whether someone managed to do something or not. In all these cases, there is some unspoken *tertium comparationis* (to borrow a phrase from Abraham [390]) which induces the contrast. Let us call this sense of *but* the 'tertium comparationis' *but*.

Finally, there is what Robin Lakoff [411] calls the 'semantic opposition' *but*:

(50)   John hates ice cream, but I like it.
(51)   John turned left, but Bill turned right.
(52)   He spoke Spanish, but she spoke Italian.

Here, the contrast between *and* and *but* is minimal: *and* could replace *but* with only the slightest difference in nuance. Other natural paraphrases are *whereas* and *while*.

Now what could be common to all these uses of *but*? My answer is based on the following statement of the dialogue game rule for *but*:

(D.but)   When a player has addressed a move to a given topic, any player may rejoin to it by a sentence beginning with *but*, addressed to a coordinate but contradictory topic.

Two auxiliary definitions are needed. First, by addressing a topic I mean making a *countermove* to it: as the topic is a question, a response to it will be a (partial or complete) answer to it, including an inductive argument for one.

What is meant by coordinate topics in (D.but) is easiest to show by means of an example. Let us look at a likely dialogue structure of one of the simplest examples:

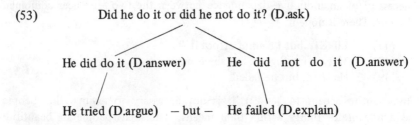

(53)   Did he do it or did he not do it? (D.ask)

He did do it (D.answer)   He did not do it (D.answer)

He tried (D.argue)   – but –   He failed (D.explain)

The motivation of *but* is graphically evident in (53). The main topic of the dialogue admits of two contradictory answers to which the two sides of (49) are addressed. The first half of (49) constitutes evidence for the positive answer, while the second half verifies the negative one. The structural condition of (D.but) is satisfied, and the sentence passed.

The same structural explanation is easily extended to the other instances of tertium comparationis *but* in (47)–(48). For (48), we might propose the topic

(54)   Is she a first-rate secretary?

and for (47)

(55)   Will you buy it?

What is meant by coordinate topics in (D.but) is now diagrammatically shown in (53): two topics are coordinate if they represent functionally similar countermoves to one and the same superordinate topic.

The rules (D.and) and (D.but) seem to capture the gist of Leibniz' suggestions concerning the use of *but* as contrasted to *and*, distilled by Goddard [409] as follows: [7]

The basic idea is that in saying a clause, and following it with another clause, preceded by the word *and*, one signals that the second clause is a continuation (something more), added to the first clause.

In saying *but*, however, it is suggested that one signals that what follows is *not* a continuation of what went before, that it is not something more.

(D.and) and (D.but) capture this insight quite literally: *and* continues a move addressed to a topic, while *but* moves to a coordinate but contrastive topic.

5. APPLICATIONS OF (D.BUT)

The contrary-to-expectation examples had as their defining feature that the two sides of *but* are in inductive conflict. How does this come about? Likely topics for (44)–(46) are (56)–(58), respectively:

(56)   Who are you? Are you a boy or a girl?
(57)   Is the president in full possession of his buttons?
(58)   What did she say? Can we count on her?

These topic proposals have one important feature in common. It is that the *but* clause actually constitutes a decisive answer to the topic it addresses – an answer which entails a direct answer to the question. This observation is nicely confirmed by the syntactic fact that it is the *but* clause that forms the main clause when *but* is paraphrased by *although* or *despite*.

The dialogue structure of (44) might be

(59)

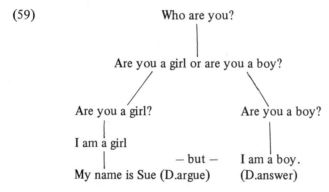

A crucial point about (59) is that the *but* clause constitutes a decisive answer to its topic. As a consequence, any argument for a conflicting answer on the left side of *but* disconfirms the *but* clause itself. Compare this to the situation in (53), where there is no necessity of inductive relevance between argument and counterargument.

Another example of a slightly different character confirms the observation. Consider

(60)   She is exceptional. She is busy, but she helps us.

Clearly, the author (60) has in mind an inductive generalization like

(61)   Busy people do not help.

to which someone forms a brilliant exception. Here, the left side of the *but* sentence, in virtue of the conditional probability statement (61) strongly suggests a negative answer to the question

    (62)   Does she help us or not?

On the other hand, the *but* sentence immediately clinches the argument contrary to common expectation: that's where she is exceptional. The structure of the dialogue could be described by something like

    (63)   What is she like?
                                  She is exceptional.
                                  How?
                                  She is busy — *but* — she helps us.

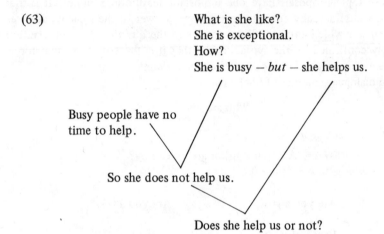

    Busy people have no
    time to help.

         So she does not help us.

                                  Does she help us or not?

The structure of the dialogue here is hard to lay out graphically without repetition, as certain sentences play multiple roles in it. The left side of *but* has the converse roles of raising the topic of the *but* clause and providing an argument for a negative answer to it. The whole *but* sentence (or the subdialogue which describes its function) provides an explanation of the woman's exceptionality by answering a *how* question.

    To sum up, a contrary-to-expectation *but* seems to arise in that special case where the *but* clause constitutes a complete answer to its topic. In that case, an inductive relation of disconfirmation between the two clauses conjoined by *but* logically follows. In other *but* sentences, such an inductive tie is quite coincidental. For *yet*, it is essential, that is why *yet* would serve to disambiguate *but* here.

    The 'semantic opposition' *but* is not difficult to subsume under (D.but). Likely topics for (50)–(52), respectively:

(64)   How do you people like ice cream? Do you like it or not?
(65)   Which way did they go? Did they turn left or right?
(66)   What language did they speak? Was it Spanish?

What is common to (64)–(66) is a presupposition of shared taste, destination
or language: the first conjunct of the *but* sentence is consistent with the
presupposition of the question, the second conjunct falsifies it. It is instructive to compare the topics in (64)–(66) to

(67)   Who hates ice cream and who likes it?
(68)   Who turned where?
(69)   Who spoke what language?

Unlike (64)–(66), these questions make no assumptions about sharing;
accordingly, there is no need to resort to *but* in answering them:

(70)   John hates ice cream and I like it.
(71)   John turned left and Bill turned right.
(72)   He spoke Spanish and she spoke Italian.

Logically, the difference between (64)–(66) and (67)–(69) is quite
subtle; it is essentially a matter of quantifier ordering. In (64)–(66), the
job of singling out individual members of *you* and *they* is left to the answerer,
whereas in (70)–(72), distributivity is already suggested in the question.
The questions in (64)–(66) carry a stronger presupposition, for in them
the choice of answer is not assumed to depend on the choice of individual
subjects in the manner of (70)–(72). It is this quite subtle presupposition
that *but* addresses in the 'semantic opposition' examples.
    If this explanation is right, we should expect the 'semantic opposition'
but to be odd when care is taken to cancel such presuppositions. This prediction seems borne out in

(73)   This is Wimbledon, the final in men's singles.
         The finalists and Björn Borg and Jim Connors.
         Borg is playing from left to right but Connors from right to left

Everybody knows that tennis players in singles matches play on opposite
sides. There is no need of *but* to point that out. As predicted, *but* does sound
oddly out of place here.

6. IMPLICATIONS OF (D.BUT)

A peculiarity of *but* as compared with *and* which is of particular interest
is the following. While a whole sequence of sentences can naturally be con-
catenated by *and*, several successive *but* sentences are rare and when they do
occur, appear curiously erratic. Here are some live specimens of each from
Marilyn French's best-seller *The Bleeding Heart:*

(74)   No, if we were together all the time, I'd get to resent quitting
        my work whenever he decided to come home. *And* he'd get to
        resent my resenting quitting my work. *And* besides, if we lived
        together all the time, he wouldn't quit early. *And* I'd get to
        resent that he worked late. *And* then, if we were together all
        the time, it wouldn't be a holiday *and* he'd expect me to cook
        him dinner. *And* I'd resent cooking dinner every night, *and* he
        wouldn't be happy with a cheese sandwich, as I am. *And* of
        course, he'd expect me to do the marketing.

(75)   I don't want to burden you, but it's a terrible marriage, but I
        can't leave because of the kids (. . .).

(76)   And I love Edith, but I love the kids more, but I love you more
        than that.

(74) does sound repetitive, but it still concentrates on one definite topic,
while (75) and (76) seem to jump from one thing to another. This intuition
is explained by (D.but): each occurrence of *but* in (75) and (76) requires a
new topic arrangement.

The topic which exercised the author of (76) in the book could be
phrased as

(77)   Who do I love most?

Three likely answers are weighed in (76) in turn: Edith (the speaker's wife),
his children, and the addressee.

However, the structural conditions of *but* do not allow construing (76)
as a three-term conjunction addressed to (77). (D.but) demands that the
three alternatives in (78) are actually taken up in two successive pairs, each
addressed to a different pair of complementary alternatives.

Thus, an admissible (and quite likely) dialogue reconstruction for (76)
is

(78)

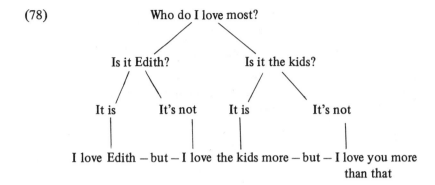

I love Edith – but – I love the kids more – but – I love you more
than that

(78) graphically shows why (76) sounds somehow shilly-shallying or out of focus: there is a change of topic mid-sentence, the middle clause straddling two topics at once.

Observe, too, that (76) can not be abbreviated by leaving out the first *but* as a sequence of *and*'s could:

(79)   I love Edith, I love the kids more, but I love you more than that.

(79) can not represent a three-way contrast either. There is one major cutoff in it at *but*, dividing the first two sentences into one argument and the *but* clause into a counterargument. If the first comma needs to spelled out by a conjunction, that conjunction will be *and*. Then a possible topic for (79) would be

(80)   How about divorce?

family ties being a *con*, the new-found love a *pro*.

Another peculiarity of *but* that is explained by our formulation of (D.but) are its implications of contrast. Consider the example

(81)   This man is black, but that man is Polish.

On cursory inspection, (81) seems to suggest strongly that being black and being Polish are contradictory characteristics: no Poles are black. This implication does arise if (81) is construed as disconfirming evidence to either of the suggestion

(82)   Are those men black?
(83)   Are those men Polish?

However, it is easy to cook up a context for (81) where there is no such implication. A simple one would be

(84)   Is this man black and that man Italian?

It is easy to see that the left side of (81) confirms a positive answer to (84) while the right side of (81) suggests a negative answer. There is no trace of any inductive relevance between the conjuncts of (81) here, as there is none in (84).

7. *BUT* IN DIALOGUE

The last mentioned example is a good reminder of the fact that *but* is an entry in dialogue grammar. The acceptability of *but* cannot be decided by looking at sentences actually conjoined by it in abstraction of assumptions about dialogue context. With suitable background assumptions, sense can be made of any concatenation. Take for instance

(85)   Two and two is four but Hitler was Austrian.

Though somewhat puzzling out of context, (85) makes perfect sense as spoken by a teacher going over a test with a student. The student got the arithmetic right, but made a blunder with Hitler's nationality. The topic might be:

(86)   Is everything right here?

Let us look more closely at the behavior of *but* in dialogue. In contrast with *and, but* need not begin a continuation move. A *but* sentence may well be meant to question or contradict its premise:[8]

(87)   A: He is extremely good.
         B: But he is slow.

(87) leaves it open whether B accepts A's claim or not. B may think that anyone extremely good should also proceed rapidly; in that case, his contribution may be a counterargument against A on the topic

(88)   Is he extremely good or not?

Alternatively, he may consider the quality and the dispatch of a person's work independent considerations relevant to some third topic, say

(89)   Should we give him tenure?

In this case, he may well accept A's contribution as well as his own. Incidentally, the two interpretations are disambiguated by ellipsis. The elliptic dialogue

(90)   A: He is extremely good.
        B: But slow.

only has the latter interpretation. *Yet*, too, will disambiguate in favor of acceptance, which points out another difference between *but* and *yet*.

In contrast, a *but* sentence may downright contradict its premise:

(91)   A: Nobody can do that.
        B: But he did it.

What *but* does only in extreme circumstances is introduce a flat denial:

(92)   A: He is dead.
        B: But he is not dead!

Use of *but* in this context seems to indicate extreme surprise, indignation, or bafflement. Why?

As comparison of (91) and (92) shows, the relevant difference is not one between logical contradiction and inductive conflict, but concerns rather the directness of the argument.

I submit that the reason why *but* is marked in (92) is the availability of a simpler dialogue reconstruction for the exchange which does not satisfy the structural description of (D.but). (92) is most likely to form a typical assertion-reply dialogue with the structure

(93)   A: He is dead.
        B: He is not dead. (D.reply)

Here, the successive moves by A and B are not parallel but sequentially ordered as assertion and reply.

Yet *but* can occur in (92), indicating surprise. Why? I suggest that what the author of *but* is surprised at (and takes exception to) here is not what his addressee says but that he should *say* it, given its patent falsity. The use of *but* in (92) is motivated, not by the simple question *Is he dead*? but by the strategical question *Should one say (accept) that he is dead*? A says so; that is prima facie evidence that one should — given that A is generally a rational player. B, who knows better, is surprised at A's mistake, and points it out by bringing the recalcitrant fact to his attention, prefaced by *but* as is fitting given (D.but).

This explanation also accounts for the difference between (91) and (92). There is nothing wrong with (91), for B's contribution does not have to constitute a direct reply to A's claim here. Rather, the likely topic is whether someone did some remarkable feat or not:

(94)

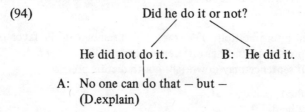

He did not do it.   B: He did it.

A: No one can do that — but —
(D.explain)

(D.but) is neutral with respect to the mood of the *but* clause. However, the requirement that the two sides of *but* address contradictory topics does rule out certain combinations. As a result, coordinate questions do not get conjoined by *but*:

(95)   Who are you but who is he?
(96)   Did he try but did he fail?

The situation is different if time is allowed for a response to the first question:

(97)   A: Who are you?
         B: I am Jack.
         A: But who is she?

(97) is intuitively quite well-formed. But what is the meaning of *but* in it? The following is a possible reconstruction:

(98)

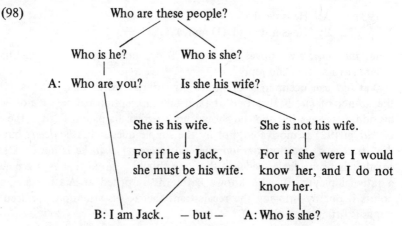

Here, the fact that A still has to inquire about the identity of the woman casts doubt on B's answer. For a slightly different case, consider

(99)   This is a dandelion, but what is that?

with the analysis

(100)

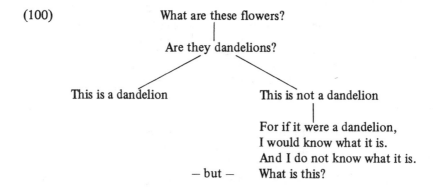

This reconstruction shows why (99) seems to convey a suggestion that the other flower cannot be a dandelion too. The suggestion is easily cancelled, however, by another reconstruction:

(101)

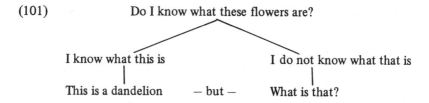

Here, *but* no longer contrasts dandelions to other kinds of flowers, but knowledge to ignorance.

8. *BUT* AND THE ABSTRACT PERFORMATIVE HYPOTHESIS

The ability of *but* to depend for its motivation on dialogue context has been construed by Robin Lakoff [411] as evidence for the *abstract performative hypothesis* of generative semantics. The hypothesis and the general form of argumentation for it have been spelled out neatly by Sadock [175]:

In its simplest form, the abstract-performative hypothesis provides that every sentence contain as its highest deep-syntactic (and semantic) clause a structure like those that give rise to explicit performatives. This contains a subject that refers to the speaker, an abstract performative verb that specifies the force of the sentence, an indirect object that refers to the addressee, and a clausal direct object. In the case of explicitly performative stentences, no drastic changes affect the performative clause during the syntactic derivation. In the case of utterances that are not explicitly performative, the highest clause is eventually deleted. (p. 17)

The greater number of syntactic arguments that have been offered in support of higher abstract performative clauses are of a single form: First, it is shown that some particular property of embedded sentences is directly traceable to some property or properties of the matrix sentence. Next it is shown that the facts that held for embedded sentences also characterize certain highest surface clauses. One therefore concludes that a higher matrix structure with the appropriate structural properties is present at the stage of derivation at which the property of the embedded sentence is determined. (p. 21)

R. Lakoff's argument from *but* follows precisely the same lines. The examples she bases her argument on are the likes of

(102)   George likes Peking Duck, but all linguists are fond of Chinese food.

She notes that

An accurate paraphrase of [102] entails bringing into discussion a number of elements that have no superficial representation in this sentence: a likely candidate is a sentence like [103].

(103)   I say to you that George likes Peking Duck, but I really don't have to say this, because all linguists are fond of Chinese food.

The other sentences of this type are also reducible to similar paraphrases. In fact, if someone says, *George likes Peking Duck*, a second speaker can say, as a rejoinder, *But all linguists are fond of Chinese food*. The purpose of his rejoinder, in its normal conversational use, is to ask politely why the first speaker bothered to say anything, rather than to contradict anything the first speaker said.

(Compare another possible reply: "But he refused to eat any at the restaurant last week.")

From this observation, it is concluded, in accordance with the general strategy of argumentation used, that the material made explicit in the paraphrase (103) must appear in the deep structure (semantic representation) of (102).

To evaluate the argument, it is important to notice that it is not logically conclusive, but an inductive one. The abstract performative hypothesis is offered as one possible explanation for the similarity of (102) and (103). In this work, another approach has been taken. It consists of (i) defining an independent set of structural descriptions of contexts of use (theory of dialogue games) as an autonomous level of description; and (ii) devising a set of rules which interpret certain aspects of the syntactic structure of sentences with respect to contexts of use. In this framework, the functional equivalence of (102) and (103) is captured by identity of appropriate dialogue contexts. In order to make sense of *but*, both (102) and (103) must be embedded in a context which provides the structural configuration required by (D.but). What distinguishes (102) in this respect is that the necessary context arises via dialogical inference (conversational implication). Thus a natural topic for (102) would be

(104)   Who likes Chinese food?

Assume someone answers

(105)   George likes Peking Duck.

If the author of (105) makes no reservations, one is justified to assume that he is putting forward (105) as his epistemically optimal answer. His interlocutor then has good reason to point out to him that he should be able to say more. The structure of (102) will then be

(106)

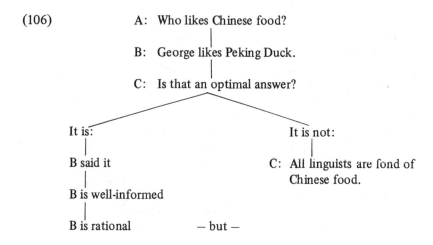

A: Who likes Chinese food?

B: George likes Peking Duck.

C: Is that an optimal answer?

It is:

B said it

B is well-informed

B is rational   – but –

It is not:

C: All linguists are fond of Chinese food.

The second speaker's *but* thus indicates his surprise at the first speaker's caution, lack of information, or irrationality.

Another possible context for (102) is the following:

(107)   Who ate the Peking Duck?

Here, the second speaker's rejoinder is directed against the supposition that George's partiality to Peking Duck is evidence for his guilt any more than for that of any other linguist. The structure of the dialogue:

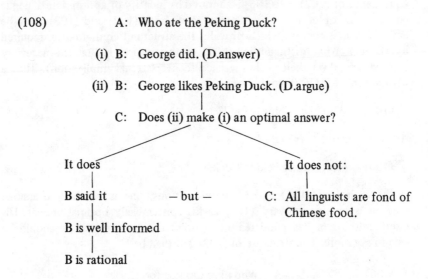

(108)   A: Who ate the Peking Duck?

       (i) B: George did. (D.answer)

      (ii) B: George likes Peking Duck. (D.argue)

           C: Does (ii) make (i) an optimal answer?

It does   It does not:

B said it   — but —   C: All linguists are fond of
                                            Chinese food.
B is well informed

B is rational

To sum up, the crucial feature of these examples of *but* is that the implicit topic addressed by it is a dialogue implicature based on the assumption that players are following optimal strategies. The main difference between the present account of such uses and the abstract performative hypothesis concerns at what level of description such implicatures are captured. In the present account, such implicatures are not part of the structure of the individual sentences of a dialogue, but rather the other way round: individual sentences and their implications become part and parcel of the structure of a dialogue. Where the abstract performative hypothesis tends to build features of implicit dialogue context into an abstract structural description of individual sentences, the dialogue approach takes the opposite route and uses the implicatures of explicit performatives to reconstruct the dialogue context they describe. Thus the paraphrase (103) too is embeddable into the following dialogue context:

(109)

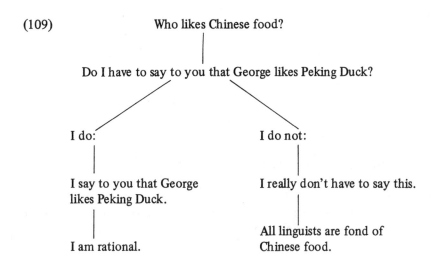

Comparing (106) to (109), we can observe that the only essential difference (102) and (103) is that (103) is less ambiguous than (102): part of the implicit structure that was postulated in (106) to make *but* interpretable is said explicitly in so many words in (109).

Another frequent species of a dialogue motivated *but* could be dubbed the *subject-changing but*. Compare the dialogues (110)–(111):

(110) A: Hi, how are you?
       B: I am fine, but how are you?
(111) A: Hi, how are you?
       B: I'm fine, thank you. I'm through with my thesis. We're going to have a baby in a month's time. Best of all, we expect to be back in Finland for Christmas. – But how are you?

(110) curiously suggests that there should be something wrong with A. This suggestion is absent from (111), where *but* just effects a timely change of topic from B's rather voluble answer to the polite reciprocating question. What B seems to be taking exception to by *but* in (111) is not what he says but rather his choice of dialogue subject: he is indicating that – despite his obvious eagerness to tell his own news – he actually ought to be asking how things are with A. The implicit topic structure which motivates *but* is something like

(112)   What is the dialogue about?

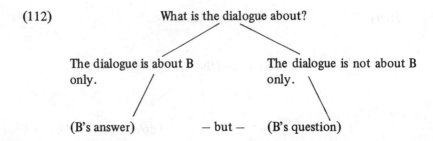

The dialogue is about B   The dialogue is not about B
only.   only.

(B's answer)   – but –   (B's question)

The difference between (110)–(111) in conversational implications is in good accordance with this analysis. B's answer in (110) is conventional enough not to create any presumption for B's favor as the subject of the dialogue, so that cannot be what explains *but* in (110). The most likely reason for *but* here is that it suggests a denial of the conventional expectation

(113)   We are both fine.[9]

9. THE LOGICIAN'S *BUT*

A particularly intriguing dialogue use of *but* was registered by John Locke:

(114)   All Animals have Sense; But a Dog is an animal. Here *but* signifies little more, but that the latter proposition is join'd to the former, as the Minor of a Syllogism.[10]

A similar use of *but* is often encountered in modern expositions of logical proofs.

How is this use of *but* to be subsumed under our general characterization in (D.but)? (D.but) already predicts that *but* indicates a topic change. But what topics? In particular, to do justice to the contradiction requirement of (D.but), we need to find two *contradictory* topics which the two lines of argument conjoined by the logicians' *but* are respectively addressed to. Note that here there need not be any explicit contradiction between the actual conjoined premises; there is none in Locke's own example. This again suggests that we are dealing with a dialogue use of *but*.

My suggestion is that the logicians' *but* is used in logical exposition to connect two prima facie unconnected lines of reasoning which on closer consideration turn out to lead to a common conclusion after all: but serves to signal that surprising turn of the argument.

This suggestion provides the necessary implicit topic for *but*. The problem of a proof is whether a certain assertion follows from given premises. To a certain point in the argument, that the conclusion follows is not at all obvious: it may be difficult to see the relevance of the preceding lemmas to the conclusion. At this point, the *but* sentence serves to resolve the doubt by bringing in a missing link in the argument: the proof does go through after all!

This element of surprise is of course minimal in Locke's trivial example. It is likely to be more perceptible in remote lines of argument such as the following one concerning the properties of large cardinals from Shoenfield's *Mathematical Logic* (p. 310):

We claim that EC is an isomorphism of I and J. In view of (14) and the definition of U_J. It is only necessary to prove

(15) $x \in_I y \longleftrightarrow EC(x) \in_J EC(y)$

The implication from left to right is obvious. Suppose that $EC(x) \in_J EC(y)$. Then $EC(x) = EC(x')$, $EC(y) = EC(y')$, and $x' \in_I y'$. By (14), $x =_I x'$ and $y =_I y'$. Thus we need only prove

$$x =_I x' \ \& \ y =_I y' \ \& \ x' \in_I y' \to x \in_I y.$$

But this is the interpretation of a theorem of ZF.

The last line is likely to come as a relief to Shoenfield's readers.

Out of historical curiosity, one may ask why this sort of *but* should have become a favorite stylistic device of syllogistic reasoning. The following conjecture might be more than just amusing.

In the last chapter of *Topics*, Aristotle offers strategic advice for a dialectician who wants to extract the premises of a proof from a critical audience. He warns especially against committing the mistake of *begging the question*, i.e., asking the audience for too immediate premises to establish the conclusion (the extreme being 'begging the question' itself). The chances are that

the answerer refuses to admit them because they are too close to the point of departure and he foresees what will result from this admission.[11]

Among other tricks to avoid this, Aristotle mentions that

it is also a useful practice not to establish the admitted propositions on which the reasonings are based in their natural order but to alternate one which leads to one conclusion with another which leads to another conclusion; for, if those which are closely related are set side by side with one another, the conclusion which will result from them is more clearly foreseen.[12]

Now let us see how these precepts apply to Locke's example. It seems fair to take as the topic of a syllogism the validity of the conclusion it tries to establish; in Locke's example, the question is

(115)   Does a dog have sense?[13]

A careless questioner would not stop to establish his premises separately, but would simply state the whole syllogism as in (110):

(116)   A dog does have sense, for dogs are animals, and all animals have sense.

An Aristotelian dialectician, in contrast, will not reveal the whole argument at once, the premises laid 'side by side' with *and*. He proceeds piecemeal, obtaining acceptance for the major premise first under the guise of irrelevance, and only then lashing out the middle premise prefaced by *but*:

(117)

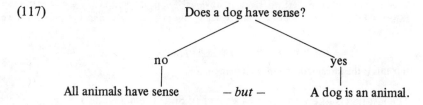

Putting the major premise first creates a confusion about the subject of the discussion: how is a fact about animals relevant to the properties of dogs? So far, it is not obvious that the conclusion follows. What the *but* sentence does is provide the missing link in the argument: despite initial appearance, the proof does go through after all.

In support of this analysis, two further peculiarities of the use of *but* in syllogism can be mentioned. First, the two premises conjoined by *but* in (114) must be spoken as separate intonational phrases, as reflected in the use of semicolon in writing. These devices serve to set off the two premises as ostensibly independent lines of argument. Second, note that the order of premises and conclusion in (114) cannot be inverted as in (116): the conclusion follows the argument as an ostensibly unforeseen result.

10. RUSSIAN ADVERSATIVE CONJUNCTIONS

In Section 6 above, we remarked that *but* cannot serve to conjoin more than two sentences around one and the same topic. From the point of view

of language typology, it is interesting to find in Russian an adversative conjunction which can do that. This remarkable conjunction is *a* 'and, yet,
whereas'. Besides *a*, Russian has a more well-behaved counterpart of *but*,
namely *no*. *No* seems to follow the same constraints as *but*, so (D.no) can
copy (D.but) without more ado.

In order to watch *a* in action, let me first list a number of representative
examples.[14]

(118) Eto jejo karandash, a ne tovoi

This is her pencil, and not yours.

(119) On ne prid'ot sevodn'a, a zavtra

He won't come today, but tomorrow.

(120) Ona zan'ata, a pomogajet nam

She is busy, yet she helps us.

(121) Eto moj syn, a eto moja doch'

This is my son, and this is my daughter.

(122) Detej bylo v sem'e troje: Sasha xodil v politexnikum, Tonja v
konservatoriju, a Lilja konchala desjatiletku.

There were three children in the family: Sasha went to Tech,
Tonja to a conservatory, and Lilja was finishing high school.

As examples (118)–(122) show, the Russian *a* overlaps with English *but*
(instead), *yet*, and *and* (*whereas*).

Example (120) is an already familiar sort: here, *a* pretty well equals the
contrary-to-expectation *but* (*yet*).

The examples where *a* does duty for *and* are more interesting. Unlike
but, *a* is symmetric in (118)–(119). It conjoins coordinate answers to multiple
questions in (121)–(122): in (121), the implicit question is who is who, in
(122) it is who does what in the family.

On the other hand, *a* is not found in the rest of the natural environments
of the English *but*, but is replaced in them by *no* 'but, however'.

So what is the difference between *a* and *but*? My proposal is that there
are three differences. First, the notion of contradictory topics must be
weakened into a concept of disjointness of topics. Call two questions *disjoint*
if they share no direct answers: their presuppositions share no true disjuncts

or substitution instances. The contradictory disjuncts of a polarity question are obviously disjoint. So are the two simple questions answered by (121), i.e.,

(123)   Kto jest' kto? Kto eto? A kto eto?

          Who is who? Who is this? And who is this?

For obviously, no one can be two different individuals at once. Similar comments apply to example (122).

In order to obtain a dialogue game rule for *a*, we need rewrite (D.but) only slightly:

(D.a)   When a player has addressed a move to a given topic, he may con-
          join to it a sentence beginning with *a* addressed to a coordinate
          but disjoint topic.

The disjointness condition ensures that sentences conjoined by *a* will imply a definite *contrast*, absent from sentences conjoined by *i* 'and'. Consider examples

(124)   Ja ljublju tebja, i ty ljubish' menja.

          I love you and you love me.

(125)   Ja ljublju tchaj, a ty ljubish' kofe

          I love tea, but you love coffee.

In (124), *a* would sound odd, while it is quite natural in (125). The reason ought to be clear: *a* tells that our objects of love are disjoint, while *i* allows them to overlap. *A* in (124) would imply that we do not love ourselves, just as it implies in (125) that we love different drinks. The semantic opposition *but* in the English translation of (125) creates the very same implication.

The weakening of contradictory to disjoint topics allows *a* to conjoin a plurality of answers to a multiple question. Although there can be only two contradictories, there may be any number of disjoint questions.

The second difference between *but* and *a* is already registered in (D.a): *a* must begin a continuation move. As a result, *a* like *and* or *yet* but unlike *but* or its Russian equivalent *no* implies acceptance of its premise. For instance, in the dialogue

(126)   A: Ja pokushalsja na ubijstvo.

               I attempted murder.

B: A tebja ne arestovyvajut!

Yet they do not arrest you!

B's response indicates surprise but not disbelief. *No* would allow construing B's response as a counterargument or rebuttal.

The third difference between *but* and *a* is what prevents *a* from covering the *tertium comparationis* use of the English *but*. The following restriction would seem to do the job:

(127)   (An addition to (D.a):) A sentence begun by *a* must constitute a decisive answer to its topic.

This formulation evidently admits answers to multiple questions as in (121)– (122), as well as the correction sentences in (118)–(119). As for (120), it suffices to refer back to our analogous findings about the contrary-to-expectation *but*.

(127) rules out the use of *a* when one is just weighing independent arguments *pro* and *con* concerning some independent question, as in

(128)   Ja ljublju Natashu, eto tak, no inogda mne kazhetsja ona udivitel'no poshloj.

I love Natasha, it's true, but sometimes she seems terribly banal to me.

The author of (128) uses *no* instead of *a* in order not to suggest that his love for Natasha should make him blind for her faults. Rather, his two sentences from independent arguments as to, say, whether he is happy with her. As no direct conflict is implied between the two sentences conjoined by *no, no* sounds less impetuous or lively than *a*.

CHAPTER 3

OLD AND NEW INFORMATION

1. SENTENCE GRAMMAR VS. FUNCTIONAL SYNTAX

Developing a theory of functional syntax is like planning a route across a difficult terrain with lots of criss-crossing paths, some of them worn wide by a multitude of wanderers. To stretch the simile, one who wants to make good headway may be wise not to follow the footsteps of his predecessors before he has cast an independent eye on the scenery. The path of least resistance may soon peter out, while the straight route goes elsewhere.

Following the advice of my simile, I shall proceed into the field paying little explicit attention to earlier approaches before I have developed my own to some degree of detail. After that, I shall retrace some of my steps and relate my proposals to main trends in the literature.

Consistently with the theme of this essay, I shall only pay attention to such aspects of syntactic structure as directly serve the function of text organization, i.e., indicate the role of a sentence in a dialogue. This means that I shall have to assume a lot of syntactic and semantic information for granted. I shall not worry about explaining choices of word order or syntactic configuration which are dictated by sentence grammar (syntax and semantics). Rather, I assume that sentence grammar tells me at the outset what choices of word order (or syntactic structure) are available given a choice of words (or lexical-functional structure), and how to compare them in terms of structural complexity or stylistic markedness.

It may be good to mention some hypotheses I am not making here. I do not mean to assume that there is, in English or other languages, a basic word order or canonical surface structure guaranteed to produce context-free sentences whatever the choice of words. Neither do I assume that functionally unmarked sentences always represent syntactically underlying forms. Such assumptions would actually disconfirm the autonomy thesis.

Let us look at some of the exceptions to these assumptions. Trivially, most sentences are context-bound because individual words in them are in need of context:

(1)   But then you would need some of those, too.

More to the point, some choices of words require derived syntactic configurations to obtain their idiomatic sense: (3) cannot replace (2) nor (5), (4).

(2)   There was a riot.
(3)   A riot was (there).
(4)   John was killed in action.
(5)   They killed John in action.

Some constructions are at best very marked if a transformational rule fails to apply: (6) is less marked than (7).

(6)   What did I say?
(7)   Did I say what? I said what?

Far from getting depressed about these and other similar examples, I consider them somewhat exceptional instances of a general rule. The general rule is that in English (and in other languages) some set of rules, syntactic, semantic, or both, not only determines for any given meaningful choice of words (lexical-functional structure) its admissible syntactic realization(s) but, also, indicates differences of structural complexity or stylistic markedness among them.

The essential feature of the rules which define such grammatical word order constraints is that they are independent of dialogue context: the notions referred to in those rules are chosen from the primitives of syntax and semantics. There is no a priori reason to assume that they will bear any resemblance to the rules which will govern the choice among the stylistically marked word orders; actually, the autonomy of dialogue grammar would be weakened by such findings.[1]

In English, a configurational language, grammatical constraints on word order are induced by phrase structure grammar, by obligatory or lexically governed syntactic processes exemplified by (2)–(7), and by minor semantic ordering principles of the sort studied, e.g., in Green [452]. For languages with freer word order, principles referring to diathetic concepts (agent, patient, instrument) have been cited as central.[2]

What I want to emphasize here is that sentence grammar is not assumed to imply contextual judgments *directly*. What it does is induce some ordering of complexity among logically equivalent variants of a lexical-functional structure: it may be stated in terms of complexity of syntactic structure, markedness of diathesis (semantic case linking), or the like. The main thing is that there is a distinction between simple straightforward versions of a sentence, and those which, while not ungrammatical, require some further reason to be resorted to. What dialogue functional rules do is provide some of the reasons.

2. STYLISTIC RULES

In transformational grammar, it is customary to make a distinction between properly grammatical and merely stylistic rules. Stylistic rules are said to share a number of *formal* characteristics. They follow all other syntactic rules, including agreement and case assignment; they are not conditional on the presence or absence of specific morphemes in the sentence (i.e., not lexically governed); above all, they are *optional*, i.e., their applicability is at best constrained by functional considerations (contextual appropriateness, avoidance of ambiguity).[3]

These criteria eliminate many putative candidates for stylistic rules from the class. In particular, any structure-preserving cyclic rules will belong to grammar proper, e.g., wh-movement, passive and existential sentences exemplified in (2)–(7); yet another such rule is the lexically governed rule of dative alternation exemplified by (8)–(9):

(8)   We read Bill books.
(9)   We read books to Bill.

Although all of these rules are exploited for textual purposes, they do not count as stylistic rules in the syntactic sense of recent transformational grammar.

Supposing that a division of syntax into proper "core" grammar and an independent stylistic component can be justified on autonomous syntactic grounds, the thought is close that one might characterize grammatically unmarked sentences as sentences generated by core grammar. This set would then be extended by the stylistic component into a set of marked variants.

The foregoing observations cast doubt on such a syntactic characterization of stylistic markedness. It seems to me that the existence of grammatically simpler equivalent variants makes a sentence a functionally marked variant, whatever the character of the rules which are responsible for the added complexity. For instance, passives are functionally marked as compared to actives because of their marked case linking. Thus the supposed division of labor within syntax does not seem alone sufficient to define stylistic variance.

I shall not pay any further attention to the particular syntactic distinction discussed here in the sequel. It suffices to suppose that sentence grammar as a whole presents discourse grammar with a range of options between different wordings of any given sentence, indicating what variations in structural complexity or stylistic markedness obtain among the variants.

Insofar as the autonomy of dialogue grammar can be upheld, this is also all the information about sentence structure which functional rules need access to. Dialogue grammar need not care *how* word order variants or markedness judgments are generated.

Before embarking on functional problems, let us become clearer about what structural options exist in English. English sentence structure can be described schematically by the following formula:

$$
\begin{array}{cccccccccc}
& \text{(i)} & \text{(ii)} & \text{(iii)} & \text{(iv)} & & \text{(v)} & \text{(vi)} & \text{(vii)} & \text{(viii)} & \text{(ix)} \\
(27) & \cdots {}_{\bar{S}}[\cdots & {}_{S}[\cdots & \text{AUX} & {}_{VP}[\cdots \text{V} \cdots] \cdots] \cdots] \cdots
\end{array}
$$

In the schema (27), everything has been left out except the heads of the major constituents S (whose head I assume to be AUX) and VP (head V). The empty spots indicate landing sites for movement rules. From left to right:

(i)   This position, outside of the sentence to the left, belongs to such to such sentential satellites as attitude adjuncts (*frankly*) and topic introducers (*as for you*). Probably nothing ever *moves* here by grammatical rule. I assume that left dislocated phrases are not dislocated at all but simply adjoined in this position.

(ii)   Topic position. The landing site for question formation, topicalization, and VP preposing.

(iii)   Subject position. The landing site for such lexically governed rules as passive and raising to subject.

(iv)   Sentential adjuncts are intricately interspersed here adjacent to auxiliaries.

(v)   Preverbal position in English occupied by adverbial adjuncts. In Finnish, this position is heavily trafficked.

(vi)   Postverb position, the home for the complements and adjuncts of the main verb. The order of complements, if not grammatically fixed, is thematically significant.

(vii)   Sentence end position. There is debate as to which of the positions (vi)–(viii) form landing sites for extraposition. Another slot for sentential adjuncts.

(viii)   Postsentential position. See (vii).
(ix)   Outside of the sentence, to the right. I assume that right dislocated
           phrases are base-generated here.

These structural positions figure, as indicated, in various grammatical rules
or alternations which, where meaning-preserving, can be exploited for the
purposes of functional grammar. We already mentioned a few structure-
preserving processes which are so exploited (passive, raising to subject,
existential sentences, dative alternation).

Among stylistic rules proper are usually counted such rules or configurations as topicalization (10), left (11) and right (12) dislocation, it-cleft (13)
and wh-cleft (14) sentences, VP preposing (15), word order inversion (this
sentence), tag formation (16), extraposition (17)–(19), and certain reshuffl-
ings of complements and adjuncts (20)–(23).

(10)   These steps I used to sweep with a broom.
(11)   This room, it really depresses me.
(12)   It leaves a nasty taste in the mouth, this scheme.
(13)   It is driving carelessly that upsets me.
(14)   What upsets me is driving carelessly.
(15)   Growl you will, but go you must.
(16)   I guess he likes foreign beers, doesn't he?
(17)   A person has arrived who we all like very much.
(18)   It is a waste of time to read so many magazines.
(19)   A new book has appeared by Chomsky.
(20)   I send every letter I receive to my lawyer.
(21)   I send to my lawyer every letter I receive.
(22)   It is not necessary on this campus to be very smart.
(23)   It is not necessary to be very smart on this campus.

In addition to these constructive processes, there are a number of proposed
stylistic rules of ellipsis. I shall not discuss ellipsis at all in this work. To
illustrate the structural effects of the stylistic rules in (10)–(30), let me
classify the examples in terms of the scheme (27):

(10)   These steps I   used to sweep with a broom.
           (ii)   (iii) V   (vi)

(11)   This room, it   really depresses me.
           (i)   (iii)   V   (vi)

(12)   It   leaves a   nasty taste in the mouth, this scheme.
        (iii) V   (vi)   (ix)

(13)   It   is   driving carelessly that upsets me.
        (iii) AUX (vi)   (vi)–(viii)

(14)   What upsets me is   driving carelessly.
        (iii)   AUX (vi)

(15)   Growl you will, but go you must.
        (ii)   (iii) AUX   (ii) (iii) AUX

(16)   I   guess he   likes foreign beers, doesn't he?
        (iii) V   (vi)   (ix)

(17)   A   person has   arrived who we all like very much.
        (iii)   AUX V   (vii)

(18)   It   is   a   waste of time to   read so many magazines.
        (iii) AUX (vi)   (vii)

(19)   A   new book has   appeared by   Chomsky.
        (iii)   AUX V   (vii)

(20)   I   send every letter I receive to   my lawyer.
        (iii) V   (vi)   (vi)

(21)   I   send to   my lawyer every letter I receive.
        (iii) V   (vi)   (vi)

(22)   It   is   not necessary on   this campus to   be very smart.
        (iii) AUX   (vi)   (vii)   (vii)

(23)   It   is   not necessary to   be very smart on   this campus.
        (iii) AUX   (vi)   (vii)   (vii)

3. FUNCTIONAL DEFINITIONS

Grammatical markedness considerations contribute to determining the class of *context-free* sentences in English: sentences which, as far as syntax and semantics can tell, are free to appear in the absence of a preparatory dialogue context.

In particular, such context free sentences serve as discussion openers or news headlines. They are, in other words, able to function as "all-new sentences", sentences which answer such generic questions as

(28)   What is new?
(29)   What happened?
(30)   What do you want?

Comparing possible answers to (28)–(30), say

(31)   I have been fired.
(32)   There was a riot.
(33)   Has anyone seen my hat?

to the respective questions, one fact immediately suggests itself: none of the answer is present in the question, but the whole answer is *new* relative to the question.

This intuition is of course common to all approaches to functional sentence perspective. A functional articulation of a sentence should determine what part(s) of a sentence constitute *old* (given, thematic) information in it and what part(s) *new* (rhematic) information.

The crucial question is *new in what sense*: what it is really that 'old' and 'new' are said of, and what does it mean for that something to be old or new.[4]

As for the first question, I take a hard line and construe *old* (thematic) and *new* (rhematic) as properties of (occurrences of) surface structure constituents of sentences, be they lexical, syntactic or phonological.

As for the second question, it is important to realize that *old* and *new* are *relational* concepts: more specifically, a constituent of a sentence is old or new relative to some other sentence in a dialogue, to which the former constitutes a countermove in that dialogue. It follows that a constituent of a sentence may be old with respect to one premise of the sentence and at the same time new with respect to another premise. (However, it will follow from the definitions of *old* and *new* that no constituent can be both old and new with respect to one and the same premise.)

The actual definitions of *old* and *new* in my approach will be quite formal, with no explicit reference to meaning or dialogue function. They are based on the familiar algebraic notion of *substitution*.

For my purposes, a substitution can be thought of as an arbitrary transformation between sentences, a homomorphic mapping in the set of all strings in the alphabet of surface structure representations. It helps to think of that alphabet as consisting of an arbitrary number of tokens of every symbol type and of surface structures as containing no repetition of symbols: every copy of *he* or the empty string in a sentence is considered a distinct token of its type.

Given a pair of surface structures, there is an infinite number of substitutions which include that pair. There is no interest in distinguishing substitutions which differ in their values for strings absent from either member of the pair. We can limit attention to the finite number of substitutions which differ in their assignments of substrings of the input sentence to substrings of the output sentence. In some of them, a substring of the input sentence is mapped to an identical string in the output sentence. We say that the substitution *repeats* that string. In others, the value of the function is distinct from its argument; then the value is said to *replace* the argument string. Some special cases of replacements may be singled out: if only the input string is empty, we have an *addition* of a string; if only the output string is empty, we have a *deletion*. If one and the same constituent is added in one place and deleted in another place, we have a *movement*. It makes sense to consider movement another instance of repetition. These concepts of repetition, replacement, and movement will figure in the functional rules and definitions.

Armed with these concepts, let us investigate a diagnostic pair of sentences:

(34)   A: Who would trust an idiot?
         B: An idiot would trust an idiot.

Intuitively, it is clear that if the B sentence is construed as an answer to the A sentence, the first occurrence of *an idiot* in B is new information, while the second occurrence is old information. This would be puzzling, if we simple-mindedly defined a phrase as old if it makes an appearance in a premise sentence and new if it does not. The noun phrase (type) *an idiot* obviously occurs in the question, yet one of its occurrences in the answer is old and one new.

What we do instead is relativize old and new to substitutions. In order to form a direct answer to A's question, B's sentence in (34) must be a substitution instance of it by (C.wh-e) or (C.wh-u). There is one substitution transformation which satisfies this requirement, namely one which replaces *who* from the question by the first occurrence of *an idiot* in the answer and repeats the rest of the question in the answer.

Generalizing from the example, I arrive at the following definition of thematicity and rhematicity:

(35)   A constituent $h(C)$ in a sentence $h(S)$ is *thematic* relative to a
         sentence $S = XCY$ and a substitution h if and only if $h(C)$ repeats
         C.

(36)   A constituent $h(C)$ in a sentence $h(S)$ is *rhematic* relative to a
         sentence $S = XCY$ and a substitution h if and only if $h(C)$ replaces
         C.

The choice of substitution is controlled by dialogue functional considerations. A player will try to choose a substitution which makes best functional
sense of a move-countermove pair: in the example (34), the obvious choice is
dictated by the formulation of the question rules. In the following examples,
it is equally easy to glean from the formulation of other dialogue rules:

(37)   Someone lives here. Who lives here? (D.question)
(38)   Someone lives here. For Bill lives here. (D.explain)
(39)   Everyone lives here. So Bill lives here. (D.infer)
(40)   Bill will live here. No, Bill will not live here! (D.reply)

In these examples, the natural substitution is defined by some dialogue
game rule or other. Less obviously, perhaps, the same is true in the following
conjunctive example.

(41)   I turned left but you turned right.

It seems almost compulsory to arrange the subjects and complements of (41)
into contrastive pairs of rhematic constituents. This tendency comes from
ascribing to (41) the role of an answer to the multiple question

(42)   Who turned where?

whose question words are regularly replaced by the respective constituents
in (41). However, it is easy to convince oneself that (41) admits of other
construals too. If (41) is offered as a reply to

(43)   Did you turn right?

then it is natural to construe *right* as thematic in (41).
    Sometimes what looks like partial deletion will turn out to be a replace-
ment, given the functionally best motivated substitution. For instance, one
who answers

(44)   Will you have tea or coffee?

by

(45)   I'll have tea.

is not just deleting *coffee* from the question but rather replacing the whole disjunction *tea or coffee* by one of the disjuncts in accordance with (C.or). As a result, *tea* is rhematic in the answer in spite of its presence in the question.

An important special case of this kind of instantiation is the rhematicity of the auxiliary in a positive answer to a polarity question:

(46)   Will you come or not?
         I will come.

Will is rhematic in the positive answer as one of the two alternatives *will* and *will not*.

In the foregoing examples, rhematic constituents appear as it were islands of new information in a wealth of thematic material. The converse relationship is quite as common:

(47)   They used to admire each other.
         Now they hate each other's guts.

The thematic noun phrases *they* and *each other* appear surrounded by new information here. I see no reason to draw a theoretical distinction between the two kinds of cases.[5]

4. MATCHING

In the above definitions, the concepts of old and new depend on a straightforward syntactic match between two sentences constituent by constituent. That is often quite sufficient, as in all of the foregoing examples. Thematic and rhematic constituents can be put into a one-one correlation with corresponding constituents in a premise sentence as in the structural description of a syntactic transformation, as in

(48)   Who — said — what — to — whom
         Bill — said — *boo* — to — *a goose.*

In the general case, however, this is not good enough. We need to know more about the underlying structure of sentences. On the syntactical side, obligatory transformations can cause trouble. Actually, they often don't

when they could. For instance, there would be nothing wrong functionally
with matching question and answer in the following way:

(49)   What do — we have — e —   in our pockets?
            e   e —   we have — *precious things* — in our pockets.

Here, preposed material is simply omitted and the gap left by the question
word replaced by the answer. This match gives just the right predictions
about old and new information.

Generally, however, the definitions (35)–(36) must be allowed to see
through a certain minimum of syntax and morphology. For instance, to
match the question and answer in (50), the sentences need to be brought to
the (possibly underlying) forms (51):

(50) Where did he go?   (51) where — e — do — past — he — go — e
       He went home.   e   — he — do — past — e — go — home

where *past* is a familiar abstraction for the shared tense of the question and
the answer.

For another example, consider the exchange in

(52) He went home.   (53) he — do — past — e — go — home
       Did he go home?   e — do — past — he — go — home

The thematicity of *did* in (52) makes it advisable to assume the dummy
auxiliary *do* to be underlyingly present in the premise as shown in (53).

A more radical departure from simple-minded syntactic matching might
seem to be the possibility of relating syntactically and even lexically dissimilar
sentences on grounds of similarity of content:

(54)   Janet likes beans.
            She seems partial to all sorts of yukky legumes.

Intuitively, only *all* in the second sentence need be new information, given
the first sentence as premise. However, this intuition needs a lot of inferential
backing. One has to assume, in particular, that the author of the second
sentence considers beans to be a repulsive sort of legume — a matter of
taste rather than a conceptual necessity as far as repulsiveness is concerned.
This is an important observation, for it at once shows that matching is not
a mere matter of meaning any more than a syntactic process. What is involved
in just the sort of enthymematic inference that the first Part of this essay is
concerned with.

This observation makes it clear that we already have a general solution of the matching problem in (54) and in similar examples. The point is to realize that the second sentence in (54) need not be directly matched with its immediate predecessor, but that implicit steps of inference may intervene. The following is as natural a reconstruction of (54) as any:

(55)   Janet likes beans.
        She is Janet. (antecedency assumption)
        She likes beans. (D.infer)
        She seems partial to beans. (D.argue)
        Beans are a sort of yukky legume. (assumption)
        She seems partial to a sort of yukky legume. (D.infer)

The last line of (55), arrived at by steps of deductive inference and inductive reasoning, provides a syntactic match to the second sentence in (54), which bears out the intuitive judgment of thematicity relations we started from.

Predictably, the more far-fetched the background assumptions and the less warranted the inductive inferences that one has to interpolate in order to bridge the gap between two sentences, the less natural become thematicity assumptions based on them. A simple example:

(56)   A: We have roaches.
        B: We have no pets.

In order to construe *pets* as thematic, one would have to consider cockroaches as pets rather than pests. It is more natural to interpret *pets* as new to the dialogue.

The device of interpolated steps of inference allows us to adhere to the basic idea that thematicity is a property of expressions rather than of their meanings. An interesting plausibility argument for the syntactic nature of thematicity comes from the so-called echo questions. These questions (discussed in the first Part) are used in particular when "we do not understand a statement and ask for the repetition of it: 'He went where?' = 'Where did you say he went?'" (Curme [331], p. 353). Echo questions, unlike normal questions, match the structure of their premise constituent by constituent. This is apt to expedite finding the premise if a syntactic matching principle of the sort we have defined is right.

A more straightforward argument is the fact that the definitions of thematicity and rhematicity need to be able to apply even where there is no semantic relation between move and countermove, as when one is correcting a misprint:

(57)   This should read 'context', not 'content'.

As the example shows, thematicity contrasts do not respect quotation marks. They go all the way down to phonology, to corrections of pronunciations:

(58)   Don't say "pronounciation" but "pronunciation".

The second syllable of the last word is new information given the mispronounced premise.

5. WORD ORDER

So far, we have presented matters as if players had nothing but their familiarity with the context to help determine the intended function of sentences they hear. Of course, matters are not that bad. For one thing, the syntactic struture of a sentence, featuring linear order and specific grammatical constructions, may prejudge its thematic structure and so restrict its functional options.

As everybody has observed who has given any thought to the matter, the general word order tendency is as simple as it seems universal: thematic constituents tend to appear early in a sentence, while rhematic ones are left late. It is another thing to formulate this tendency in terms of grammatical rules so as not to do injustice to the many real or apparent exceptions.

Two insights seem essential for a correct appraisal of the situation. The first is that word order judgments are *relative*; the second is that they are *cancellable*. Let me explain these ideas in turn.

What functional word order rules do is make *relative word order comparisons*: they check whether a given constituent in a sentence appears to the left or to the right from its position in some given premise. If the point of comparison is not obvious from context, it is usually assumed to be a stylistically neutral, context-independent variant of the same lexical-functional structure. This is where syntactic markedness considerations enter the evaluation.

The relativity of word order comparisons already explains some failures of the left-to-right tendency mentioned in the second paragraph of this section. If a sentence copies the syntactic structure of its premise, no inferences from its word order to its information structure are warranted, for nothing has moved:

(59)   A: This gazebo was built by Sir Christopher Wren.
         B: Which gazebo was built by Sir Christopher Wren?

While it is a fair guess that A is using the passive to introduce the famous architect, nothing of the sort follows from B's similarly structured sentence. B is simply echoing A, with no textual intent of his own in mind. All of his sentence is thematic with the exception of the question word.

There is a second way in which inferences from word order to theme-rheme structure are subject to failure. This pitfall is the fact that word order does have other stylistic functions than indicating theme-rheme articulation. The most conspicuous examples come from poetry, whose requirements of rhyme and metre may effectively stamp out any thematic implications. In prose, too, there are certain stylistic preferences which may explain the choice of ordering of constituents. Behaghel's *Gesetz der wachsenden Glieder*, i.e., the preference to order complex constituents late irrespective of their thematic nature is one such competing factor.[6]

We thus have to take care to formulate word order rules so that they do not elbow out other possible explanations for word order choices. The way I choose to do it is to write word order rules as *optional rules of text strategy*:

(D.left)   Move a thematic constituent to the left.
(D.right)   Move a rhematic constituent to the right.

In all their terseness, (D.left) and (D.right) capture the salient points we have been making. First, the dynamic formulation ('move') presupposes a comparison (mapping) between an input structure (comparison sentence) and an output sentence. I do not want to suggest that each application of (D.left) or (D.right) matches a syntactic movement rule; actually, I have expressed doubts about that. What is essential is that (D.left) and (D.right) refer to a mapping between two sentences which can be functionally interpreted as changing the linear position of a designated constituent.

Second, the rules do not say *where* constituents move or *how* they are moved: that is a matter of sentence grammar.

An archetypal example of the application of (D.left) and (D.right) helps to appreciate these points. Consider the dialogue

(60)   Who arrested Pongo?
         Pongo was arrested by the constable.

In order to match question and answer as indicated in (C.wh-e), we may unpack the passive transformation by an interpolated move of explication:

(61)   Who   — arrested   — Pongo
         1   2   3

         The constable — arrested   — Pongo
            1'   2   3

         Pongo   — was arrested by — the constable
           3   2   1'

As (61) shows, the passive paraphrase of the direct answer repeats the verb (up to predictable differences of morphology) and moves the remaining constituents in opposite directions. Inspecting the question, it is easy to ascertain that these movements are accounted for by the thematic word order rules (D.left) and (D.right).

Third, the rules are optional. Therefore, there is no way for the *audience* of a sentence to know for sure that a thematic word order rule has applied in any given sentence. As a result, thematicity inferences from word order have the logic of an inductive *what else* argument. (D.left) or (D.right) can be assumed to have applied if there is no better explanation for a given word order. Thematicity inferences thus constitute instances of *dialogical* (*strategic*) reasoning.

This insight explains an intriguing observation registered by Susumu Kuno as a principle of

(62)   Penalties on Discourse Rule Violations: An intentional (active) violation of a discourse principle produces an unacceptable sentence, but a nonintentional (passive) violation of a discourse principle does not affect the acceptability of the sentence.[7]

To see (62) in action, compare the dialogues in (63)–(66):

(63)   Who did the constable arrest?   (passive application)
         The constable arrested Pongo.
(64)   Who arrested Pongo?   (passive violation)
         The constable arrested Pongo.
(65)   Who arrested Pongo?
         Pongo was arrested by the constable.   (active application)
(66)   Who did the constable arrest?
         Pongo was arrested by the constable.   (active violation)

Intuitively, dialogue (66) is clearly the odd man out: the use of the passive

voice seems completely unmotivated and confusing. Comparing (66) with
(64), we see that the answerer has gone out of his way to violate the left-to-
right tendency: instead of leaving well alone and copying the active voice
of the question, he has opted for a construction which puts rheme before
theme. True, (64) violates the left-to-right tendency too, but only passively,
for the answer copies the structure of the question.

This intuitive account uses the left-to-right tendency itself as an explanatory principle. Our account of (63)–(64) is slightly different, though the
spirit is the same. In (63)–(64), no word order principle need be assumed to
have applied or failed to apply. Nothing has been moved: the form of the
answer is dictated by the form of the question in accordance with the game
rules for questions.

The situation is different in (65)–(66), where the diathesis of the answer
has been changed. In (65), this change can be attributed to applications
of (D.left) and (D.right). That explanation is impossible in (66), for the
structural descriptions of the thematic rules are not met. Unless some other
explanation for the use of the passive is in the offing, the choice of word
order is not only left unmotivated but appears confusing and inappropriate,
as it only complicates the application of question-answer rules.

6. TOPICALIZATION

Besides the left-to-right tendency of thematic organization, specific structural
configurations have specific textual function. A conspicuous case is the
topic position, the presentence position filled by the first constituent of the
examples (67)–(73).

(67)   Of himself Heraclitus no doubt had quite a good opinion.
(68)   About his life we know little of interest.
(69)   Tomorrow I think she said she had an exam.
(70)   These examples I found in Gundel.
(71)   This picture I like.

Somewhat surprisingly, perhaps, I propose to capture the textual function
of topicalization by the following rule of interpretation:

(D.topic)   A constituent in the topic position is rhematic.[8]

Yes, it reads rhematic, not thematic. (D.topic) predicts that a topicalized
constituent cannot enter into a dialogue except as a replacement for a corresponding constituent in some premise or other. But recall: old and new in

our approach are not exclusive concepts, for they are relative to premises. A constituent which is new with respect to one premise may at the same time be old with respect to another.

That a topical constituent frequently if not typically is old information as well is already predicted by the linear rule (D.left), given the unmistakable fact that topicalization moves a constituent earlier in a sentence in addition to hanging it higher in the constituent structure tree. If one wishes, (D.topic) can be thought of as accounting for the promotion in constituent hierarchy while (D.left) takes care of linear precedence.[9]

The foregoing leads one to expect that two premises are relevant for figuring out the textual role of a topicalized sentence. What could these premises be? It is not difficult to come up with very natural candidates for each of (67)–(71). Let (70) serve as a representative. As the author of (70), I have maker's knowledge of the context I had in mind for it:

(72)   Where did I find which examples?

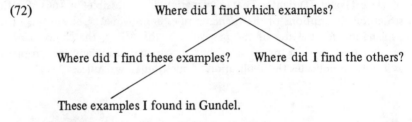

Where did I find these examples?   Where did I find the others?

These examples I found in Gundel.

The topicalized sentence here constitutes a partial answer to a multiple question by directly answering a simple question entailed by it. It is these two questions that the topic construction of (71) harks back to. The double question provides the premise for (D.topic) to relate to, while the simple question is what makes the preposed constituent appear thematic.

To appreciate the fact that topicalization indeed manages to make reference to the underlying multiple question, it is instructive to compare how one would answer the simple question in isolation:

(73)   A: Where did you find these examples?
           B: I found them in Gundel.

It would be odd to answer with

(74)   B: Them I found in Gundel.

if one wants to avoid suggestion of further examples whose source one might talk about. To make intuitions sharper, choose an example where it is vital to avoid such a suggestion:

(75)   A: What did you hit the victim with?
        B: Him I hit with a bicycle-chain.

Here, topicalization embarrassingly suggests that the defendant did some
more hitting with other tools as well — a very unwise suggestion to make
to a court of justice.[10]

Thus we see how a very natural suggestion of *contrast* arises precisely from
the fact that (D.topic) helps place a topicalized constituent as a partial answer
to a multiple question. As a partial answer, a topic constituent immediately
suggests a contrast to further answers to the same question.

The feeling of contrast is very clear in the following literary examples from
Walpole:

(76)   His life had been entangled with women; some he had loved,
        others he had been in love with, others again had loved him.

and Dickens:

(77)   Talent, Mr. Micawber has; capital Mr. Micawber has not.

But as expected, the feeling of contrast disappears if the topicalized
sentence alone forms an exhaustive answer:

(78)   Each part John examined carefully.

There are no further parts to talk about, hence no contrast to other parts
is implied.[11]

The importance of the contribution of (D.left) in topicalization is evident
when (72) is juxtaposed with a dialogue where the scope relations of the
question words are reversed:

(79)   Which examples did I find where?
        Which examples did I find in Gundel?
        In Gundel, I found these examples.

As soon as the order of unpacking of the question words is reversed, the
natural choice of topicalized constituent changes. What gets topicalized is the
answer which already appears instantiated in the intervening simple question,
just as (D.left) leads us to expect.[12]

Structurally the same explanation applies for the remaining examples in
(67)–(71). Thus (67) might be a partial answer to

(80)   What did Heraclitus think of whom?

contrasted, perhaps, to

(81)   Of others, Heraclitus had a low opinion.

Similarly, (68) could answer

(82)   What do we know about his life and writings?

and (71) either of

(83)   What do you think of which picture?
         Which picture do you like and which picture not?

7. VP PREPOSING

A particularly interesting special case of topicalization is found in the phenomenon called in transformational literature VP preposing or fronting.[13] It is exemplified by

(84)   "If you telegraph at once, he can be stopped," said the Inspector. And stopped he was.
(85)   Growl you will, but go you must.
(86)   John tried to find his hat, but find it he could not.
(87)   She needs to be free, so free she must be.
(88)   She expects to be respected, and respected she will be.
(89)   She seems to have left. Well, left she may have.

Very intuitively, the function of VP-preposing would seem to be *affirmation or denial of a suggestion*, whether that suggestion be put in so many words (84); inferred from observation (85) or implicit in previous discourse, as in the rest of our examples.

This intuition can be explained if VP preposing is assumed to be nothing but a special case of topicalization. Let us see how. It is easiest to start with example (85), as it makes the dialogue context of a topicalized verb phrase most apparent.

Assuming that (D.topic) and (D.left) both apply to the preposed verb phrases in (85), what would be a dialogue context which would satisfy their structural descriptions? The following seems to be appropriate both structurally and intuitively.

(90)   What will you do and what must you do?

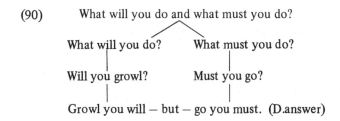

What will you do?   What must you do?

Will you growl?   Must you go?

Growl you will — but — go you must. (D.answer)

As (90) graphically shows, both conjuncts of (85) furnish a partial answer to the main topic of the sentence. An important subordinate issue is whether you go or not — this is what motivates the use of *but* between the conjuncts. Growling is notoriously a bad sign, but on the other hand, what a man must do a man must do. As for the word order, (D.topic) is accounted for by the main question, while (D.left) is taken care of by the explanatory moves immediately above the answers. The answers seem to affirm a suggestion for the simple reason that this is precisely what they do in (90): the auxiliary is rhematic in each case. All the VP preposing examples share this characteristic information structure.

Structurally similar reconstructions are easy to provide for the rest of the VP preposing examples. I take just one more example:

(91)   What did John do?

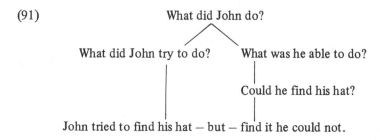

What did John try to do?   What was he able to do?

Could he find his hat?

John tried to find his hat — but — find it he could not.

I have proposed that functionally, at least, there is no obstacle to subsuming VP preposing under the same principles as other cases of topicalization. The question then arises, are there grammatical reasons for distinguishing two rules here. One possible argument could be to show that the structural description of VP proposing must specify which sort of VP can be preposed by the rule, some choices of VP not being available for topicalization.

Such an argument has in fact been put forward in Akmajian, et al. [428], based on the acceptability difference between (87)–(89) and the sentences in (92)–(94):

(92)   She needs to be free, so be free she must.
(93)   She expects to be respected, and be respected she will.
(94)   She seems to have left. Well, have left she may.

These examples are out because a copular or passive *be* or an aspectual *have* has illicitly been preposed along with a smaller phrase. This seems to call for restricting VP preposing to such specified phrases which are allowed to move. At the other extreme, sometimes too little seems to have moved: (95) is also starred in Akmajian, et al. [428].

(95)   They claimed he would be very shrewd, and very shrewd he looks.

A good affirmative sentence is obtained if the main verb is preposed along wih its complement:

(96)   They claimed he would be very shrewd, and look shrewd he does.

This seems to establish a lower bound for the size of preposable VP's.

True, unless there is an independent functional explanation for the restrictions. It seems to me, in fact, that there may be one. For the upper bound, it starts from the observation that English (like all languages I know of) has no question words for verb phrases. There are no anaphoric, question, or quantifier words ranging over predicate phrases.[14] Hence, the only way to ask for a VP is to question the complement of some suitable semantically noncommittal verb. Unfortunately, no verb in English is noncommittal enough for all intents and purposes. As a result, there are a number of different VP questions, which all in some respect prejudge the aspect and diathesis of their answers:

(97)   Who was John?   John was the baby.
(98)   What was John?   John was a doctor.
(99)   What was John like?   John was nice.
(100)   How was John?   John was ill.
(101)   What did John think?   John was pleased.
(102)   What was John up to?   John was reading.
(103)   What did John do?   John built a house.
(104)   What happened to John?   John was fired.

Any permutations of the questions and answers produce odd or indirect replies.

In particular (and this is important), there is no way of forming a question which would question copular *be*, the passive voice, or the perfect aspect. There are no non-elliptic questions like

(105)   What must (will, may) she?

which could be answered by

(106)   She must *be free*
(107)   She will *be respected*
(108)   She may *have left*.

Admissible topics for (106)–(108), e.g.,

(109)   What must she be?
(110)   What will happen to her?
(111)   What may she have done?

already incorporate the semantic contribution of the copula, the passive, or the perfect. Hence there is no way of accounting for the presence of these items in the topic position, which according to (D.topic) is reserved for new information.

The converse restriction in (95) has to do with the interaction of the auxiliary system with rhematicity. It is a peculiarity of English that polarity contrasts are carried by auxiliary verbs. A sentential polarity question is formed by preposing an auxiliary verb (a dummy one, if necessary):

(112)   Did you see it?

and it is answered — emphatically or elliptically — by stressing the auxiliary, not the main verb:

(113)   I did (see it).

It would sound quite foreign to reply with *I saw*. To put the point generally, if the sign of an English sentence is singled out for new information, an auxiliary must appear to carry the stress. And this is precisely the case in our VP preposing examples.

For some speakers, (95) may be questionable even in a context where *look* is rhematic. For these speakers, topicalization of predicative complements is likely to be restricted to copular or near copular verbs such as *be; remain*, as in (114)–(116), is likely not to be too bad either:

(114)   I am glad to see you free, and trust that free you will long remain.
(115)   If a person cannot be happy without remaining idle, idle he should remain.
(116)   She found him perfect; and perfect in her sight he remained.[15]

It might be argued that the functional specialization of VP topicalization to affirmative repetition constitutes an argument for treating VP fronting as a syntactic rule on its own. However, not only would such a conclusion go counter to the autonomy thesis, it would be simply false to fact.

In the following example, VP topicalization places a sentences in a list of alternative plans of action:

(116)   "Well, I'm going to tell you the truth. I was in a hole for money. . . . I tried my uncle. He'd no love for me, but I thought he might care for the honour of his name. Middle-aged men sometimes do. My uncle proved to be lamentably modern in his cynical indifference. . . . I was going to try and have a shot at borrowing from Dortheimer, but I knew there wasn't a hope. *And marry his daughter I couldn't*. She's much too sensible a girl to take me, anyway." (Agatha Christie, *Thirteen at Dinner*, Ch. 21)

Consider next (117):

(117)   Burrell picks only four new shows as "potential hits", and gives only two others a "fighting chance". Four shows are given a "fair" chance of success, and the rest are listed as "likely failures".
Given a "fighting chance" are "Today's FBI", an ABC update of "The FBI", starring Mike Connors, and "Shannon", with Kevin Dobson as a police detective who moves from New York to San Francisco with his young son after the death of his wife. (*Boston Globe*, August 1981)

This recent newspaper cutting exemplifies current use of VP topicalization to rhematicize a subject. In this example, there is no feeling of affirmation at all, as it is the subject and not the auxiliary that constitutes the rheme of the sentence. Again, what topicalization does is organize the sentence as a partial answer to a multiple question, one easily recoverable from the structure of the paragraph:

(118)   Which show got which ranking?

For the purposes of the next section, I want to draw attention to one important property of the topicalization examples in this and the preceding section. As we have emphasized, most of these examples have answered double questions. Consequently, the sentences have two rhematic constituents, one in the topic position and another further down in the sentence. While the topical constituent repeats an answer to a subordinate question word in a multiple question further up in the dialogue, the sentential rheme answers an immediately preceding simple sentential or search question.

8. FOCUS TOPICALIZATION

It is in the just mentioned respect that the above examples differ from another natural class of topical sentences. This class is exemplified by

(119)   John he called.
(120)   Our daughters we are proud of.
(121)   Very grateful they were for my offer.
(122)   Now I see what you mean.
(123)   This also I have taken notice of.
(124)   Only at sunset did I leave the house.
(125)   Not another word did Mr. Dick utter on the subject.
(126)   Pretty silly she made him look last night.
(127)   A fine loyal bunch of pals they've turned out to be.
(128)   It'll kill me; but a fat lot you care about that.

It these sentences, the main news comes first, in the topical constituent; if there are further rhematic constituents in the sentence at all, they are subordinate to the topical rheme. Intuitively, when compared to the previous examples, these sentences sound even more affirmative, sometimes even insistent or challenging. The last three examples seem emphatic to the extent that they can be classed as exclamations, sarcastic or otherwise.

Thus again, we face the task of figuring out what sort of dialogue context would allow the dialogue rules (D.topic) and (D.left) apply so as to justify the above intuitive judgments.

Again, we do not have to look very far. For instance, our first example is very naturally embedded in the context of a choice question following a guess at an answer to it:

(129)   He called John.
         Did he call John or Mary?
         John he called.

John at the same time instantiates the choice question and repeats its earlier mention, which provides the foothold for the dialogue rules. As for the function of the topical sentence in (129), it is a very common and typical one. The topical sentence here pushes forward a certain alternative answer to a choice question at the expense of other suggestions.

Thus the reconstruction (129) explains why a focused topic sentence is particularly apt to be used as a corrective reply to a declarative premise, as in

(130)   A: The chief called Mary.
         B: John he called, not Mary.

For the dialogue reconstruction of (130) would be

(131)   Who did the chief call?

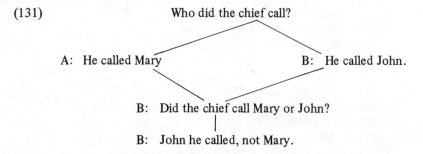

A: He called Mary   B: He called John.

         B: Did the chief call Mary or John?
                           |
         B: John he called, not Mary.

A, who answers first, has no reason to use a topical construction: he is answering a simple search question, whose most fluent answers simply leave the answer constituent at the end of the sentence where it belongs syntactically as well as functionally.

B would have answered with the same word order if he had gone first, only he would have suggested John instead of Mary. But hearing A's answer, B is induced to doubt: there are two answer alternatives, both supported by one witness. Which one is true? Inspecting the disjunctive question, B once more convinces himself that it is his answer that prevails, and puts it forward. The topicalized form of his answer gives away his awareness of the rejected alternative by referring back to the interpolated disjunction.

Now notice an important presupposition of the reconstruction (129). We assumed straight away that acceptance of one of the alternatives in (129) implied rejection of the remaining alternative. In other words, we assumed that the disjunction in (129) was exclusive, presumably because the underlying search question carried a presupposition of uniqueness. (Recall that any direct answer to a unique-answer question is at once a complete answer to it and excludes any other alternatives.)

If this presupposition is rejected, there is no need for B to consider his answer and A's proposal as alternatives to each other. They may as well form two partial answers to a universal question. But if that is the case, there is no need to use topicalization, either:

(132)   A: The chief called Mary.
         B: And he called John.

Using focus topicalization in the addition would actually be quite odd:

(133)   And John he called.

Topicalization is also unnecessary if A's answer is obviously short of being a complete answer. In that case too, it does not present a challenge to B's more informative answer:

(134)   A: The chief called Mary.
         B: He called everybody.

The two answers obviously cannot be construed as exclusive alternatives, as B's answer even entails A's contribution.

Topical word order can make a comeback, however, if the incomplete answer is offered as an exhaustive answer. As an example of this, consider (135):

(135)   What have you taken notice of?
         You have taken notice of that (only).
         This also I have taken notice of.

The topical sentence is in order here, for here the answer and reply constitute two candidates for complete answerhood and as such will exclude each other. In that case, it makes sense to weigh them against each other as alternatives of a choice question.

The presence of other alternatives in the disjunctive question explains the clear feeling of *contrastiveness* of focus topicalization. The accepted alternative contrasts with other proposals which are turned down. Thus, (120) is likely to contrast with, say,

(136)   You must be proud of your sons.

Similarly, (121) can reject the expectation

(137)   They resented your offer.

In the same vein, (122) is the natural order of words if the speaker wants to contrast his sudden flash of understanding with

(138)   I have seen what you mean all along.

(124) again creates a contrast with a more expected

(139)   I left the house before sunset.

and (125) emphasizes the falsity of

(140)   Mr. Dick broached the subject again.

Conversely, if one wants to avoid suggestion of rejecting alternative answers, it is wiser to shun topical word order. For this reason, it is more polite to correct one with direct word order:

(141)   A: You'll have tea, won't you?
         B: Well, I'll have coffee, actually.

Topical word order would surely drive the point home as well or better, but a little too forcefully for a polite occasion.

By the same token, a quiz contestant who is not supposed to overhear other contestants' answers would give away his unfair advantage if he used topical word order:

(142)   Q: When is Fathers' Day?
         A: It is in June.
         B: In November it is.

The examples so far have been easy to characterize as *corrections* of (implicit or explicit) suggestions. The rest of our examples have a slightly different feel. They rather represent emphatic *affirmations* of some more or less obvious suggestion. For them, I propose a very similar dialogue reconstruction. Let us take (126) as a representative:

(143)   She made him look pretty silly last night.
        Now how did she make him look last night again?
        Yes, pretty silly she made him look last night.

Here, the topicalized sentence *affirms* a suggested answer to a search question by (D.reply). The topicalized constituent thus in effect puts forward a given answer to a search question a second time around. The message of topical word order could be conveyed by such expressions of emphatic assent or approval as *indeed, right you are* or *you can say that again*. If I am right, this is just what one is doing with topicalization in the examples (126)–(128): one in effect *is saying something again* in order to affirm it with emphasis.

Why should saying something repeatedly underscore its importance? One might refer to affective causes. It is a law of behavior that exciting things get repeated, whether in speech or in other action. Here is a case in point:

(144)   "Yes," he said, "the mark is there." There was jubilation now in his voice and he came back to the table. "Good girl," he said, "good girl, good girl! She managed it!" (Agatha Christie: *So Many Steps to Death*)

That aside, there seems to be a quite rational connection between repetition and emphatic affirmation. Whenever an answer has been called into question, a player has the chance of amending it. If the best a player can do on second consideration is repeat an earlier answer, the implication is that he finds that answer hard to improve on. The confidence the speaker has in the answer shows in the fact that he "can say that again" even on second, more careful consideration.[16] Conversely, using a form of words designed for repetitions, a player can show that he accepts what he is saying with great confidence.

If he is being sarcastic, the indication is that he rejects what he says with equal emphasis, as is the case in (127)–(128).

For later reference, again, it should not be missed that topic as a main rheme does not exclude the possibility of subordinate rhemes further down in the sentence. For instance,

(145)   A fat lot you care about that.

can very well have *you* as a subordinate rheme; in that case, (145) actually affirms an answer to a double question:

(146)   Who cares what about that?

There may be even three rhemes if it answers the question

(147)   Who cares what about what?

9. OTHER USES OF TOPICALIZATION

(D.topic) and (D.left) thus together explain why topicalized sentences are particularly apt to confirm suggested answers to simple or multiple questions. However, the rules do not require that topicalized sentences can only refer back to such questions. Any context which allows the rules to apply would be as welcome. With this in mind, consider the example

> (148) "I shall kick your spine through your hat!" shouted the invalid. This threat he was quite unable to carry out.

It seems to me that topicalization is quite natural in (148) without any necessity of contrast to other implied threats.

The point of this example, too, is that the topicalized constituent is both old and new. The preposed constituent makes reference to an implied threat but describes it for the first time as a threat. These intuitions are accounted for if (148) is expanded so as to allow (D.topic) and (D.left) to apply directly:

> (149) "I shall kick your spine through your hat!" shouted the invalid. What was this? This was a threat. This threat he was quite unable to carry out.

The simple explanatory identity interpolated in (149) suffices to give foothold for (D.left), while (D.topic) uses the interpolated question. As confirmation of this textual analysis, note that nothing would be more natural than actually inserting the explanation parenthetically in the topicalized sentence itself:

> (150) This threat — for this was a threat — he was quite unable to carry out.

A real-life example of this sort of explanatory topicalization is the following passage from Agatha Christie's novel *So Many Steps to Death* (p. 91):

> (151) Towards both Mrs. Baker and Hilary she displayed a certain amount of contempt as towards people unworthy to associate with her. This arrogance Hilary found very irritating.

The first sentence (whose topicalization is not relevant here) describes the arrogance which the last sentence points out by name.

Instantiation by topicalization is involved in the following sentences from the same novel:

(152) The fact that Morocco was a French colonial possession did not seem to count much with Miss Hetherington. Hotels anywhere abroad she regarded as the prerogative of the English travelling public.

(153) It seems possible that we may in the end so condition a human being that while his powers of intellect remain unimpaired, he will exhibit perfect docility. Any suggestion made to him he will accept.

In these examples, a universal phrase is topicalized as an instance of a wider generalization made in the foregoing sentence. (153), for instance, could be reconstructed into the following argument:

(154) . . . He will exhibit perfect docility. This will show in his reaction to suggestions. Any suggestion made to him he will accept.

Another sort of case where no appreciable feeling of contrast is involved was pointed out to me by Susumo Kuno (private communication). An example is the following passage from Agatha Christie's novel *They Came to Baghdad*:

(155) "You'll want the necessary visas," said Mr. Clipp, taking the passport. "I'll run round to our friend Mr. Burgeon in American Express and he'll get everything fixed up. Perhaps you'd better call round this afternoon so you can sign whatever's necessary."
       This Victoria agreed to do.

All the preposed demonstrative seems to do is connect the last sentence to the previous paragraph. Or is that really all? Compare the effect of replacing the last line of (155) by

(156) Victoria agreed to do this.

My spontaneous reaction is that (156) would make more of Victoria's acquiescence than the topicalized sentence in (155). Whereas the girl's consent comes through as more or less as a matter of course in (155), it becomes news in (156). If so, why?

My explanation is this. Mr. Clipp makes a certain suggestion. This raises the question, how does Victoria react to it? Does she agree to do what she

is told? Yes, that (is what) she does. Here again, topicalization thus has the
function of confirming an expectation created by the context:

> (157)   This is what Mr. Clipp proposed.
>   What did Victoria do?
>   Did Victoria agree to do this?
>   This Victoria agreed to do.

10. FUNCTIONAL DEFINITIONS REFINED

The foregoing analysis of topicalization suggests drawing a further functional
distinction among thematic and rhematic constituents of a sentence. What
we want to do is register the clear functional contrast between the two
uses of topicalization, Gundel's 'topicalization of topic' and 'topicalization
of focus', in evidence in the following pair of dialogues from Gundel [453],
p. 137:

> (158)   A: Did you see any kangaroos?
>   B: No.
>   A: What about monkeys?
>   B: A monkey I saw.
> (159)   A: What did you see?
>   What was it you saw?
>   B: A monkey I saw.

If our analysis of topicalization is right, the functional difference of the two
occurrences *A monkey I saw* should be evident in a reconstruction of the
dialogues (158)–(159) along the lines explained in previous sections:

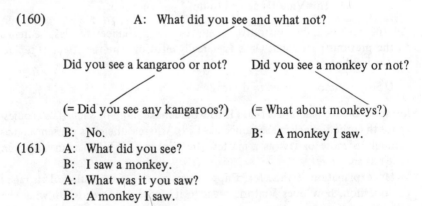

> (160)   A: What did you see and what not?
>
>   Did you see a kangaroo or not?   Did you see a monkey or not?
>
>   (= Did you see any kangaroos?)   (= What about monkeys?)
>   B: No.   B: A monkey I saw.
> (161)   A: What did you see?
>   B: I saw a monkey.
>   A: What was it you saw?
>   B: A monkey I saw.

The reconstruction (160) for (158) construes the latter as a fragment of a dialogue whose topic is a universal question: what did the addressee see on a trip to the zoo, say. The reconstruction (161) brings out the feeling of insistence in B's answer in the dialogue (159), and explains why Gundel lets A ask what seems the same question twice: what B is doing in (159) with his topicalized sentence is repeating his answer after a doubtful checking question.

Now there is a significant difference in the structural position of *a monkey* in the two reconstructed dialogues (160)–(161). In (160), it repeats from an immediately preceding premise an instantiation of the double question one move up; in (161), it instantiates the immediately preceding checking question by repeating an answer already given one move earlier. This observation suggests refining the definitions of thematicity and rhematicity as follows:

(162)   A constituent C of a sentence S is a *rheme* in S iff C is rhematic with respect to an immediate premise of S.

(163)   A constituent C of a sentence S is a *theme* in S iff C is thematic with respect to an immediate premise of S.

These definitions of course do not supersede the earlier definitions of thematicity and rhematicity. On the contrary, they depend on the earlier definitions. What they do is effect a further dichotomy within the categories of thematic and rhematic constituents on the basis of immediacy of premises.

Let us apply the new definitions to (160)–(161). The first thing to note is what is common to both uses of topicalization in (160)–(161): in both cases, the topical constituent is functionally bivalent, both thematic and rhematic. It is interesting that these cases constitute examples of what in the literature is frequently referred to as *contrastiveness*. In our approach, we can thus characterize the intuitive notion of contrastiveness by functional bivalence.

However, there is an important difference too. What distinguishes the two cases is that in (160), *a monkey* is thematic with respect to an immediate premise, hence it is a *theme*. In (161), the topical constituent is rhematic with respect to an immediate premise, i.e., a *rheme*.

Applying the definitions further, we find that the predicate *saw* is unambiguously thematic in (161), but a rheme in (160). This explains the intuition that it is the verb which carries the nub of the message in (160) while in (161), it is the topical constituent.

It is also interesting to compare the two answers of B in (161): while on the first occurrence, *a monkey* is an unambiguous rheme, it is thematic as well the second time around. This accords well with our word order findings.

The new definitions of theme and rheme extend the earlier functional dichotomy into a fourfold functional classification: we distinguish

    (i)   (simple or thematic) theme: *saw* in (161)
    (ii)   rhematic theme: *a monkey* in (160)
    (iii) thematic rheme: *a monkey* in (161)
    (iv) (simple or rhematic) rheme: *saw* in (160).

11. KUNO'S CLASSIFICATION AND JAPANESE *WA* VS. *GA*

The resulting fourfold classification bears a striking likeness to the four functional categories introduced in Kuno [468] to account for a number of functional phenomena. This is how Kuno ([468], p. 269) describes his categories:

The English sentence *John kissed Mary* can be interpreted at least in four different ways:
    (i)   theme: 'Speaking of John, he kissed Mary'
    (ii)   contrast: 'John kissed Mary, but Bill did not'
    (iii) exhaustive listing: 'John (and only John) kissed Mary; among those under discussion, it was John who kissed Mary'
    (iv) neutral description: 'What happened next? John kissed Mary.'

The description is repeated, with slightly different paraphrases, on p. 297:

It is clear, given appropriate contexts, that sentences such as *Alexander kissed Mary* can represent any of the following four meanings:
    (i)   theme: 'Speaking of Alexander, he kissed Mary'
    (ii)   contrast: 'As for Alexander, he kissed Mary.' as in *Alexander kissed Mary, but Bill didn't.*
    (iii) exhaustive listing: 'It was Alexander who kissed Mary.' as in *Who kissed Mary*? (*Only*) *Alexander kissed Mary.*
    (iv) neutral description: 'It happened that Alexander kissed Mary.' as in *What happened next? Alexander kissed Mary.*

These descriptions seems to match nicely our functional definitions. A theme, in our terms, is a constituent which is repeated from an immediate premise: Kuno's paraphrase 'Speaking of' for his theme provides the necessary previous mention. Kuno's paraphrase for contrast adds beside the previous mention another instance of the same sentence structure. In our terms, this instance serves to induce a common underlying question with respect to which the contrastive constituent is rhematic:

(164)   Who kissed Mary and who did not?

For exhaustive listing, the it-cleft construction seems to provide the best paraphrase. Later on, we shall find that it-clefts indeed feature thematic rhemes. In a footnote, Kuno mentions that in the exhaustive listing sense, *John hit Mary* implies 'no one else did'. This implication of a thematic rheme was found and explained in the section on focused topics.

The category of neutral description is illustrated by all-new sentences, a special case of our notion of simple rheme. Kuno does not consider other cases of simple rheme, apparently for the reason that he is only concerned with different functional interpretations of subjects. It is easiest to distinguish the neutral description use of a subject constituent from the exhaustive listing use if the rest of the sentence is new as well. However, in the footnote we mentioned, Kuno admits that English rhematic subjects are not restricted to the exhaustive listing interpretation even if the rest of the sentence is thematic. Apparently, then, such cases of rhematic subject will also belong to Kuno's fourth category.

With this proviso, it seems that Kuno's four categories can be mapped one to one on our functional distinctions.[17] Considering the different routes by which the two classifications have been arrived at, this is a remarkable convergence. It benefits the present approach by turning Kuno's observations into evidence for our functional definitions. It also consolidates Kuno's findings by offering them a systematic theoretical basis in the theory of dialogue games.[18]

As an example of the advantages of our definition of the four functional categories, consider Kuno's analysis of the Japanese subject markers *wa* and *ga*. He finds that

(i)   *Wa* marks either the *theme* or the *contrasted element* of the sentence.

(ii)   *Ga* as subject case marker is either for *neutral description* or for *exhaustive listing.*

Why just these natural classes of functional categories? The answer is anticipated by Kuno who proposes that

(165)   *Ga* as subject marker in matrix clauses always signals that the subject conveys new information.

For some reason, Kuno refrains from making the complementary hypothesis that *wa* always conveys old information. Given our definitions, it seems safe to go all the way and write for Japanese the functional principles

(D.wa)   Mark a main clause subject with *wa* if it is a theme.
(D.ga)   Mark a main clause subject with *ga* if it is a rheme.

The simplicity of the rules for *wa* and *ga* in our approach supports our functional definitions. The functional definitions do not only single out a number of functionally important categories, but also make correct predictions about the natural classes these categories fall into.[19]

CHAPTER 4

GIVEN VS. KNOWN INFORMATION

1. SUBORDINATION AND THEMATICITY

It might seem at first that syntactic subordination too serves the purposes of theme-rheme organization. I think that this impression is misleading. Subordination has another important function in textual organization.

The way our dialogue rules are defined, *subordinate clauses cannot act as independent dialogue moves*: they can answer questions, supply explanations or draw inferences at best indirectly, by implication. For example,

(1)   Did he win?

is not directly answered by (2) like it is by (3):

(2)   It is obvious that he won.
(3)   Obviously, he won.

Understandably enough, (2) seems to change the topic if only slightly, as it directly answers not (1) but

(4)   Is it obvious that he won?

In order to obtain a direct answer to (1) from (2), the addressee must remember that *obvious* has a success grammar, i.e., (2) sustains the inference of

(5)   He won.

Yet the fact that subordinate clauses thus supply information only indirectly, or by inference, should not be confused with calling that information thematic. *Won* is rhematic in (2) if (2) is offered as an answer to (1).[1]

Thematicity and subordination between themselves account for a large share of the much-discussed pretheoretic distinction between *presupposed* and *asserted* information in discourse. In our terms, a declarative sentence S *asserts* (whatever is expressed by) another sentence S' if S constitutes a direct answer to the interrogative form of S'. Thus (3) asserts (5) because it directly answers (1); in contrast, (2) entails but does not assert (5).

219

Two frequently encountered senses of 'presupposition' are approximated by the following characterizations: Sentence S *logically presupposes* S' if the interrogative form of S entails S'; S *pragmatically presupposes* S' if S' is a necessary dialogue premise for S. These characterizations, if appropriate, suggest that the notion of presupposition is not needed as a primitive concept of our theory of discourse.

2. FACTIVITY

Thematicity and subordination alike should be kept separate from *factivity*. It seems to me a fair description of certain intensional words that they are predicated (true or false) of true sentences only: *reveal* and *odd* are such words. If their sentential argument is not true, the question of their truth or falsity does not even arise.[2]

There is a clear difference in the behavior of *obvious* and *odd* in this respect. Both have a success grammar. Yet while (4) is noncommittal as to the truth of its complement, (6) must assume that its complement is true:

(6)   Is it odd that he won?

It has been argued that factivity is a myth.[3] If factive words can only be predicated of true sentences, how can it be that one hears sentences like

(7)   It is not odd that he won, for he did not win.

Actually, (7) does not prove much, for we can also say

(8)   Friday is not in bed, it is a date.

to point out a category mistake. Although (8) serves to correct a conceptual error, it does not show that it is sensible to ask whether Friday is in bed or not. If there are any category mistakes at all, (7) may quite well involve one too.

What is more important, I find (7) slightly uncomfortable in a way absent from, say,

(9)   It is not true that he won, for he missed.

The difference cannot be in mere entailments, for *true* surely entails truth if anything does. But unlike *odd*, it does not presuppose it.

To capture these intuitions, I join the school of presupposition theorists which recognize a *tertium quid* in *odd* sentences and their ilk, and the two sentences of negation which go with it: that of a *denial* of a sentence (true if and only if the sentence is false) and its *rejection* or categorical denial (true if and only if the sentence is not true). The crucial difference between ordinary and categorical denial is that categorical rejection of an ordinary negative sentence does not amount to the same as dropping both denials: one who categorically denies

(10)   It is not odd that he won

where *not odd* equals *natural*, does not wish to imply

(11)   It is odd that he won.

All that is needed to recognize categorical denial in our approach is to be careful not to apply the law of double negation in such cases. This proviso will be assumed to be worked into the syntactic definition of denial.

Categorical denial is surely a marked option, but so are category mistakes. However, that it is a live option is shown by the consistency of such apparently contradictory sentences like

(12)   It is neither odd nor not odd that he won, for he did not win.

I assume that the factivity of *odd* is captured in the semantic component of grammar along with other sortal restrictions on predicates.

All of the foregoing establishes no direct connection between factivity and thematicity. In fact, I do not believe there is one. What was said of subordination already accounts for the fact that it is odd to announce urgent news as the subordinate clause of an *odd* sentence:

(13)   It is odd that your house is on fire.

However, that does not show that an *odd* clause could not introduce new information. It clearly does in the following example:

(14)   It is not odd that math can be difficult for some people. What is odd is that there are mathematical truths that no one can prove.

(14) could open a popular exposition of Gödel's results. The main news is construed as an answer to the question

(15)   What is odd?

which clearly shows that the subordinate clause is rhematic.[4]

3. CLEFT SENTENCES

In our approach, the question-answer relationship plays an important role in organizing the structure of a dialogue. Questions serve to state the *topic* of a dialogue, in other words, what the dialogue is about or what it wants to accomplish. An information sharing dialogue is aimed to create a common understanding about its topics, expressed as questions which the dialogue participants are interested in (accept). The topical questions determine, by means of the dialogue rules and the definition of answerhood, which further questions and declarative sentences are relevant to the dialogue.[5]

The importance of the question-answer relationship for dialogue structure is confirmed by the existence, in English and in other languages, of peculiar grammatical constructions which serve the purpose of articulating a sentence as an answer to a particular question. In English, they are of course the much-discussed cleft sentences, the *wh-clefts*, exemplified by (16)–(17), and the *it-clefts*, represented by (18)–(19).

(16)   What David wants is his wallet.
(17)   His wallet is what David wants.
(18)   It is his wallet that David wants.
(19)   It is David who wants his wallet.[6]

At first blush, (16)–(19) do not seem to add very much by way of logical force to the simple sentence

(20)   David wants his wallet.

The near-synonymy of the cleft sentences (16)–(19) with (20) has actually encouraged nearly every conceivable proposal for syntactically deriving (16)–(19) from (20), from one another, or from yet other textual variants of (20).[7]

Faithful to the autonomy of dialogue grammar, I shall not pass judgment on the syntactic derivation history of (16)–(19). It suffices to be clear about certain syntactic and semantic properties of the resulting configurations, however generated.

We start from wh-clefts. Wh-clefts have the structure of a copular sentence, whose subject has the superficial form of a simple subordinate search question, and whose complement is a syntactically and semantically appropriate substituend for the question word in the subject phrase.

Certain well-chosen sentences of this superficial form allow no less than three readings:

(21)   What I am looking for is a good question.

If the subject of (21) is construed as a subordinate question, the sentence can be paraphrased by

(22)   One may well ask what I am looking for.

If, alternatively, the subject of (21) is construed as a free relative clause, two further readings emerge depending on what is being referred to: a particular question as in

(23)   The question I am looking for is good.

or – most relevantly to our present topic – good questions in general, as in

(24)   A good question is what I am looking for.

On this last reading, (21) is a simple identity between two noun phrases.

This last interpretation seems to me to capture precisely the logical force of (21) as a wh-cleft sentence. There seems to be no objection to saying that, as far as their syntactic and semantic properties go, wh-clefts are simply *identity sentences with free relative subject.*

Their semantic interpretation can then be accomplished by a logical game rule copying the semantic game rule (G.free wh) of Hintikka [130], p. 147. The rule instantiates a free relative by a phrase of the category of its initial constituent, so as to explain (16) by (25) and to infer (26) from it.

(25)   This is his wallet, and David wants this.
(26)   If David wants that, that is his wallet.

This interpretive move seems to capture the salient points about the semantics of (16). It correctly predicts that (16) implies the simple sentence (20). What is more, it also captures the slight nuance that sets off (16) from (20): (16), unlike (20), implies that his wallet is *all* David wants. This difference in entailment is due to the fact, registered in the duality of outcomes (25)–(26), that the quantifier character of free relatives is left open between existential and universal force.

On the existential interpretation, (16) guarantees that one thing David wants is his wallet; on the universal interpretation, it says that all David wants is his wallet. By conjoining the two interpretations, we obtain the uniqueness entailment which distinguishes (16) from (20).

Akmajian [489] is a good source for arguments that wh-clefts are identity sentences with free relative subject. Let me mention some of them.

(i) Wh-clefts have free relative subject. Like other free relatives, they cannot be done on sentential, *which*, or multiple questions:

(27)   Which book he read was *War and Peace*.
(28)   Whether he will go is yes.
(29)   Who kissed whom was John kissed Mary.

Or on prepositional phrases:

(30)   To whom I spoke was John.

(ii) Wh-clefts are identity sentences. Unlike predicative sentences, they freely tolerate reversal of subject and complement:

(31)   Bill is the fool. The fool is Bill.
(32)   What Bill is a fool. A fool is what Bill is.
(33)   Bill is a fool. A fool is Bill.[8]

In a wh-cleft, as in any identity sentence, the subject must match the complement in category:

(34)   What he turned out to be was a fool.
(35)   Who it turned out to be was Bill.

Exchange of *what* and *who* in (34)–(35) will destroy the wh-cleft reading.

However, not all free-relative identities qualify for use as cleft sentences. In addition to the syntactic and semantic constraints, there will be further restrictions of a functional sort.

Among the further restrictions are the following.

(iii) The question phrase of a cleft cannot be modified by *else*:

(36)   What else he did was a mistake

Clefts cannot be formed from attributive *what* relatives:

(37)   What mistakes remain are mine.

A cleft free relative cannot house negative polarity items:

(38)   Whatever he did was a mistake.

Note a certain feeling of 'iffiness' about the free relatives in (36)–(38): they seem to make universal claims without existential commitments, unlike *bona fide* clefts.

(iv) There are certain restrictions on the tense and mood of the copula in cleft sentences. For instance, (39) does not qualify for a cleft, although (40) does:

(39)   What I propose will be a new approach.
(40)   What I propose is a new approach.

We shall see later if these further constraints are not entailed by independently motivated functional properties of wh-clefts.

What is the function of wh-clefts anyway? I already gave away my proposal in the beginning of the section: a wh-cleft is nothing else than a *question-answer dialogue condensed into a sentence*. The free relative subject introduces a question, and the complement constituent answers it.[9]

To capture this simple insight, I propose the following dialogue rule for wh-clefts:

(D.wh-cleft)   A wh-cleft sentence of the form
$$(\text{wh-word} - X - t - Y) - \text{be} - A$$
answers the question
$$i(\text{wh-word} - X - t - Y).$$

For instance, the dialogue function of our example

(41)   What David wants is his wallet.

can be explained by expanding it into the following small dialogue:

(42)   What does David want?
         What David wants is his wallet.

This explication of (41) makes an important prediction about its information structure. As (41) makes explicit, the complement of a cleft sentence constitutes a main rheme with respect of its subject. It cannot but be new information, for it carries along a dialogue context which makes it so. By the same token, the question premise in (42) designates the subject of (41) as inherently thematic.

Something equally important is predicted about the subject of a wh-cleft. To justify the use of a wh-cleft in a dialogue, a direct question structurally identical to the subject free relative has to have a place in the dialogue. In other words, to accept a wh-cleft is to accept its subject as a topical question worthy of interest, or relevant to the dialogue.

This requirement suggests an explanation to the restrictions registered in (i) above. It follows from it that the existential presupposition of the cleft

subject question must be established in the dialogue context, whether independently or as a consequence of the cleft sentence itself. This, I suspect, is
why the free relatives in (iii) do not admit of a cleft reading. As we noted,
these free relatives do away with existential commitments, and this mili-
tates against the existential presupposition imported by (D.wh-cleft).

Another corollary of (D.wh-cleft) is that the cleft sentence must constitute
a *bona fide* answer to its subject question. If I am not mistaken, this is what
distinguishes (39) from (40) in (iv). An application of (D.wh-cleft) to (40)
spells it out as

(43)   I propose this, and this is a new approach.

(C.be) applies to (43) to give

(44)   I propose a new approach.

which is a good answer to the question raised by (40):

(45)   What do I propose?

In contrast, (D.wh-cleft) takes (39) into

(46)   I propose this, and this will be a new approach.

But this time, the promissory identity in (46) does not warrant substitutivity,
so (46) gives no clue to what 'this' counts as now. In other words, (40)
answers the question it raises, but (39) does not.[10]

(D.wh-cleft) makes cleft sentences a powerful tool for organizing the topic
structure of a discourse. A wh-cleft sentence at once indicates what question
it is addressed to. Hence it will be appropriate to a context only if its subject
is a question that naturally arises in that context.

This prediction is confirmed by the painstaking study of the textual
function of cleft sentences in Prince [531]. Prince summarizes her findings as
the following:

(47)   Discourse condition on wh-clefts: a wh-cleft will not occur
         coherently in a discourse if the material inside the (subject)
         wh-clause does not represent material which the cooperative
         speaker can assume to be appropriately in the hearer's conscious-
         ness at the time of hearing the utterance.

It remains obscure in (47) what is meant by material inside sentences, and
what is it for that material to be appropriately in anyone's consciousness. The

dialogue reconstruction suggests a simple explication: the subject question must occur among the premises of the cleft sentence in the dialogue game.

Let us look at some of the evidence. Sometimes, the premise is put into so many words in the dialogue context:

(48)   There's no question what they are after. What the committee is after is somebody at the White House.

(Here, the idiom "there is no question" of course does not dismiss a question but serves to introduce one.)

Another example:

(49)   H: I'm really very sorry to disturb you. It's just that we're making a few inquiries about Margery Phipps.
K: What's this all about?
H: What I'd like to know is exactly what you did after shooting finished on the day that Margery Phipps died.

Example (49) is taken, with abbreviations, from Patricia Moyes' novel *The Falling Star*. The first speaker's cleft is clearly a polite paraphrase of the witness' abrupt inquiry.

Often, the informational interest which motivates the cleft can be inferred from the presence of alternative answers to the same question:

(50)   He did not fall accidentally. What happened was someone pushed him.

Obviously, if it is worth while denying one account of the event it is of interest to know what really happened. Other examples of this character are

(51)   Nikki Caine, 19, does not want to be a movie star. What she hopes to do is to be a star on the horse-show circuit.

and

(52)   Precisely how pseudo-clefts are formed need not concern us. What is relevant is their dialogue function.

(52) is particularly interesting, as its underlying question is motivated by properly dialogical considerations. A cleft like (52) can occur anywhere in a dialogue, as it is addressed to a question which is part and parcel of the decision problem of every dialogue game:

(53)   What is relevant and what is not relevant?

Another constitutive question in any dialogue is what players mean by what they say. Hence any dialogue move can prompt a cleft like Nixon's

(54)   What I mean is we need something to answer somebody.

One more case of this sort: any dialogue overture immediately raises the question of the author's aims. It is therefore natural to start a discourse by answering that implicit question. This covers informal appointments as well as lectures or scientific essays:

(55)   What I wanted to ask you is could you read this draft for me.
(56)   What we shall be talking about today is cleft sentences.
(57)   What we have set as our goal is the grammatical capacity of children — a part of their linguistic competence.

When asked for an opinion, one is entitled to clefts like

(58)   What is appealing about your approach is its artlessness; what makes it suspect is that it is not fully thought out.
(59)   What I think is you should rewrite it.

Conversely, it is quite out of place to cleft where no one is interested in your opinion.

(60)   A: Hello, operator. I'm trying to dial this number. Could you please check it for me?
         B: What I think is the exchange is overloaded. Hold on while I check it.

Here, a rude caller might point out that no one had asked what the operator thought.

Another telling example of a misplaced cleft is the following dialogue opening:

(61)   Hi! What I heard is you are expecting a baby.

There is no reason to suppose that the addressee of (61) is wondering what the author has heard. So there is no explanation for the cleft. (61) contrasts nicely with the following opening:

(62)   Hi! What I am calling about is we just had a baby.

It is a justifiable assumption that the receiver of a phone call wonders what gives him the honor.

All the above properties of wh-clefts can be traced back to (D.wh-cleft). But of course clefts are not exempt from the application of other textual principles either. Intuitively, it is a complement of a cleft sentence that annouces its main news, while the relative clause houses subordinate information. This intuition is already accounted for by the fact that the relative clause is a subordinate clause. No wonder it is odd to hide the answer to a question in the subject clause of a cleft as in

(63)   A: Wasn't that incredible when Mary called the boss a pig?
         B: Yeah, what really shocked me was that she called him that.

An acceptable answer will make the answer a main clause:

(64)   B: Yeah, it really shocked me that she called him that.

Another expectation is that (16)–(17) will differ in dialogue function because of their different linear order.

(16)   What David wants is his wallet.
(17)   His wallet is what David wants.

(16) has its inherently rhematic complement on the right side of the copula, where it syntactically belongs. No further thematicity predictions are warranted. Consequently, as we saw in (55)–(57) and (62), direct word-order wh-clefts can quite well open a dialogue.

In contrast, in (17) the predicate complement is markedly early. A likely explanation is that (D.topic) and (D.left) have been applied, marking the complement as thematic as well as rhematic. We would expect, then, that inverted wh-clefts share environments with topicalized sentences. Indeed, they do:

(65)   Does David want his passport?
         No, his wallet is what David wants.

The cleft structure of the last line of (65) indicates that what the author wants is at issue; the inversion contrasts his answer to the interlocutor's suggestion in the same way as topicalization or it-clefting would do:

(66)   His wallet, David wants.

(67)   It is his wallet that David wants.

Inverse wh-clefts are particularly idiomatic with a demonstrative or anaphoric *this* or *that* as the preposed complement:

(68)   "It doesn't seem real. Tom." ... "There are so many things, silly little everyday things, you don't even know about. *That's what seems so odd.*"

(69)   No need to go outside ever again. No chance of ever going outside again. ... The well-appointed cage! Was it for this, she thought, that all these varying personalities had abandoned their countries, their loyalties, their everyday lives? *Was this what they wanted?*

4. *IT*-CLEFTS

Let us proceed to *it*-clefts like (18).

(18)   It is his wallet that David wants.

I make the relatively uncontroversial (or at least naive) syntactical assumption that they feature obligatorily extraposed relative clauses: in (18), the *that*-clause is bound to the subject *it* as its modifier, whether or not it originated next to its head.

As for the semantics of (18), I sympathize with Bolinger's thesis in [496], p. 66. He claims that "Sentences with *it* differ in meaning from sentences without *it*, and that the difference can be assigned to *it* as a member of the set that includes *he, she,* and *they.*"

In accordance with Bolinger's thesis, I assume that (18) means just what it would seem to mean: the subject *it* is a pronoun which picks out something that David wants, and the rest of the main clause identifies that something as his wallet.

This interpretive strategy can be captured by the following game rule for *it*:

(C.it)   Explain a sentence of the form
$$X - it - Y (\text{Comp} - Z - t - W) - V,$$
where *it* is the head of the parenthetical clause (if any), by a sentence
$$X - A - Y \text{ and } Z - A - W,$$
whereupon infer any sentence
$$(\text{if } Z - B - W,) \text{ then } B \text{ is } A.$$

An application of (C.it) to (18) produces an explanation like

(70)   This is his wallet and David wants this

and allows any inference of the form

(71)   If David wants that, then that is this.

It seems to me that this game strategy brings out all that is noteworthy about the logical force of the it-cleft (18). We capture the fact that (18) entails the simple sentence

(20)   David wants his wallet.

but we can also point out the logical difference between (18) and (20): (18) makes it clear that his wallet is *all* David wants. This uniqueness entailment, missing from (20), is due to the final uniqueness clause of (C.it) which registers the well-known fact that *it* is a definite pronoun.

The rule (C.it) succeeds in capturing Bolinger's observation that the uniqueness entailment of the it-cleft construction is due to the inherent meaning of *it*. To illustrate this, note that (C.it) applies equally well to explain the uniqueness entailments of the answer in

(72)   — What are these things on my desk?
         — It is my stone collection.

It indicates that only one object is present. (Cf. *one*.)

An application of (C.it) explains the second line of (72) by something like

(73)   What you were pointing at is my stone collection.

and uniqueness of reference is ensured by the validity, wherever one might point, of

(74)   What you are pointing at is what you were pointing at.

The uniqueness implication of *it* also explains why the following dialogue example from Bolinger [496] is wrong-headed:

(75)   — Who came?
         — It was John.
         — Who else came?
         — It was Mary.

Since *it* makes clear that only John came, one should not inquire about other comers, even less answer such inquiries.

There is one important respect in which the subject of an *it*-cleft is more versatile than other occurrences of *it*: it is not sensitive to person, gender or number. *It is* stays put, whatever follows:

(76)   It is us that he means.

An equally topic-neutral *it* is found free-standing in (77), where it *identifies an answer to a question*:

(77)   — Who is calling?
             — It is us.

The last observation, I believe, is diagnostic. The topic-neutral *it* in cleft sentences — and in (77) — identifies *an answer* — an abstract object: that is why *it* is not sensitive to person, gender or number here any more than in, say,

(78)   — What is the last word of the previous example?
             — It is *us*.

The affinity of (77) to cleft sentences is close: the answer can be reconstructed into an it-cleft by appending the topical question to it:

(79)   — Who is calling?
             — It is us who is calling.

The following example sentences could equally easily be completed via it-clefts to question-answer dialogues:

(80)   Something is still bothering me. It is how he got in.
(81)   If he had a friend, it was Winnie Nelson.

The same idea seems to explain the turn of phrase in

(82)   I am afraid that we have to let you go. It is not that we do not
         like you. It is just that we can no more use you.

What this sort of it-sentence does is identify reasons or explanations. That is, they supply answers to questions like

(83)   What is the reason (explanation) for this?

This underlying question is nicely in evidence in the following dialogue:

(84) H: Did you take the letter?
      S: Why ever should I do that?
      H: It is just that we can't lay hands on it at the moment.

The second speaker is in effect wondering

(85) What is the reason for that question?

— at any rate this is the question H addresses his answer to.
Similar topical constraints seem involved in the difference between

(86) It was John who called

and

(87) Only John called.

as answers to the question

(88) What is wrong? What happened?

Intuitively, (86)–(87) report different worries. If (86) is used, the author probably expected just one caller, but not John. If (87) is used, the author may be disappointed at just one caller instead of a number.

In popular terminology, (86) seems to presuppose uniqueness while (87) asserts it. In dialogue terms, this amounts to the simple fact that (86)–(87) constitutionally answer different questions: (86), unlike (87), is limited to address

(89) Who called?

while (87) can also answer, among other questions,

(90) How many people called?

Multiple questions bring in further evidence:

(91) Now, who wrote what again?
      It was Jack who wrote the preface, it was Ernie who wrote the text, and it was Tex who wrote the appendix.

It would be quite odd to cleft the other way round:

(92) It was the preface that Jack wrote, it was the text that Ernie wrote, and it was the appendix that Tex wrote.

To sum up, our data seems to suggest the following dialogue rule for it-clefts:

(D.it-cleft) An it-cleft sentence of the form
          it be A (Comp $X - t - Y$)
     answers a question of the form
          i(Wh-phrase $- X - t - Y$)

The condition (D.it-cleft) immediately explains what is wrong with (92) as an answer to the question in (91): *what* is a secondary question word of the multiple question in (91), whose instantiations constitute rhematic themes.

The formulation of (D.it-cleft) is sufficiently loose to make room for certain atypical uses of clefts. The following are pertinent examples:

(93)   It was a fine performance that he gave.
(94)   It is not every man who makes his own meals.
(95)   It is a good divine that follows his own instructions.

What is peculiar about (93)–(95) is that not *all* of the predicate complement is rhematic, as is shown by the questions which they are likely to address, respectively:

(96)   What sort of performance did he give?
(97)   How many men make their own meals?
(98)   What sort of a divine is a good divine?

An even more intriguing example is the following:

(99)   It is not I who have lost the Athenians: it is the Athenians who have lost me.

(100) clearly addresses a double question with a unique pair presupposition:

(100)   Who has lost (and) what?

An example which seems not to be an example at all is Prince's

(101)   If I see a train crossing, I keep going. It's a game you're playing.

It seems to me more natural to interpret *a game you're playing* in (101) as one constituent. The sentence is not a cleft sentence at all but an ordinary predicative sentence whose subject refers to the preceding sentence and whose predicate complement is a noun modified by a relative clause.[11]

As with wh-clefts, we can see the workings of other dialogue principles in the textual use of it-clefts. It-clefts are currently perhaps the most popular device for corrective remarks:

(102)   Does David want his passport?
         No, it is his wallet that David wants.

This is explained by reference to (D.left) exactly as in the section on focal topicalization.

The application of (D.left) also explains why clefts are useful reminders. By moving an answer early in a sentence, it can be marked as old information. This explains Bolinger's contrast

(103)   A: When will we know?
         B: It's tomorrow we will know.
(104)   A: When will you tell me?
         B: It's tomorrow I shall tell you.

The cleft is queer in (104) if it is assumed that B is revealing new information to A; in (103), it is motivated if it reminds B of something he should already know. Focus topicalization of *tomorrow* would create the same effect.

Yet clefting stays functionally apart from focus topicalization, as topicalization does not entail uniqueness (it only suggests a contrast to possible alternatives). As a result, (105)–(106) are not at all interchangeable functionally:

(105)   Now I understand!
(106)   It is now that I understand!

While (105) only suggests that the author did not understand earlier, (106) restricts understanding to the present, excluding past as well as future.

(D.it-cleft) predicts that the relative clause of a cleft is inherently thematic, as it repeats material from an implicit question. However, (D.it-cleft) does not require that the underlying *question itself* be familiar to the audience. To the contrary, a cleft sentence can actually be used to suggest it as a topic worthy of attention. In fact, clefts have an important function as rhetorical openings of literary texts:

(108)   It was just about fifty years ago that Henry Ford gave us the weekend.

Ellen Prince, to whom this observation is due, also neatly describes the dialogue intent of this sort of all-new it-cleft:

Their function, or at least one of their functions, is to mark a piece of information as a fact, known to some people although not yet known to the intended hearer.

This it-clefts accomplish by the simple trick of embedding an assumption in the subordinate clause of the cleft. As we have noted, what is said in a subordinate clause is not called into question: subordinate clauses cannot constitute dialogue moves without intervening steps of inference.

CHAPTER 5

ABOUTNESS

1. A TRADITIONAL AMBIGUITY IN THE NOTION OF 'THEME'

Despite individual differences, most approaches to text grammar or functional sentence perspective share a number of basic insights and distinctions.

A fundamental commonplace is the distinction between structure (means of expression) and function (choice among means of expression). This distinction is accepted in principle by all writers, although in practice confusions occur.[1]

Further, there is a consensus that the main problem of text grammar is the characterization of functional notions. Behind confusing terminology, there seems to be much more convergence on answers to this problem too, than first meets the eye. A case in point is a traditional distinction between two notions of theme, *theme as givenness* and *theme as aboutness*. It is this distinction that I shall try to examine and vindicate in this and following sections.

The roots of the distinction go back to the forerunners of functional grammar. According to Firbas [552], the true pioneer of text grammar was the nineteenth-century French classicist Henri Weil [600].

According to Firbas, it was Weil who concluded from his comparative word order studies that

A sentence contains a point of departure (an initial notion) and a goal of discourse. The point of departure is equally present to the speaker and to the hearer; it is their rallying point, the ground on which they meet. The goal of discourse presents the very information that is to be imparted to the hearer.[2]

Referring to these functional notions, Weil described unmarked word order, which moves from the point of departure to the goal of discourse, as the proper movement of the mind. The inverse order which puts the goal of discourse before the initial notion Weil described as the "pathetic" order — a vehicle of emotion.[2]

From Weil, the basic functional division of a sentence into a familiar point of departure and the newly introduced goal of discourse has been inherited by most modern approaches.

Weil did not fix his ideas in technical terms. Other nineteenth-century grammarians referred to the terms of the dichotomy by the Protean names 'psychological subject' and 'psychological predicate'. For all its simplicity, this dichotomy was riddled by a crucial ambiguity, brought out lucidly by Jespersen [569:145—146] in his discussion of the received notions of subject and predicate:

The subject is sometimes said to be the relatively familiar element to which the predicate is added as something new.
  Another definition that is frequently given is that the subject is what we talk about, and the predicate is what is said about this subject.

The same duality of definition is in evidence in the work of the founder of the Czechoslovak school of functional grammar, Vilem Mathesius [581—2].
  Attributing the observation to Daneš, Firbas [552] notes that

Mathesius in fact offers two conceptions of the theme. Roughly speaking, according to one of them the theme expresses something that is spoken about; according to the other it expresses something that is known or at least obvious in the given situation. (p. 23)

Daneš himself [547] elaborates his point as follows:

(. . .) the distinctions [known (given) information—new information and theme—rheme] go back to V. Mathesius. In his well-known paper from 1939 he defines the "starting point of the utterance (východisko)" as "that which is known or at least obvious in the given situation and from which the speaker proceeds", whereas "the core of the utterance (jádro)" is "What the speaker states about, or in regard to, the starting point of the utterance."
  The same author defines (in 1942) "the foundation (or the theme) of the utterance (základ, téma)" as something "that is being spoken about in the sentence", and "the core (jádro)" as what the speaker says about this theme. (p. 106)

A similar duality has been recognized by several authors, including Beneš [542], Halliday [562], Sgall [592], Sgall, et al. [594], not to forget Daneš himself. In the American tradition, a similar distinction has been made in the duality of term pairs *topic-comment* (Hockett [566]) and *given-new* (Chafe [432], [543]). Chomsky [434] has added to the terminological confusion by yet another pair *presupposition-focus*, in function similar if not identical to Chafe's given-new distinction.[3]

All of the above authors seem to agree that two independent dichotomies are involved here, and that both play a part in text organization. This thesis is listed as the first item of "Main points of Agreement" among text grammarians in Sgall, et al. [594], p. 17:

The distinction between topic and comment is autonomous, in the sense that it cannot be derived from the distinction between "given" (i.e., known from the preceding context or situation, contained among the presuppositions) and "new" (not given).

Our definitions of theme (thematicity) and rheme (rhematicity) have been contextual, i.e., based on the idea of given vs. new information. A few sections later, I shall join the consensus and claim a place for another distinction independent of the contextual notions, based on the intuitive idea of 'aboutness'. Before doing so, however, I shall examine some fallacious arguments for the duality of distinctions.

2. INVALID ARGUMENTS FOR INDEPENDENCE

As Daneš ([547], p. 108) points out,

(...) what makes the investigators differentiate between "known" and "theme" is the fact that there exist cases where [theme] does not convey known information (...) or where the ranges of both do not fully coincide.

However, the success of such applications of the Padoan principle depends on how the relevant predicates are defined in the first place. If the definitions are deficient, the independence argument may be fallacious. In this section, I want to show that our contextual definitions of theme and rheme are immune to certain arguments offered in the literature.

A case in point is the argument offered by Sgall, et al. [594], p. 17–18:

What is perhaps most decisive as an argument for the autonomy of [topic-comment articulation] is that the preceding context does not always determine uniquely the choice of topic and comment of a sentence; for instance the statement $(1-1)$ can be followed in a quite natural way either by $(1-2)$ or by $(1-3)$ – not to speak of other possibilities:

$(1-1)$ Yesterday was the last day of the Davis cup match between Australia and ROUMANIA.
$(1-2)$ Australia WON the match.
$(1-3)$ The match was won by AUSTRALIA.

In such cases the speaker is free to choose any of the previously mentioned names of countries or a word referring to the match itself as the topic of the next sentence. If he is Australian, the choice of the name of his country readily occurs, but this is not the only type of situation in which the country is "in the speakers' minds" or is spoken about.

Similarly, after the statement $(1-4)$ it is possible to choose either $(1-5)$ or $(1-6)$:

(1–4)   On Christmas Eve we expected our RELATIVES.
(1–5)   Uncle Fred came FIRST.
(1–6)   First came Uncle FRED.

Here one either speaks about Uncle Fred and states when he came, or one speaks about the one who came first, and states who he was.

The argument is somewhat inexplicit, but its point seems clear. In the first example, both *Australia* and *the match* have been mentioned previously, yet either can be chosen as the first constituent of the next sentence. In the second example, neither *Uncle Fred* nor *first* have been mentioned, yet either can begin the next sentence. It is assumed that in these examples at least, the first constituent indicates the topic of the sentence. In each case, the choice of topic depends on what the speaker wants to speak about and not on the preceding text.

What is wrong with this argument is its overly simplistic construction of the notion 'given (new) relative to context'. It misses the following insights of Daneš [547], p. 109–110:

It is evident that the notion "given (known)" is relative and very broad (if not vague):

(1) Given or known is that information which is derivable or recoverable (to use Halliday's wording) from the context, situation and the common knowledge of the speaker and the listener. Certainly, there exist individual divergences between the two, due to differences in their experience, memory, attention, etc. But after all, it is the speaker's evaluation that is the determining factor; this does not exclude, of course, that the speaker takes, more or less, into account the presupposed position of the listener.

(2) The communicative feature of "givenness", assigned to particular sentence elements, is a graded property.

(3) "Givenness" depends on the length of the portion of preceding text in relation to which the evaluation is being carried out. The upper limit of such a portion should be empirically ascertained. We may tentatively assume, that these portions or "intervals" are in a way correlated with the segmentation of text into paragraphs, groups of paragraphs, chapters, etc. We may even expect a kind of hierarchy or stratification of the feature "given": taking for granted that not only particular utterances but also the sections of text, as paragraphs, etc., and the whole text have "themes" of their own ("hyperthemes"), we can expect that, e.g., the theme of a chapter will be evaluated as "given" throughout the chapter, so that the "interval of givenness" in respect to the information carried by this "hypertheme" will be the whole chapter.

(4) The contextual determination of givenness is far from being a simple phenomenon. We might tentatively suggest that as "contextually given" may be regarded such semantic information that has been somehow mentioned in a qualified portion (interval) of the preceding text. It can be mentioned directly, or indirectly. In the first case, it can be mentioned not only with the identical wording, but also with a synonymous

expression, or with a paraphrase (cf. Pike's "hypermeaning" or "verbalized concept"). The indirect mentioning is based on semantic inference (or semantic implication, if viewed from the opposite point).

In this important passage, Daneš makes a number of observations that have inspired the present approach to text grammar:

(i) Textual notions are relative to dialogue structure, not just to previous text. What an appropriate reconstruction of a dialogue context is depends on previous text, but only in part. Further structure can be gleaned from the context, situation, and the common knowledge between the participants.

(ii) What is given to one participant may be new to another. Every player of a dialogue game uses his own representation of the dialogue situation as his guide in planning his dialogue strategy. Yet players aim at common understanding. It is in their interest to frame their moves so that their relation to earlier moves is obvious to the audience.

(iii) Thematicity is a relative notion. What is old information relative to one premise may be new with respect to another premise. In that sense, it is a graded notion. What is thematic with respect to a smaller dialogue may be rhematic with respect to a larger one, and vice versa.

(iv) Previous mention may be indirect or implicit. Thematicity may depend on implicit interpolated premises instead of the explicit sentences of the preceding text.

Let us now see how these insights apply in Sgall's examples.

As the capitalizations in the example sentences indicate, these sentences are clearly informationally distinct. In (1–2), the verb conveys the main news of the sentence, in (1–3) it is *Australia*. Correspondingly, the two sentences address quite different informational interests, or topical questions. If one is Australian, one is indeed likely to wonder.

(1)   How did Australia fare in the match?

in which context (1–2) is the expected form of answer, given our contextual definitions. However, a more objective observer would put another implicit question, duly answered by (1–3):

(2)   Who won the match?

Given these quite natural expansions of the implicit dialogue context, we are able to tell apart the textual functions of (1–2) and (1–3) in terms of contextual notions.

A similar explication fits the second example as well. Sentence (1–5) is appropriate as a move in the implicit context of

(3)   When did each relative come?
         When did Uncle Fred come?

whereas (1—6) fits the context of

(4)   In which order did the relatives come?
         Who came first?

Again, the textual roles of *Uncle Fred* and *first* can be distinguished in terms of contextual notions: one of them is a rhematic theme, the other a simple rheme.

3. ABOUTNESS

Yet it is impressive how many writes on functional grammar agree that one question of great importance to text organization is what sentences intuitively are *about*. The following is just a small selection:

An old maxim says that [topic-comment articulation] consists, first of all, in the distinction between "what is spoken about" and "what is said about it" in a sentence. (Sgall, et al. [594], p. 10)

Man wird also zugeben, dass die einfachste und oft benutzte Charakteristik der Thema-Rhema-Gliederung — worüber man spricht, is das Thema, was man darüber aussagt, is das Rhema" — im Grunde richtig ist. (Sgall [593], p. 55)

The subject is that which is spoken of. (Curme [331], p. 1)

Theme means what I am talking about now. (Halliday [562])

I suggest . . . making explicit the notion that the fundamental division of a sentence is between the *topic*, the element that identifies what the sentence is about, and the *comment*, the predication which is made of that object. (Gundel [453], p. 10)

So far as I can see at present, the best way to characterize the subject function is not very different from the ancient statement that the subject is what we are talking about . . . (Chafe [593], p. 43)

The concept of 'theme' cannot be given any precise formulation. I can only say that the theme is what the rest of the sentence is about. (Kuno [470], p. 277)

Good, but how is one to characterize the notion 'about'? Sgall, et al. [594], p. 15) feel that "for many sentences it is fairly easy to ascertain that something is talked about in them and some (other) thing is stated about it there". Unfortunately, things are not always that easy. I let Jespersen point out the difficulty with an appeal to intuition here.

This is true about many, perhaps most, sentences, though the man in the street would probably be inclined to say that it does not help him very much, for in such a sentence as "John promised Mary a gold ring" he would say that there are four things of which something is said, and which might therefore all of them be said to be "subjects" namely (1) John, (2) a promise, (3) Mary, and (4) a ring.[4]

An interesting refinement of unschooled intuitions of aboutness is suggested in Reinhart [587]:

To the question what sentence (1) is about, or what is its topic, both (2) and (3), among several others, are appropriate answers.

(1)   Mr. Morgan is a careful researcher and a knowledgeable semiticist, but his originality leaves something to be desired.

(2)   (1) is about Mr. Morgan.

(3)   (1) is about Mr. Morgan's scholarly ability.

Intuitively, it is not the same sense of aboutness that is used in (2) and in (3). (1) is about Morgan because it predicates something of Morgan. On the other hand, (1) does not explicitly predicate anything of Morgan's scholarly ability, though it provides some information about it (. . .).

It is only the first of these uses of aboutness that the technical term *sentence-topic* is intended to capture in linguistic theory. For convenience, we will label the aboutness relation expressed in (3) *discourse topic*, although this is not a commonly accepted terminology.

Let us examine this proposal more closely. According to Reinhart's explanation in the quote, Mr. Morgan is (or can be) the sentence topic of her example (1) because (1) explicitly predicates something of Morgan. Presumably, this is because the grammatical subject of (1) actually refers to him. In contrast, there is no explicit mention of Mr. Morgan's scholarly ability in (1).

On the other hand, Mr. Morgan's scholarly ability is a (possible) discourse topic for (1) because (1) provides information about it though (1) does not make actual mention of it. In other words, (1) is an informative although indirect answer to the following question, whose grammatical subject does refer to Mr. Morgan's scholarly ability:

(5)   What is Mr. Morgan's scholarly ability?

This observation suggests that a reduction of Reinhart's two concepts of aboutness to one is possible given our notion of topic (or topical question) of a dialogue.

What we have to do is make aboutness too depend on dialogue context. We may say that (1) is about Mr. Morgan in virtue of constituting a well-formed answer to the topic

(6)   What is Mr. Morgan like?

while it is about Mr. Morgan's scholarly ability in virtue of constituting
an answer to (5). What accounts for the feeling that (1) is somehow more
directly about Mr. Morgan is the simple fact that (1) is a direct answer to (6)
but an indirect answer to (5).

This relativization at once sets to rest the question of how the same sentence can be taken to be about a number of different things at once without
compromising the conflicting intuition that we are dealing with a functional
notion ('the' topic of a sentence). A sentence can be about different things
with respect to different topical sentences, yet about some one thing with
respect to each one topic.

So let us set about developing this insight. To fix our terminology, let us
call what a sentence intuitively is about its *dialogue subject.*[5]

As with thematic notions, the first question to ask is: what sort of thing
are dialogue subjects? For the thematic notions, our answer was simple:
thematic notions are properties of (structural) constituents of sentences.

For the notion of dialogue subject, a different answer seems forced upon
us. Sentences are not about their structural constituents. What they are about
— what they speak of — are things: objects in the domain of discourse of
language which the constituents of sentences may pick out, refer to, or stand
for.

The notion of picking out or standing for is a tricky notion. Let us become
a bit clearer about what it involves. Actually, objects are not picked out
by noun phrases. Rather, players of semantic games pick out objects following semantic game rules for noun phrases. For instance, the subject of

(7)   Lennon lives.

is agreed by players of a semantical game of verification to designate a particular person, say the late Beatle. In the rest of the game, 'Lennon' stands for,
or refers to him. In the game connected with

(8)   A madman killed Lennon.

the proponent picks out an individual he thinks killed Lennon; for the
rest of the game, the subject of (8) is replaced by some designation of that
individual. It would be misleading to ask simply who *a madman* refers to in
(8): that is up to the proponent to decide. If there is one and only one
individual for which the game connected with (8) has a winning strategy,
one might say that he is who (8) refers to, or picks out. But if (8) is false,

one is puzzled: should one for instance root for an individual which satisfies the main clause of (8)

(9)   he killed Lennon

on one who satisfies the subject description

(10)   he is a madman.

Let us take a third example.

(11)   No one wanted Lennon to die.

Who does the subject of (11) refer to? Here, no satisfactory answer is forthcoming: (11) is about everyone in general or no one in particular, take your pick.

Certain insights emerge from these examples. First, what a noun phrase refers to is a function of the more fundamental question of who does the referring. An objective sense to the notion is available when one can point to a unique winning strategy, the rational player's choice in a game of verification. In the absence of an objective basis, a subjective interpretation prevails: what a noun phrase refers to is what, if anything, its user refers to by it. What is that, then? Not necessarily any particular thing, as (11) shows. One who puts forward (11) is not under any obligation to provide substitution instances for it — that is a job for an opponent of (11). The proponent of (11) is not likely to be speaking of — or referring to — any particular individual at all.

But compare again (8). One who maintains (8) must accept that its predicate is true of one particular individual. Does it follow that he is speaking *about* any one object whenever he puts forward (8)? My intuition says: yes and no. He *is* speaking about a particular individual, namely the supposed murderer of John Lennon. No matter if he knows nothing further about him, it suffices that he believes him to exist and to be unique. No matter if he is wrong: he is still talking about the murderer, whatever others may say.

Yet, to do justice to the contrary intuition, he need not have any particular person in mind, anyone he knows or could name or describe. If he does, all the better; but that is not necessary. The object he has in mind may well be just an individual concept, not an individuating function, to use the distinction made in Part I, Chapter 3.7.

This will henceforth be my construal of the objects of *about* ascriptions: what players speak are about individual concepts, represented by functions from epistemic alternatives to descriptions of individuals in them as explained in Part I of this essay.

This reconstruction sheds some light on the question of when two dialogue participants can be said to speak about the same thing. Two detectives who agree that a murder was committed but differ on the identity of the murderer can naturally be said to talk about the same person in two senses and about different persons in one. If a murder was actually committed, there is an objective sense in which both speak of the same flesh-and-blood individual, viz. the real murderer. Even if they are mistaken, they still speak of the same person in a loose but quite colloquial sense; they both speak of the imaginary murderer, an individual concept which spans both participants' epistemic alternatives. At the same time, they would emphasize that they refer to different persons when they speak about the murderer, for the concept 'the murderer' coincides with different well-defined individuals in each speaker's epistemic alternatives. It seems the present reconstruction of aboutness does justice to all of these aspects of ordinary usage.[6]

To avoid conceptual confusion at the expense of proliferation of terminology, let us call what (if anything) an author of a sentence refers to by a noun phrase in a dialogue move, the *value* of the noun phrase. It is understood that the value of a noun phrase may depend on the author and the dialogue context of the move. For instance, in

(12)   A: Your wife is very pretty.
         B: Actually, she is not my wife.

the second speaker is not likely to be meaning to contradict himself: he is not speaking about his wife, but his companion, who he assumes his interlocutor is referring to as well. The value of *B's wife* is different for A and B, but the value of *your wife* for A can be cross-identified with the value of *she* for B: the two are speaking of the same person after all.

4. DIALOGUE SUBJECTS

With the help of the notion of value, we are in a position to formulate the following partial definition of the *dialogue subject* of a sentence relative to a premise:

(13)   The dialogue subject of a sentence S with respect to a sentence S' is the value of the grammatical subject of S'.

A dialogue subject of a sentence is what the sentence intuitively is *about* — or better, what its author speaks about in the sentence. Formally, this connection would be made by letting the rule of interpretation for the preposition *about* refer to the notion of dialogue subject so as to imply

(14)   A sentence S in a dialogue D is *about* an object V if V is a dialogue subject of S in D.

I shall not try to define the meaning of *about* further than (14) here. (14) will suffice for a good intuitive test for dialogue subjecthood.[7]

Now (13) does not (nor is it meant to) define more than a partial function from pairs of sentences to individual concepts. As we have seen, not all grammatical subjects of sentences have a value. Such sentences cannot introduce dialogue subjects directly (though they may indirectly, by implying further sentences whose subjects do refer). A case in point would be

(15)   It was raining.

whose grammatical subject refers to nothing.

Note that (13) does not care whether S makes explicit reference to its dialogue subject. Hence (15), although it has no referring noun phrases, may have a dialogue subject. It is a good answer to the question

(16)   How was the weather?

whose subject *the weather* does refer. Accordingly, in the context of (16), (15) can perfectly well be said to speak about the weather, though it does not mention the weather.

It was suggested in the preceding section that Reinhart's notions of sentence topic and discourse topic might be reduced to one. (13) effects such a reduction. In its full generality, (13) seems to do justice to Reinhart's notion of discourse topic. Her notion of sentence topic can be defined in terms of (13): a noun phrase in a sentence indicates its sentence topic if the value of that noun phrase is its dialogue subject.

It is fair to ask if this notion of sentence topic, even as a definable rather than a primitive concept, still ought to be singled out as a unit of dialogue grammar. Reinhart [587] has an ingenious though inconclusive argument that it should. Compare again Reinhart's (1) to (17) and (18):

(5)   What is Mr. Morgan's scholarly ability?
(17)   Mr. Morgan has a clear handwriting and he is punctual.

(18)   My Aunt Rosa has a clear handwriting and she is punctual.
         My Aunt Rosa is a careful researcher, but her originality leaves
         something to be desired.

While all of (17)–(18) are rather unsatisfactory as responses to (5), there is
a clear difference. While (17) is ungenerous, (18) seems simply irrelevant to
the question. In Reinhart's terms, the difference is that

although [17] fails to assert anything about Morgan's scholarly ability, it does assert
something about Morgan, while the answers in [18] fail even that. In other words,
[17], but not [18], sticks to the sentence-topic specified by the request.

The contrast between (17) and (18) is suggested to depend on this theoretical
difference, although it is left unclear just how.

Actually, it turns out that the difference between (17)–(18) can be
explained without reference to dialogue subjects at all. It suffices to pay
closer attention to the relation of (17)–(18) to the dialogue topic (5). It is
true that none of (17)–(18) form a direct answer to (5). However, (17)
but not (18) answers directly a related more general question:

(19)   What qualifications does Mr. Morgan have?

This more general question implies the question (5) on the condition that the
presupposition of the latter is true: (19) entails

(20)   What is Mr. Morgan's scholarly ability, if any?

If (19) is the fundamental question, (5) arises only if the conditional 'if any'
is fulfilled. If not, (5) can be left unanswered. Now, to understand why (17)
as the sole response to (5) tends to be read as a belittling remark on Mr.
Morgan's scholastic ability, it suffices to construe it as a complete answer to
(19) rather than to (5). The addressee dismisses the more specific question
(5) by finding (17) a sufficient answer to the more general question (19).

Now compare (18). In order to obtain an analogous reconstruction for
(18), one should be able to figure out how Aunt Rosa's abilities might have
the least bearing on Mr. Morgan's aptitude. Then, perhaps even (18) might
be redeemed as replies to (5). Be that as it may, a clear difference still remains
between (17)–(18).

Better evidence for the need for Reinhart's distinction will emerge in the
chapter on dislocations. For its purposes, we spell out the requisite notion
of *direct dialogue subject* in

(21)   A dialogue subject of a sentence is a *direct dialogue subject* if
         it is the value of some constituent of the sentence.

What, the question now arises, is the relation of the new concept of
dialogue subject to thematicity. One fact at once meets the eye: with the
relativization of dialogue subject to dialogue premise in the manner of (13),
a reference to a dialogue subject is unavoidably thematic with respect to that
premise. We shall see consequences of this thematicity prediction in the sequel.

But where do these premises for dialogue subjects come from? This
question will be asked and answered in the next section.

5. SUBJECT AND TOPIC

An important distinction about *about* is reflected in the very syntax of
the preposition. The English preposition *about* (and its synonym *of*) admits
of two syntactically distinct constructions, nicely brought together in Lewis
Carroll's familiar poem:[8]

> "The time has come", the Walrus said,
> "To talk of many things:
> Of shoes — and ships — and sealing wax —
> Of cabbages — and kings —
> And why the sea is boiling hot —
> And whether pigs have wings."

In the first construction, discourse is about *things*; the object of *about* is
then syntactically a noun phrase like *shoes* or *kings*. In the second, talk is
of *topics*, represented by subordinate questions like the last two lines of the
poem. That this distinction does amount to a genuine ambiguity can be felt
in an example like

(22)   We were talking about what you had suggested.

The object of *about* in (22) can ambiguously represent a free relative clause
or a subordinate question. In the first case, the object is referential, and
can be specified in virtue of the rule for free relatives by some sentence like

(23)   We were talking about this new approach, and you had suggested
         this new approach.

In the second case, the topic of discussion is not any particular suggestion:
indeed, the speakers are wondering what the addressee did suggest. This
interpretation of (22) is nicely disambiguated by

(24)   We were talking about what it was that you had suggested.

Any further doubt about the reality of the question construction is dispersed
by observing that questions like the last line of Carroll's poem could not
possibly be anything but subordinate questions: there are no free relative
whether clauses. (Compare also the other tests for free relatives in the section
on wh-clefts.)

This syntactical distinction nicely tallies with the duality of concepts of
a *dialogue subject* and a *dialogue topic*. The subject of a dialogue, as we have
defined it, is some thing or other, an object the dialogue participants have
in mind. The topic of a dialogue is a problem, represented by a question
which dialogue participants are interested in (accept).[9] It seems that the
syntactic ambiguity of *about* already provides indirect evidence for the
importance of this distinction.

However, on a deeper level of analysis, I think the two senses of aboutness
are again connected in a definite way. (They are senses of one and the same
word, after all!)

A clue to the connecting link is the phenomenon of concealed questions.[10]
Noun phrases sometimes do duty for subordinate questions, as in Grimshaw's

(25)   Bill asked me the time, but I did not know.
(26)   John refused to tell the police the fellows who were involved.

The phenomenon is no surprise to Hintikka's analysis of direct object
constructions with epistemic verbs. According to him, such constructions
go back to 'concealed' questions anyway: even a straight-forward direct
object construction like

(27)   I know Bill

goes back to an identity question:

(28)   I know who Bill is.[11]

The most significant difference between (27) and (28) concerns, for Hintikka,
the sort of cross-world identification involved: for (27), it is likely to be
what Hintikka calls identification by acquaintance, while (28) suggests
descriptive cross-identification.

Let us adopt Hintikka's analysis. We need a rule which takes direct object
constructions with certain epistemic words back to identity sentences in the
style of

(C.wh-object)   Explain a sentence of form
                X – epistemic word – NP – Y
                by the sentence
                X – epistemic word – wh-word NP be – Y
                where 'wh-word' is of the category of NP and *be* agrees with
                NP.

(I won't try to spell out instructions on the method of cross-identification
associated with the direct-object construction here.)

Now just as (C.wh-object) takes (27) to (28), it will take the concealed
questions (25)–(26) to appropriate explicit questions:

(29)   Bill asked me what the time was, but I did not know.
(30)   John refused to tell the police who the fellows were who were
        involved.

Now assume that *about* constructions too conceal questions, i.e., (C.wh-
object) applies to sentences like

(31)   This sentence is about Mr. Morgan's scholarly ability

with the output

(32)   This sentence is about what Mr. Morgan's scholarly ability is.

Given this assumption, we have found a connecting link between the two
senses of *about*. According to (C.wh-object), that a sentence is *about* a
particular object means that it is addressed to a particularly simple topical
question whose subject is that object, viz. the question *what that object is*.
This simple question of identity is thus found concealed in the notion of
dialogue subject. *A sentence is about an object if it is addressed to the question what that object is.* Such identity questions, then, constitute premises
S' which definition (13) makes a reference to.

Identity questions are exceptionally well suited for their versatile role.
Exceptional among search questions, identity questions are *safe*, in terms
of Harrah's erotetic logic:

(33)   What is A?

is safe to ask, for its presupposition

(34)   A is something

is provable from a minimum of assumptions about A: to deny (34) will contradict the self-preservation principle (C.self) of Part I as soon as A is as much as mentioned in the dialogue.

Note, too, that sentences of the form (33) are generated by the logical game rules from other search questions as well. To answer a question by instantiating it with A immediately makes A a dialogue subject with respect to a follow-up question about its identity.

6. EVIDENCE FOR DIALOGUE SUBJECTS: (D.SUBJECT)

Well, so we have a concept of dialogue subject. What is it good for?

To find unambiguous evidence for the need for the new discourse notion, it seems best to devise a controlled experiment. What needs to be controlled is the implicit dialogue structure: specifically, we have to make it absolutely clear, what is actually thematic or rhematic with respect to what. If we succeed, keeping contextual properties of constituents constant, in discerning further functional differences, we have evidence for a new distinction.

For this purpose, let us construct a set of textual variations on a simple theme. Consider a simple business transaction, the sale of a useful all-around brush to a housewife by a travelling salesman. What happens can be described informally by the sentences

(35)   The brush goes from the man to the woman.
(36)   A dollar goes from the woman to the man.
(37)   The man prefers the brush with the dollar to the dollar and that to the brush.
(38)   The woman prefers the brush with the dollar to the brush and that to the dollar.
(39)   The woman brings about (36).
(40)   The man brings about (35).

The transaction can be looked upon as a simple bargaining game. The salesman's strategies are (40) and its negation: he may give or not give the brush to the woman; the woman's strategies are (39) and its negation: she may give the man a dollar or not. Given the player's preferences in (37)–(38), the game has a solution in (39)–(40).

Now how would one describe the transaction more colloquially? By any of the following textual variants:

(41)   The man sold the brush to the woman. He charged her a dollar for it.

(42)   The woman bought the brush from the man. She paid him a dollar for it.

(43)   The man sold the brush to the woman. She paid him a dollar for it.

(44)   The woman bought the brush from the man. He charged her a dollar for it.

In each case, the man and the woman are equally thematic as far as our contextual definitions go: whatever difference there is between the variants, it will not be due to differences in thematicity.

Is there any functional difference among (41)–(44)? I think there is. (41) considers the transaction consistently from the man's point of view, describing his choices of strategy. (42) takes as consistently the woman's point of view, while (43)–(44) feel more objective or impartial. These feelings can be sharpened by considering (41)–(44) in turn as answers to the questions

(45)   What sort of a deal did the man make with the woman?

(46)   What sort of a deal did the woman make with the man?

(47)   What sort of a deal did the man and the woman make?

It seems undeniable that (41) is the best form of answer for (45) and (42) for (46), while (43)–(44) are more apt to answer (47). (44) seems the least felicitous of all, for its unmotivated use of the diathetically marked converses of *sell* and *pay*.

Intuitively, these most fluent combinations appear to follow consistently one particular perspective. Other combinations are not excluded by any means, but they seem to involve a slight change of subject in mid-dialogue.

Let us try to clarify some of these further nuances by making the changing topics explicit. For example, consider the variant

(48)   A: Did the man give the brush to the woman for free?
        B: No, the woman bought the brush from the man. She paid him a dollar for it.

This combination suggests that A sides with the man and B with the woman. A is worried about the man:

(49)   Did the man lose in the deal?

B in turn fixes upon the nearly equivalent suggestion

(50)   Did the woman take advantage of the man?

and takes pains to point out that the woman kept her side of the bargain.

What gives away the auxiliary premises (49)–(50) in (48)? The choice of grammatical subject, obviously. The dialogues seem to follow a rule of dialogue strategy to the following effect:

(D.subject) Indicate the dialogue subject of a sentence by its grammatical subject.[12]

Let us apply (D.subject) to our experimental dialogues. (41) and (42) preserve the dialogue subject; this property extends throughout the dialogue if (41) is paired with (45) and (42) with (46). The dialogues are about the man and the woman, respectively, in virtue of the rule of meaning for *about* in (14).

The situation is more interesting in (43). If (43) is addressed to (47), is there a change of subject or not? The intuitive answer is, yes and no: the dialogue subject of (47) is a pair of people, while each sentence in (43) speaks of one of them in turn. The structure of a dialogue is made clear by noting that (47) implies a conjunction of two sentences with the desired subjects:

(51)   What did the man do and what did the woman do in the deal?

(51) has two dialogue subjects, one of which is pursued by the first sentence of (43) and the other by the second sentence of (43). Thus each sentence of (43) preserves a dialogue subject introduced by the topical question, albeit indirectly by inference. This is why (43) seems intuitively to preserve the subject of (47) despite first appearances.

Finally, the partiality of the participants in (48) is explained by interpolating (49)–(50) as topics for each player to pursue independently. The fact that the choices of subject in (48) can tease out implicit premises like (49)–(50) is good evidence for the reality of the new discourse notion.

(D.subject) together with the definition (13) of dialogue subject can be considered a tribute to "the ancient statement that subject is what we are talking about".[13] For consider a sentence like (52) in abstraction of dialogue context:

(52)   Charles married Diana.

Who is (52) about? The unschooled intuition is clear: about Charles. For if one wanted to talk about Diana, nothing could be easier than putting it the other way round:

(53)   Diana married Charles.

These *prima facie* impressions are explained given (D. subject).

It goes without saying that (D.subject) cannot be an obligatory rule. For one thing, we already recognized that some sentences refer to nothing, for instance,

(54)   It was raining.

The resultant failure of (54) to conform to (D.subject) does not render it useless. Or consider the dialogue

(55)   A: Why is Bill flustered?
         B: I hurt his feelings.

Surely, B is not changing the topic here: his comment is as much about Bill as the question. Here, other, independent considerations of subject choice overrule the recommendation of (D.subject). The first consideration is the choice of wording. There is no word-preserving paraphrase of B's explanation which would get Bill in the subject position. Even if this obstacle is removed, by substituting *nose* for feelings:

(56)   He was hurt on the nose by me.

the resulting sentence may still violate other preferences (say a preference for agentive subjects or to have first person first).[14]

The logical conclusion from these observations is that the status of (D.subject) is precisely like that of the thematic word order principles. They represent optional strategy choices which have to compete with other strategic considerations, with the result that they are reliable guides into dialogue structure only where they constitute the best available explanation for a choice of textual variant.

7. EVIDENCE FROM ANAPHORA

(D.subject) registers a certain referential preference: other things being equal, the subject of a sentence is likely to indicate what the sentence is about. This referential preference can be expected to show when doubt arises as to what a noun phrase refers to. Such referential ambiguities often arise with anaphoric personal pronouns.

As Smaby [595] points out, resolving anaphoric ambiguity is quite a complex decision problem whose dimensions include syntactic constraints of admissibility of cross-reference, categorial information (gender and number), discourse grammatical constraints, and last but not least a mixed bag of extralinguistic considerations of what people are likely to say and to be interested in.

This comes as no surprise to a dialogue grammarian. As we noted, what a subject does who forms a dialogue grammatical judgment on a piece of discourse is look for a likely dialogue reconstruction for it. The question he asks implicitly is "Why should anyone say this?": the answer is apt to be some specific dialogue situation which the subject finds natural as to its necessary background assumptions, the functional connections between the different sentences in it, and the characterization of the dialogue participants.

Let me illustrate this by an example.

(57)   The doctor showed the baby to her mother.

Whose mother? The baby's, of course. This is the interpretation which first springs to mind if (57) is understood to describe a childbirth. As everybody knows, babies are shown to their mothers when they are born. Could it be the doctor's mother? That would make no sense at all. Why on earth should the doctor's mother be present at a delivery? Surely, doctors are past showing off their achievement to their mothers: Look, Momma, I can deliver! Besides, the stereotype doctor is male anyway.

Now consider two possible continuations of (57):

(58)   She felt just great.
(59)   She looked just great.

Don't you agree that (58) is more likely to speak of the mother, while (59) is most likely to describe the baby? Here, we are concerned with guessing at the likeliest *focus of interest* or *topic*, of the passage given (57). Our guesses are based on commonplaces like

(60)   Mothers wonder how their babies look.
(61)   Never mind how the mother looks.
(62)   No one knows how newborns feel.
(63)   Mothers feel great about their babies.
(64)   Never mind the doctor's looks or feelings.

As Smaby points out, what we are watching out for here is not just what is likely to be *true* given a certain premise, but what is likely to be *interesting*: what questions are likely to arise. This is why

(65)   She felt depressed

in the context (57) can also describe the mother, however uncommon or shameful the feeling. (65) too is relevant in the context of (57) because it answers a question (57) is likely to give rise to, viz.

(66)   How did the mother feel?

In explanatory discourse, a leading consideration in the choice of antecedents is the search for a likely major premise. Consider for instance

(67)   Why did John hit Bill?
        Because he insulted him.
        Because he was insulted by him.

There is little doubt about antecedency, for one tries to construe the explanation as an instance of well-known laws of human behavior:

(68)   If one is insulted, one hits.
        If one insults, one gets hit.

Only if Bill is construed as the insulting party will (68) explain the hitting. Two more examples of this sort.

(69)   John and Bill fought. Who won?
        Well, John is older than Bill, so I guess he won.
        Well, Bill is younger than John, so I guess he won.

In each case, *he* seems pretty unambiguously to pick out the subject of the *Well* clause. Here, unlike the previous example, worldly knowledge amounts to little, for which explanation is likely depends on the ages of John and Bill: are they youngsters or oldsters?

What seems decisive in this example is the syntactic complexity of the necessary major premises. The intuitive antecedency is established by the interpolation of

(70)   Whoever is older (vs. younger) wins.

as an enthymematic premise. The converse antecedency would require a rather more awkward wording:

(71)   Whoever the opponent is older (vs. younger) than wins.

(71) is hard to figure out even when spelled out — not a likely major premise
to spring to mind on hearing (69).

For a final example, consider a third person report of (72)–(74):

(72)   Why do you always bother me?
(73)   You are my brother.
(74)   I am your brother.

For ease of exposition, I shall discuss the example in terms of its direct-
discourse counterpart (72)–(74). Although (73)–(74) are logically equivalent
among men, they have a quite different feeling to them. What is more, the
intuitive feeling depends on what sort of bothering is going on. If one is
offering help, (73) seems to point out brotherly rights and (74) brotherly
duties; if help is being asked for, the intuitions are reversed. Why?

Again, implicit general premises are at work. The intuitions arise from a
need to construe (73)–(74) as instantiations for the two ethical principles

(75)   People should help their brothers.
(76)   People should be helped by their brothers.

(75) points out brotherly duties, (76) their rights. Now if (72) means

(77)   Why should you help me?

it is directly explained by (74) and (75), or by (73) and (76). If it means

(78)   Why should I help you?

the direct explanation consists of (73) and (75) or of (74) and (76). This
seems as neat an explanation of the subtleties of (72)–(74) as one could wish
for.

Implicit premises also have a sway in inferential dialogue. In Smaby's
example

(79)   John tickled Bill. He squirmed.

there is a strong inclination to take Bill to be the squirmer, for this will allow
construing (79) as an inference from the premise

(80)   People who are tickled squirm.

This analysis supported by the fact that (81) makes Bill pretty unambiguously
the squirmer:

(81)'   John tickled Bill. So he squirmed.

Of course, the inclination to apply (80) can be stifled by explicit explanations to the contrary: perhaps John and Bill are an exceptional couple — when John tickles Bill, it is John who squirms. This fact only constitutes further proof of the power of intervening premises to guide inferential discourse.

All of the above shows that not too much should be expected of the force of subject choice to dictate antecedency. (D.subject) is an optional rule after all, easily overruled by more pressing considerations. To find unambiguous evidence for its operation, care must be taken to play down such other considerations.

One way to accomplish this is to make it explicit that no logical connection is intended. For instance, compare (81) to

(82)   John tickled Bill. And then he squirmed.

And shows that the two sentences in (82) are not arranged as premise and conclusion, but as coordinate answers to a common topic. The temporal *then* helps play down any causal implications. When this trouble is taken, John does emerge as the likelier candidate for antecedency in (82). Why? Because of (D.subject). (D.subject) suggests looking for the common topic of (82) among questions about John, say

(83)   What did John do?

If (83) is the topic of (82), (D.subject) is satisfied by both of the partial answers.

One more example:

(84)   The father took the daughter from the mother.
        She did not want to leave her.

Who didn't? One is pretty much at a loss to say. But the situation is cleared up when the right topical sentence is prefaced to (84):

(85)   How was the daughter treated in the divorce?
(86)   How was the mother treated in the divorce?

In the context of (85), we are speaking about the daughter, so we expect to hear her reactions. If (86) is the topic, we are talking of the mother, which makes her the likely value of *she*. Here again, (D.subject) helps determine antecedency.[15]

8. SO-CALLED DISLOCATIONS

Since Ross [590], a distinction has been made in transformational grammar between syntactic movement rules like topicalization and another group of phenomena which exhibit quite different grammatical properties, called *dislocations*:

(87)   Quine, he is a character.
(88)   He is a character, Quine.

(87) exemplifies a left dislocation and (88) a right dislocation.

The most obvious syntactic difference between movement rules and dislocations is that movement rules are subject to certain constraints on what can move where. One cannot, for instance, topicalize 'Quine' as shown in

(89)   Quine, who cares what says?

for more than one reason.[16] However, the sentence is saved if a personal pronoun is as it were "left behind" to mark Quine's place in the predication:

(90)   Quine, who cares what he says?

What Ross suggested to mark the distinction was to consider dislocations the result of a copying rule: *Quine* in (90) is copied from its original subject position outside the sentence and the source is replaced by a personal pronoun.

A simpler alternative, that (87)–(88) are base-generated, is argued for at length in Rodman [589] and Gundel [453]. A particularly straightforward argument is that the replacement is not predictable by rule: all of (91)–(93) are functioning "dislocations".

(91)   Quine, that guy is a character.
(92)   Your mother, is your darling mother coming?
(93)   Roaches, America teems with these foul pests.

What conditions there are relating the prefaced phrase to its pair inside the sentence seem corollaries of more general interpretive constraints on cross-reference.

A fact missed by most discussions of dislocations is that the simple dislocations (91)–(93) are very different from such ornate sentential satellites as

(94)   As for Quine, he is a character.
(95)   Speaking of Quine, he is a character.

For one thing, a simple dislocation requires a later cross-reference: if we leave out *as for* or *speaking of* from

(96)   As for the zoo, the animals seemed healthy enough.
(97)   Speaking of Quine, have you read *Word and Object*?

we get only false starts and vocatives, not dislocations. We do well to keep (94)–(97) clearly apart from dislocation proper in the sequel.

Also, dislocations are to be distinguished from elliptic sentences, which have the earmarks of independent dialogue moves: they have separate prosody and independent dialogue function.

(98)   — What are you looking for?
              — My pen. Have you seen it?
              — Your pen? It is in your breast pocket.

As false starts and vocatives witness, dislocations are not set apart by structural considerations alone. What makes them a natural class is some shared functional characteristic. But what is it?

Let us start our investigation from left dislocation. Traditional grammars tend to construe left dislocation as a slip of the tongue, occasioned by a speaker's eagerness to blurt out what is foremost in his mind:

A speaker begins a sentence with some word which takes a prominent place in his thought, but has not yet made up his mind with regard to its syntactical connexion; if it is a word inflected in the cases he provisionally puts it in the nom[inative], but is then often obliged by an after-correction to insert a pronoun indicating the case in which the word should have been. This phenomenon is extremely frequent in the colloquial forms of all languages, but in literary language it is often avoided. (Jespersen 1949:223)

Under the pressure of thought or feeling the subject here springs forth before the usual grammatical structure occurs to the mind, and is later repeated in the usual position of the subject in the form of a personal pronoun. (Curme 1935:4)

This seems an overly narrow characterization of left dislocation. Not all leftward satellites are false starts, though some certainly are. For one thing, the case of a dislocated personal pronoun by now is accusative, which sets off a dislocated pronoun from a false start:

(99)   Oh, him, he is an asshole. I – he's always bothering me.

For another thing, an element of design is clearly apparent in the following examples, where a phrase has been prefaced to its sentence instead of embedding to ease processing:

(100)   The Lord your God, which goes before you, he shall fight for you.

(101)   He that is without sin among you, let him first cast a stone at her.

(102)   But we indeed who call things good and fair, the evil is upon us while we speak.

(103)   Very good orators, when they are out, they will spit.

(104)   Not to follow your leader whithersoever he may think proper to lead; to back out of an expedition because the end of it frowns dubious, and the present fruit of it is discomfort; to quit a comrade on the road, and return home without him; these are tricks which no boy of spirit would be guilty of.

It would not do to accuse the authors of these sentences of careless language. Nor is there anything slipshod about the use of dislocation in poetry to satisfy metrical requirements:

(105)   For the deck it was their field of fame, and ocean was their grave.

In short, it seems fair to recognize left dislocation as a proper rule of syntax which can have purely syntactic function. However, such syntactical motivation of left dislocation seems to me incidental to its main dialogue function. It seems to me that the traditional grammarians' description, despite its defects, is on to something essential. A left dislocated phrase is indeed apt to indicate what is foremost on the mind of the author — viz. the *dialogue subject* he is speaking about in the sentence following. This is my proposal for a functional game rule for dislocation:

(D.dislocate)   A noun phrase adjoined to a sentence indicates its direct dialogue subject.

Dislocation is optional — most sentences are not explicit about their dialogue subjects. When is it advisable to be that explicit, then? Of course, when one's subject is not otherwise obvious: when one embarks upon a new subject, or changes subject in mid-dialogue. To see this effect of left dislocation, compare the dialogues (106)—(107):

(106)   — Who is Goofy's oldest friend?
           — Goofy's oldest friend is Mickey Mouse. Mickey is Disney's
           oldest character.
(107)   — Who is Goofy's oldest friend?
           — Goofy's oldest friend is Mickey Mouse. Mickey, he is
           Disney's oldest character.

What is the function of the last sentence of these dialogues? For (104), it
seems simple: the answerer hastens to answer the implicit identity question

(108)   Who is Mickey Mouse?

occasioned by his answer to the original question in virtue of (C.wh-e).
Mickey's identity is kept in low profile here, as it is only a subordinate
matter. In (107), in contrast, Mickey seems to become a main character:
the speaker drops Goofy as the subject of the dialogue and takes up Mickey.
This intention of his is conveyed by (D.dislocate). Alternatively, the questioner might have effected the change of subject by asking, instead of (108),
the dislocated question

(109)   Mickey Mouse, who is he?

whereupon the change of subject could very naturally be confirmed by
the answerer as in (107).
    Left dislocation is common in interrogation, where changes of subject
are frequent. Typically, a previous answer suggests a new subject to the
questioner, who seizes upon it by left dislocation:

(110)   — These persons who have just gone — had they anything to
           do with your quarrel?
           — Not at all — it was strictly a matter between Lizzie and
           me.
           — This girl Lizzie, how old is she?

We said that left dislocation is a means of taking up a new dialogue subject.
Does it follow that a left dislocated constituent can be all new information?
We already know that the opposite is the case: dialogue subjects are constitutionally given.[17]
    This accounts for the curious feeling of familiarity which surrounds
dislocated sentences. One cannot just go and accost an unsuspecting audience
with

(111)   Inferiority complex, what exactly does that mean?

For instance, if one wants to start a treatise with (111), one will have to think up a title which is suggestive of the subject.

Otherwise, dislocation has little to do with thematicity. The adjunction of a dislocated phrase leaves the thematic character of its intrasentential pair quite free: all of (112)–(115) are quite natural.

(112)   – What did the Bishop do in the actress' boudoir?
          – The Bishop, he admonished the actress. (theme)
(113)   – Who admonished the actress?
          – The Bishop, he admonished the actress. (rheme)
(114)   – Did you admonish the actress?
          – No, the Bishop, he admonished the actress. (thematic rheme)
(115)   – Who did what? What did the Bishop do?
          – The Bishop, he admonished the actress. (rhematic theme)

This is why left dislocation and topicalization are not interchangeable in

(116)   Our daughters we are proud of.
(117)   Our daughters, we are proud of them.

Only in the topicalized sentence does the leftward position of the object create a contrast. This is predicted by our rules. While topicalization, via (D.topic) and (D.left) marks a constituent contrastive (thematically ambivalent), dislocation does not fix thematic structure beyond the thematicity of the adjunct phrase.[18] In order to make (117) contrastive, one can topicalize the pronoun inside the sentence:

(118)   Our daughters, them we are proud of.

The fact that a dislocated constituent indicates a dialogue subject explains why it has to be referential, i.e., have a value. We do not dislocate noun phrases whose reference is not clear, e.g.,

(119)   – Did you buy anything?
          – Some books, I bought them.

There is no way for the addressee to guess which books are being discussed here. Compare

(120)   – Aren't those people disgusting?
          – Yeah, some people, they think they know everything.

where it is obvious who (what kind of people) the speaker means by *some people*. As is clear from the examples, the difference here is not a matter of syntax or truth conditions, but a question of dialogue grammar.

This property of left dislocation also serves to set it off from topicalization. Topicalization does not care about reference. So there is nothing odd with

(121)   Some Cupid kills with arrows, some with traps.

whereas left dislocation would be quite out of its depth here:

(122)   Some, Cupid kills them with arrows, some, with traps.

The cleft construction, too, remains distinct from left dislocation on this count. (123)–(127) are not interchangeable, for they answer the different questions (125)–(126):

(123)   It's a wonderful place you have here, sir.
(124)   A wonderful place, you have it here, sir.
(125)   What sort of place do I have here?
(126)   Where do I have a wonderful place?

It is only the left dislocated version (124) which must be construed as speaking of wonderful places.[19]

The above examples were carefully chosen to avoid the intrusion of more general constraints on anaphora. Thus no considerations specific to dislocations are needed to explain why (121)–(122) are unacceptable – it suffices to refer to general constraints on discourse anaphora.

(127)   No explanations, they are necessary.
(128)   Every one of my friends, he is married.

What is wrong with (128), in particular, is not the dislocation but the singular cross-reference; (129) is quite all right.

(129)   Every one of my friends, they are married.

9. RIGHT DISLOCATION

The formulation of (D.dislocate) was left vague on the direction of disloca-tion, and that on purpose. As Gundel [453] argues at length, left and right dislocations share all the properties predicted by (D.dislocate). Right disloca-tion too prejudges the dialogue subject; that is why there is a feeling of conflict in Gundel's example

(130)   — What about your nerves?
             — He's beginning to get on my nerves, that dog.[20]

The first speaker wants to talk about nerves, but the addressee speaks of the dog.

As further evidence of the independence of dislocation from thematic word order principles, a right dislocated phrase too must be thematic, not rhematic as one would expect if (D.right) were applicable to it. One would not answer the question

(131)   What depresses you?

by

(132)   It depresses me, this room.

To answer (131), one must change the wording inside the sentence, e.g.

(133)   This depresses me, this room.

Instead of dwelling on the similarities of left and right dislocation, let us try to ferret out their functional differences. It seems to me that they are in a large measure due to a simple fact of discourse anaphora. While a leftward adjunct can serve as an antecedent to fix the reference of its sentence internal reflex, a rightward adjunct can not. Hence the user of right dislocation must assume, justifiably or not, that the context already makes clear what he is talking about.[21] It follows that right dislocation, unlike left dislocation, is not suited for indicating explicit changes of subject. Compare in this respect (130) to

(134)   — What about your nerves?
             — That dog, he's beginning to get on my nerves.

(134) suggests, but (130) simply assumes, that the dog is what should be talked about. In other words, right dislocation can not affirm a dialogue subject, it can only confirm one.

When is there a need for such confirmation? Two distinct cases may be discerned. Frequently, right dislocation secures a reference which may have remained vague to the audience after all. This sort of sentence is colloquial and intimate, particularly when the subject is elliptic:

(135)   "I'll say I'm stiff", said Mrs. Baker. "Gets you kind of cramped, riding along the way we've been doing."

(136)   Must have cost a pretty penny that thing tonight.
(137)   All, all are gone, the familiar faces.
(138)   Are they learned men, your priests?

This construction is frequent in reports of internal dialogue:

(139)   What did it do to people, she wondered, living like this.
(140)   Perhaps an hour later his nostrils began to twitch. A delicious
         aroma was being carried towards him by the breeze. Kidneys
         and bacon, he was certain. Devilish cruel to an empty stomach,
         tantalizing it with the smell of other men's breakfasts. How long
         would he have to endure this?

As Vygotsky once observed, subjectless sentences are common in internalized
speech, obviously because there is no need to spell out to oneself what one
is thinking about.[22] That information, however, may be necessary for one's
audience. This is probably why right dislocation is so common in spontaneous
speech where thoughts are outputted with less preplanning than in writing.

Right dislocation may involve quite deliberate planning, too. It is a common stylistic trick to use right dislocation to avoid the suggestion of opening
a new subject. A good example of this comes from Patricia Moyes' novel *Dead
Men Don't Ski*. A detective wants to interview a woman on the subject of a
murder without letting on that he is pumping her. This is how he proceeds:

(141)   His next objective was the Generi Misti run by Signora Vespi. He
         purchased a fresh supply of American cigarettes, and then said
         casually, in Italian, "Bad business, this death on the ski-lift."
         "Terrible, signore, terrible."

(141), unlike a straightforward subject-predicate sentence, gives the impression that the death is already established as a common subject of speculation.

In the preceding examples, the right dislocated phrase is pronounced with
moderate or no emphasis. In this respect, they contrast with another batch
of examples:

(142)   They are no ordinary houses, those.
(143)   It is entirely of the earth, that passion.
(144)   He was not going to be a snuffy schoolmaster, he.
(145)   "And yet, if you say to people, 'a leper colony' they will
         shudder and give it a wide berth. It is an old, old fear that."

In these examples, the right dislocated phrase can well be emphatic. Intuitively, the sentences sound emphatic or impressed, often admiring or boasting. Here, there is not likely to be any unclarity of reference — for instance, the right dislocated phrase in (144) adds nothing to what transpires from the preceding sentence. Rather, the subject of discussion is pointed out for contrast: the subject at hand satisfies the sentence said of it, but what about certain other subjects that might spring to mind? These further subjects are suggested by a simple strategical argument: if the present dialogue subject were the only one to consider, there would be no need to point it out; however, it is being pointed out, hence other candidates must be in the offing.

10. *AS FOR*

We already found a warning against a too easy identification of *as for* with dislocations in the contrasts like

(146)   As for the weather, I think it will rain tomorrow.
(147)   The weather, I think it will rain tomorrow.

As (146)–(147) show, *as for* is freer with its subject than left dislocation: a left dislocated phrase introduces a direct dialogue subject, whereas *as for* may broach a subject obliquely.

This is not the only difference, either. *As for*, unlike left dislocation, does not like to pick up a subject from an immediate premise:

(148)   — Where is John?
           — (As for) John, he is at home.

What is most significant, *as for* sentences are constrained as to what they can say of a subject, unlike left dislocations. Compare

(149)   — Who is Goofy's oldest friend?
           — Goofy's oldest friend is Mickey Mouse. Mickey, he is my
             favorite character.
(150)   — Who is Goofy's oldest friend?
           — Goofy's oldest friend is Mickey Mouse. As for Mickey, his
             oldest friend is Minnie Mouse.

As for would sound oddly out of place in the first dialogue, while left dislocation would do in both dialogues.
Compare also

(151)   — Holmes, who do you think is the murderer?
            — Well, Watson, the man who the police suspect is out of
            question. As for Lestrade, he is all too stupid for the job.

(151) curiously suggests that Holmes finds Lestrade (the police inspector)
among the suspects. Left dislocation would not force such a construal (although it would allow it).

Note, finally, that *as for* is nearly interchangeable with *but* in

(152)   This one will do. But the others, you may as well forget them.
         This one will do. As for the others, you may as well forget them.

To account for these observations, I suggest the following dialogue rule
for *as for*:

(D.as for)   When a player has put forward a move addressed to a topic, any
              player may address a coordinate topic by a sentence prefaced
              with *as for NP*, where NP is a direct dialogue subject of the new
              topic.

In our analysis, *as for* is not only a subject-introducer, but also a topic-
introducer: what it suggests is not just a subject of the following sentence but
its *topic* as well, the question it is addressed as an answer to. Let us consider
how it does this in example (151):

(153)   Who is the murderer?

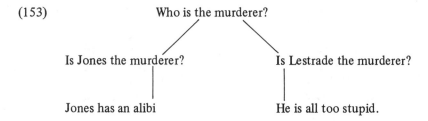

Is Jones the murderer?   Is Lestrade the murderer?

Jones has an alibi   He is all too stupid.

What (153) construes Holmes as doing in (151) is going through the suspects
one by one. Jones, the obvious suspect, has an alibi. If it weren't for the
unfortunate *as for*, Holmes' last statement in (151) could be construed as
an impatient comment on police incompetence. As it is, (D.as for) forces the
audience to look for a coordinate topic structure in which Lestrade's name
figures as a fresh substituend, only to find (153) as the simplest candidate.

Let us go through our other observations to see if they are accounted for by (D.as for). We have first the freedom of *as for* sentences with their dialogue subjects as in example (146). This freedom is allowed for by (D.as for). All the rule requires is that the sentence following an *as for* phrase can be construed as an answer to the question indicated by it — and that leaves quite a lot of leeway.

The inappropriateness of *as for* in (148) is also easily explained: (D.as for) reserves *as for* phrases for changes of topic, not for keeping one.

As for the ability of *as for* to do duty for *but* in (152), it suffices to compare the respective game rules (D.but) and (D.as for) to see that they indeed apply in overlapping dialogue environments.

A number of further observations can be predicted still. The unacceptability of

(154)   As for some people, I like them, as for others, I don't.

is explained by the requirement that the object of *as for* must have a value. (154) backfires as an attempt to address the topic

(155)   Do you like people or not?

because (155) gives no clue who *some people* and *others* might refer to. A better fit to (155) is obtained by using topicalization:

(156)   Some people, I like; others, I don't.

As we observed earlier, topicalization does not care about reference.

Finally, (D.as for) explains why objects of *as for* phrases have a contrastive feel about them, as the rule marks them thematically ambivalent by definition. To appreciate this point, consider the example dialogue

(157)   — Who invented penicillin? Was it Nobel?
            — No, penicillin was invented by Fleming. As for Nobel, he
            invented dynamite.

The following is a likely reconstruction for (157):

(158)

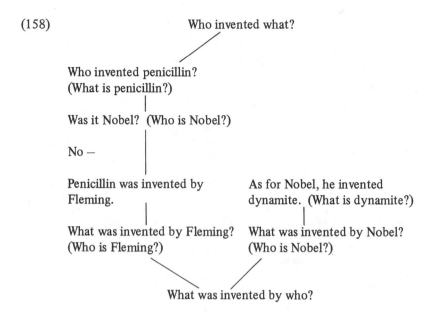

Who invented what?

Who invented penicillin?
(What is penicillin?)

Was it Nobel? (Who is Nobel?)

No —

Penicillin was invented by
Fleming.

As for Nobel, he invented
dynamite. (What is dynamite?)

What was invented by Fleming?
(Who is Fleming?)

What was invented by Nobel?
(Who is Nobel?)

What was invented by who?

The initial topic of discussion is *who invented what*. The questioner instantiates it with penicillin and conjectures Nobel as its inventor. Penicillin is indicated as a subject of the discussion by being the subject of a concealed identity question. The answerer recognizes this in his correction of the questioner's conjecture. The correction in turn suggests a new twist to the topic: echoing its syntactic form, it is now asked *what was invented by who*. This question is instantiated by the questioner's conjecture and duly answered. Nobel is recognized as a dialogue subject in virtue of another concealed identity question. The *as for* phrase serves to indicate the new topic configuration with Fleming and Nobel as coordinate subjects generated by a common topic. Note, in contrast, that

(159)   As for dynamite, it was invented by Nobel.

would be out of place in (157), if dynamite has not yet been suggested as a possible dialogue subject.

The thematic ambivalence of *Nobel* in (157) *vis-à-vis* its dialogue premises is apparent in the reconstruction (158). The name at once repeats an earlier mention and contrasts with another instance of the same common topic.

NOTES

PREFACE

[1] For surveys of the field, see Dressler [7] and Hendricks [13].
[2] Much of recent text linguistics is vulnerable to the candid criticism of Hannes Rieser [7], p. 15:

In hindsight it can be said that text linguistics tried to apply formal apparatus too early, perhaps because in general the role of formalization in theory construction was grossly overrated. Also, everybody tried to use formalisms without considering whether this was really appropriate. . . . The precise explication of one's linguistic intuitions should come first, and only then does formalization make sense. Formalization alone cannot be equated with theory . . . nor can it be used − as is frequently the case − to cover up the neglecting of empirical data.

Cf. also Pierrehumbert [367].

INTRODUCTION

[1] Hendricks [14], p. 31, quoting Archibald Hill.
[2] Quoted in Hendricks [14], p. 31.
[3] Coulthard's reference is to Labov [22].
[4] Wittgenstein [38], Part I: §134. For a dissenting opinion, see McGee [26].
[5] Wittgenstein [38], Part I: §23.
[6] For further discussion, see J. Hintikka, 'Language-games' in Saarinen (ed.) [32], pp. 1−26.
[7] Wittgenstein [37], §7.
[8] Ibid., §23.
[9] Coulthard [6], p. 7, quoting Labov [24].
[10] Grice [10].
[11] Wittgenstein [38], Part I: §29.
[12] Ibid., Part I: §32.
[13] Ibid., Part II: §11.
[14] Ibid., Part I: §33..
[15] Ibid., Part I: §140.
[16] Ibid., Part I: §140.
[17] Ibid., Part I: §137.
[18] Wittgenstein [37], §130.
[19] Ibid., §66−67.
[20] For an introduction and critical survey of game theory, see Luce and Raiffa [25].

272

21 For references, see Saarinen (ed.) [32].

22 Quoted, with minor changes of wording, from p. 297 of J. Hintikka, 'Quantifiers in Natural Language, some logical problems', in J. Hintikka et al. (eds.) *Essays on Mathematical and Philosophical Logic*, D. Reidel, Dordrecht 1979, pp. 295–314, reprinted in Saarinen [32], pp. 81–117.

23 Quoted from p. 119 of C. Peacocke's article in Saarinen (ed.) [32], pp. 119–134.

24 (In mathematical logic:) L. Henkin, G. Kreisel, V. Rantala and others; (In philosophical logic:) K. Lorenz [244], P. Lorenzen [245–6] and their associates; see also D. Lewis [167], [147], Stalnaker [34] and Harrah [11].

25 See Hintikka [16–21].

26 For further discussion, see Stenius [35], Carlson [3], Lewis [147].

27 Aristotle [2], 1355b. For a more recent definition, see Young et al. [388].

28 Aristotle [2], 1354a.

29 Charles Morris's definition. See Morris [28–9].

30 See Introduction to Searle et al. [318], p. ix.

31 See Part I, Chapter IV. 4–5, for these rules.

32 Wittgenstein [37], §24. Cf. Llewelyn [148].

33 Aristotle [2], 1403b.

34 Cf. Enkvist [8], p. 25, Enkvist [9], Andersson [1].

PART I
CHAPTER 1

1 For discussion, see, e.g., Chomsky [39], pp. 55–57.

2 Cf. Schiffer [47], pp. 30–31, Lewis [167], pp. 52–60.

3 The first sentence of *Metaphysics* (980a).

4 See e.g., Levi [46], Hilpinen [42–3], Swain [48], Cohen and Hesse [40].

5 Cf. Section 2 of Introduction.

CHAPTER 2

1 Cf. Luce and Raiffa [25], p. 269–271.

2 A better way of looking at the situation here may be to construe the players' misperceptions as illicit idiosyncratic truncations of an identical overall game. E.g., a poker player *knows* what cards other players *might* hold (as far as the rules of the game are concerned), but he may still (mistakenly) believe that they actually hold certain particular hands, and plan his strategies on his mistaken assumptions. This way of looking at the situation preserves standard game structure; however, we still need to redefine the concept of a solution of such a subjectively truncated game.

3 There is a growing literature on this problem. See, e.g., Cresswell [56–7], Eberle [58], Goddard and Routley [60], Hintikka [70–71], Purtill [90], Rescher and Brandon [94], Routley and Routley [95], and Thomason [105].

4 For these insights, see Hintikka [61–62], [65–68], [72]. Cf. Chisholm [54], Kaplan [76], Kripke [79–80], Lewis [81], Parsons [87], Quine [92], Saarinen [96], Scott [97], for a few of a legion of papers on quantification in intensional contexts.

[5] See, e.g., Hintikka [66]. For a set of model set conditions, see Appendix II.

[6] For one version, see Appendix II.

[7] For different approaches, see note 3 above. Ours seems closest to Eberle [58], Goddard and Routley [60] and Routley and Routley [95].

[8] What it means to accept or reject a question will be discussed in Chapter 7.4.

[9] A dialogue based on this game situation is described in Chapter 8.5.

[10] I call a question *true* if its presupposition is true (if it has a true answer). Cf. Belnap and Steel [113], p. 116.

CHAPTER 3

[1] See Hintikka [129–130]. For criticism, cf. Karttunen [139].

[2] J. Higginbotham (private conversation) has suggested treating question quantifiers as a type of nonstandard quantifier of its own. Rather than being ambivalent between existential and universal force, a question quantifier would be semantically vague; criteria of complete answerhood would be a function of a questioner's informational interests. In the present approach, questions are used to represent informational interests. It is therefore necessary to fix beforehand what interests they do represent. Hintikka's two-quantifier analysis is adopted for definiteness. Nothing crucial depends on this particular assumption. Cf. Higginbotham and May [240].

[3] See Hintikka [131], Kamp [137–8], Lewis [147].

[4] Cf. Hintikka [130], pp. 22–29.

[5] Cf. Appendix II.

[6] Cf. Hintikka [132].

[7] See Hintikka [65–68], [70], [72].

[8] See Hintikka [65], [68].

[9] Cf. Boër and Lycan [116]. Two senses of knowing who are nicely contrasted in the following passage from Agatha Christie's *The Clocks* (Chapter 20):

"I don't believe you know a thing, Poirot! This is all bluff. Why, nobody knows yet who the dead man is —"

"I know."

"What's his name?"

"I have no idea. His name is not important. I know, if you can understand, not *who* he is but who he *is*."

"A blackmailer?"

Poirot closed his eyes.

"A detective?"

Poirot opened his eyes. (. . .)

[10] Different methods of cross-identification are distinguished in Hintikka [127–128].

CHAPTER 4

[1] Grice's first maxim of quality is somewhat weaker: "Do not say what you believe to be false". Grice actually voices doubts whether this principle is on a par with other

conversational maxims: "Other maxims come into operation only on the assumption that this maxim is satisfied" (p. 46 of Cole and Morgan [10]).

2 Cf. Quintilian, lib. viii cap. 6 §2: "In eo vero genere quo contraria ostenduntur, Ironia est. Illusionem vocant, quae aut pronunciatione intelligitur, aut persona, aut rei natura. Num si qua earum verbis dissentit, apparet diversam esse orationi voluntatem." See also Brown and Levinson [288], Grice [257].

3 Cf. Lewis [167] for a good discussion of conventionality.

4 Searle [314], p. 66.

5 Searle [314], p. 57.

6 Here is an example from Rex Stout's novel *The Gambit*. Archie Goodwin impersonates a police officer by denying that he is one:

> "Are you from the police?"
> "No", I said, "I'm a gorilla. How often do you have to see a face?"

For similar examples and insights, cf. W. Abraham's paper in [373].

7 Wittgenstein [38], §§28−32. Of course, (D.perhaps) can be rewritten in the form of a truth definition if players' beliefs are treated as another index of context (point of reference). This does not make *perhaps* any less pragmatic, however.

8 (6) is consistent on an exclusive interpretation of quantifiers (if the range of *no one* does not include the substitution value of *a person*). This is how (6) and its likes are usually understood.

9 There is a rich philosophical literature on subjunctive and indicative conditionals. See e.g., Adams [151−2], Ayers [154], Braine [156], Chisholm [158], Goodman [163], Harper et al. [164], Karttunen [165], von Kutschera [166], Lewis [168], Pollock [170], Rescher [173], Stalnaker [177], or Tichy [179].

10 For a clear example of an elliptic subjunctive, witness the following passage from Agatha Christie's novel *The Clocks* (Chapter 26):

> "Oh dear me, I don't know what to do, I'm sure."
> "I should go home and have a nice kip", said the barman kindly.

Of course, the barman is not announcing that *he* is quitting − the implicit condition "if I were you" has appeared repeatedly in his previous exhortations to the drunken lady.

(D.earnest) and (D.subjunctive) are not mutually exclusive. Use of the subjunctive does not in itself imply that the user rejects or even doubts a supposition he is making − although he of course often conversationally implicates as much (why use subjunctive where indicative would do?). The implication is cancellable, as in the following example from Patricia Moyes' novel *The Black Widower*:

> "Tell me, sir − this is a merely hypothetical question − but what effect would it have on these talks if it came to light that certain political figures in Tampica had financial interest in the development company you mentioned yesterday?"

Despite the subjunctive, the addressee has good reason to ask,

> "Say, do you have information on this?"

11 Cf. Wunderlich [323], p. 295.

12 That conversational implicatures get conventionalized is something of a commonplace by now. See Grice (p. 50 of Cole and Morgan [10]), Searle [315], p. 76, Sadock [175], p. 78, van der Auwera [283], pp. 44−45.

[13] Repetition of a claim is not a totally pointless move. If caution is increased between repetitions, the number of repetitions indicate the strength of the player's confidence in his claim. That 'second thoughts' in fact indicate increased caution is nicely witnessed in Agatha Christie's *Funerals are Fatal* (Chapter XIV):

"She didn't take it seriously?"
"Oh, no. No, I'm sure she didn't . . . "

The second "no", Poirot thought had sounded suddenly doubtful. But was not that almost always the case when you went back over something in your mind?

CHAPTER 5

[1] According to G. Hankamer and I. Sag, 'Deep and Surface Anaphora', *Linguistic Inquiry* 7 (1976), 391–428, certain types of ellipsis require an explicit antecedent, while others don't.
[2] On the structural complexity of conversation, see e.g., Paun [210], Ritchie [214], Chapter 9, or Weizenbaum [229].
[3] "Functional diagrams" like this are for illustration only. They play no essential part in my framework. As a systematic method of representation, I prefer sequences of moves annotated in the manner described in Section 2 of this Chapter.
[4] Similar criticisms are raised in Mohan [207]. Note that the vicious circle in (13) could be widened to include any number of players.

CHAPTER 6

[1] Cf. our notion of elementary question to Bennett's [114] "basic question" and Karttunen's [139] "proto-question". Our notion is distinct from its namesake in Belnap and Steel [113].
[2] The present definition of presupposition is the only technical sense of this overwrought term in this work. For the rest, I am in sympathy with attempts like Wilson and Sperber [537] or Bickerton [491] to trade in the notion for diverse more tangible distinctions. Cf. Chapter 4 of Part II.
[3] See e.g., Chang and Keisler [237], p. 228.
[4] Hirschbühler [241], p. 49. Cf. Karttunen [243], Bennett [233], Higginbotham and May [240]. My discussion of Karttunen [243] is based on Hirschbühler [241].
[5] Carlson [236].
[6] The notion of a self-answering identity might explain the use of certain tautologies as discussion-stoppers. E.g., "war is war" as an explanation of a cruelty indicates that cruelty belongs to the very concept of war: "war is war" effectively equals "you know what war is (like)".
[7] Cf. (C.wh-id) to Belnap and Steel's notion of distinctness-claim (pp. 60–61 of [113]).

CHAPTER 7

[1] See G. E. Moore, 'Russell's "Theory of Descriptions",' in G. E. Moore, *Philosophical Papers*, Allen & Unwin, London 1959, pp. 151–195, esp. p. 175. Cf. Hintikka [63] and W. Kummer [269].

2 Dascal [159], p. 322, makes the same point.

3 Hintikka's defense of the transitivity axiom in [63] is not based on the argument from introspection. See also Hintikka [66], Chapter 1, Hintikka [260–262], and works by Castañeda, Collins, Geach, Ginet, Hilpinen, Lehrer, Pailthorp, de Sousa, and Wiggins in the references to this Chapter.

4 The failure of transitivity means that the players of a dialogue game need not have perfect information of their own epistemic alternatives. Cf. Chapter 2.1.

CHAPTER 8

1 Searle [314], pp. 16–17.

2 Ibid., p. 21.

3 Ibid., p. 19.

4 Ibid., p. 37.

5 Cf. Wunderlich [321], [323]. Ferrara [294–5] has attempted to extend speech act theory to discourse analysis.

6 Cf. Hintikka, 'Language-games', in Saarinen (ed.) [32], esp. pp. 13–14.

7 Searle [314], p. 54. Searle is actually speaking of promises in the passage quoted. I have taken the liberty of replacing 'promise' by 'question' throughout. I trust the substitution is warranted by the context.

8 A good discussion of the meaning of questions is Hudson [136], esp. p. 4–6.

9 Cf. Sadock [175], pp. 138–139, R. Lakoff [304], p. 455, Pope [310], pp. 36, 44.

10 Chapter 2.6.

11 My example is a restatement of the familiar puzzle of three wise men. I owe the example and its solution to McCarthy [307].

12 An interesting analysis of politeness in decision-theoretic terms is Brown and Levinson [288]. See also Fraser [297] and R. Lakoff [305].

13 Cf. Jespersen [357], p. 304, Pope [310], Chapter 3, Culicover [292], Chapter 2.

14 The pretheoretic characterization of rhetorical question as a question which is not in need of an answer covers a heterogeneous class of cases, including different sorts of eliciting questions (Chapter 8.4, n. 9 above), pleas of ignorance (Chapter 8.6) and sarcastic and perfunctory questions (Chapter 8.9, Chapter 8.8). For a good list of examples, see Quintilian, Book ix, Chapter II. Cf. also Pope [310], Chapter 2, Schmidt-Radefelt [313].

15 See Chapter 4.3.

16 Observe that this conversational implication can in turn be understood ironically: the author of (82) may be playfully conveying that he knows a whole lot. Such double irony is obvious in

Aren't you clever!

which actually reads

You are not clever at all.

17 See e.g., Klima [302], Culicover [292], p. 187.

18 Courtesy of Ken Hale (personal communication). Culicover, *Syntax*, Academic Press, New York 1976, p. 132, maintains that sentences like (101b) are not acceptable for most speakers of English. My informants have accepted (101b) to a man.

[19] For good discussions of tag questions, see Bolinger [117], Chapter 2, and Hudson [136].

[20] I use the term 'echo question' in a syntactic sense. Echo questions are direct questions which match their presupposition without an application of wh-preposing or auxiliary inversion.

[21] Kuno and Robinson [144], p. 466 fn. 5.

[22] Bolinger [287], p. 131.

APPENDIX I

[1] See Levi [46], Chapter 7, esp. p. 106–108. Note that caution increases in inverse proportion to the index q.

[2] See Luce and Raiffa [25], Chapter 13 for a survey.

APPENDIX II

[1] For further discussion, see e.g., Hintikka [66].

[2] Cf. Hintikka [61–8]. See also Sleigh [101].

PART II
CHAPTER 1

[1] For similar ideas, cf. Gray [343–4], Christensen [183], Young et al. [388], Clark and Haviland [437] and Warren et al. [385].

If my approach is right, there is reason to doubt any simple-minded approach to characterizing textual cohesion in terms of, say, surface repetition of lexical material or frequent anaphoric connections. I suspect that such regularities, though undeniably real, are just epiphenomena of more fundamental requirements. To put the point roughly, any nontrivial piece of discourse will exhibit logical connections among its sentences. There is a theorem in first-order quantification theory (known as Craig's interpolation theorem) which states in effect that there is no logical entailment without shared vocabulary: sentences which share no nonlogical words cannot enter into logical relations. I suspect that many regularities of lexical and anaphoric repetition in a connected text can be traced back to this simple truth of logic.

[2] Lewis Carroll, *Alice in Wonderland*, ch. VII.

[3] Cf. Bolinger [327], Householder [354], Labov [22], Enkvist [9], Dinsmore [336].

[4] For the notions of coherence and cohesion, see Halliday [349–50], Halliday and Hasan [351], Coulthard [6], p. 10, Enkvist [337], Grimes [345], p. 113, Gutwinski [348], pp. 25–33, Hendricks [14], pp. 39–41.

[5] On autonomy of grammar, cf. Chomsky [39], [544], Dascal and Margalit [333].

[6] This paragraph exhausts my intentions with the term *functional*. In particular, my explanations of functional contrasts are not functional explanations, but structural.

[7] Structuralist approaches prefer to treat of discourse phenomena on an intermediate level of representation which, as a part of the structural description of a sentence, relates

grammatical structure to context. The mapping from the discourse grammatical representations to contexts of use is often left unspecified. See e.g., Chomsky [434], Karttunen and Peters [267], cf. Williams [386]. The present approach does not make this assumption. The rules of dialogue grammar defined here relate grammatical structures directly to dialogue context. Nothing crucial depends on this issue, however.

8 Cf. K. Hale, L. Jeanne and P. Platero, 'Three cases of overgeneration', in P. Culicover, T. Wasow and A. Akmajian (eds.) *Formal syntax*, Academic Press, New York 1977, and Chomsky [435].

9 The omission is part due to the absence of a suitable phonological theory of intonational contrasts until very recently (see J. Pierrehumbert, *The phonology and phonetics of English intonation*, MIT Press, forthcoming), part to crude considerations of space. For preliminary work on this topic, see Carlson [4].

CHAPTER 2

1 Cf. Posner [421], p. 187.

2 Chapter 8.4. of Part I.

3 See McCawley [416], Gazdar [407].

4 McCawley [416] attributes this observation to Hans Reichenbach.

5 I leave out of consideration here uses of *but* in the senses of 'only', 'except' and 'instead'. The last mentioned use can probably be subsumed under (D.but). It is omitted here because an adequate discussion of it would require an analysis of elliptic sentences.

6 For other analyses of the different senses of *but*, see Abraham [390], Bellert [394], Dascal and Katriel [398], Halliday and Hasan [351], R. Lakoff [411], Spencer [486].

7 Leibniz [413], Chapter vii, §5.

8 According to Piaget [420], French *mais* 'but' is actually first acquired in countermoves.

9 On discourse uses of connectives, cf. also Halliday and Hasan [351], van Dijk [399].

10 Locke [415], Chapter vii, §5; cf. n. 7.

11 Aristotle, *Topics*, Book VIII.

12 Ibid.

13 The conclusion of a syllogism was even called 'the question': cf. Robinson [423].

14 Many of my observations and examples are due to Olga Yokoyama (lecture notes, Harvard 1980). The mistakes are my own.

CHAPTER 3

1 On the problem of basic word order, see esp. Firbas [552], p. 33–34. On this issue, I side with Isačenko [457–8] against Firbas. Firbas' primitive concept of communicative dynamism seems apt to explain *obscurum per obscurius*. Cf. also Heinämäki [456].

2 See e.g., Sgall et al. [594], p. 67, Hakulinen [455], p. 90. My term 'diathetic' is designed to cover the sort of 'deep (semantic) case' relations Jackendoff [355] infelicitously calls thematic relations. For a recent discussion of these, see Ostler [477]. For terminological priority, cf. e.g., Firbas [448], p. 112:

Very roughly speaking, thematic elements are such as convey facts known from the verbal or situational context, whereas rhematic elements are such as convey new, unknown facts.

For even more ancient history, see Danes et al. [445].

3 See Emonds [446], p. 9, Chomsky and Lasnik [436], Chomsky [435], p. 18.

4 Cf. Dahl [439].

5 Here, as elsewhere, intuitive thematicity judgments are correlated with judgments of stress prominence: rhematic constituents receive emphasis while thematic ones avoid it. Cf. Carlson [4].

6 Otto Behaghel, *Indogermanische Forschungen* 25 (1909), 110–142. Cf. Jespersen [356] §2.15.

7 Kuno (Class notes, Harvard 1980).

8 The precise interpretation of (D.topic) is somewhat tricky. Not all of a topical constituent need be new (see text for counterexamples). Yet it would be misleading to say that it suffices for some constituent of the preposed phrase to be rhematic. The right interpretation seems to be that the topical phrase must be the smallest preposable phrase containing the rhematic constituent.

9 The duality of functions of topicalization is an old observation. Sweet [384] notes that "In some of these cases (of topicalization, L. C.) the front-order is emphatic, in others connective." I differ only in claiming that topicalization always creates a rhematic constituent.

10 (D.topic), as an obligatory rule, predicts that mere thematicity does not warrant the use of topicalization: some sort of emphasis or contrast is always involved. This may explain why the constitutionally thematic pronoun *it* is ungrammatical in topic position:

As for the last example, it I invented myself.

11 On contrastiveness, see Chafe [543], Spencer [486].

12 Cf. Bolinger [287], pp. 132–5, Chafe [543], p. 49.

13 See esp. Akmajian et al. [428]. Cf. Jespersen [356], § §2.32, 2.37.

14 Ken Hale (personal communication) tells me that Navajo has question verbs (yet no interrogative predicate phrases).

15 In support of a functional explanation of the constraints on VP topicalization, consider the following facts from Finnish. The Finnish auxiliary system is radically different from the English. Yet the upper limit restriction holds in Finnish too:

*olla lähtenyt hän saattaakin cf. *mitä hän saattaa?
be   left   he   may – too   what he   may

lähtenyt hän saattaa ollakin
left   he   may   be – too

On the other hand, the lower limit restriction does not hold:

ovelalta hän näyttääkin
shrewd   he   looks – too

This is not surprising, as there is no dummy auxiliary in Finnish to carry affirmative emphasis.

[16] Cf. Part I, Chapter 4 n. 13 and Chapter 8.7.

[17] Another qualification is in order. Kuno's own characterization of his theme in [468], p. 302 rather suggests our notion of dialogue subject.

[18] According to Kuno (class notes, Harvard 1980 and private conversation) the following elliptic dialogue proves the need of distinguishing new information from another notion of important information:

A: Did you stay in a hotel in Paris?
B: No, I didn't stay in a hotel – I stayed with my friends.
A: How about London?
B: I stayed in a hotel because I didn't have any friends there.

Kuno's rule of ellipsis says that important information cannot be omitted before less important information. In the last line of the dialogue, B omits *London* though it seems newer information than *in a hotel*; this shows that importance cannot be defined in terms of new information. It seems to me that the conclusion follows only if the definitions of old and new information are applied mechanically on the surface of the dialogue. If they are applied in a well motivated reconstruction of the dialogue, it turns out that the omitted constituent *in London* is actually a theme, and the retained one *in a hotel* a rheme:

Where did you stay in which city?

Where did you stay in Paris?	How about London?
Did you stay in a hotel in Paris?	Where did you stay in London?
No, I did not stay in a hotel –	I stayed in a hotel because I
I stayed with my friends.	did not have any friends there.

[19] Cf. also Kuroda [471], Janoš [459], Oh [476].

CHAPTER 4

[1] On subordination, cf. Bickerton [491], Bolinger [495], Green [504], Ross [532], Sledd [533], and Wilson and Sperber [537].

[2] See Kiparsky and Kiparsky [520]. For the extensive follow-up literature, see the bibliography in Oh and Dinneen [527].

[3] For a recent attack, see Böer and Lycan [492], p. 28–41. I should mention that I do not think *know* is a factive verb.

[4] Cf. Bolinger [496], p. 68: "A factive verb implies the factuality of its complement in the mind of the speaker, not the shared knowledge of it between the speaker and hearer". Cf. also Prince [531], p. 897.

[5] For the role of questions in the organization and understanding of discourse, see Hatcher [508–9], Gray [343–4], Christensen [183], Warren et al. [385], Young et al. [388].

[6] Cf. Grimes [345], pp. 338–342 for a similar suggestion.

[7] Faraci [502] suggests a syntactic derivation of wh-clefts from questions. Gundel

[453] derives it-clefts from right dislocated sentences by an optional rule. This analysis is faulted for functional reasons: the two constructions are functionally quite different. (See text for arguments.) Higgins [510] defends the base generation hypothesis.

[8] To be accurate, predicative complements can be preposed in English:

> Fortunate are the parents with a strong religious faith.
> Convenient is a dressing table with a waterproof changing pad, safety strap, and storage shelves.

(These examples come from Dr. Spock's *Baby and Child Care*.) The precise difference is that in virtue of (D.topic), a preposed predicative complement must be rhematic, whereas an identity sentence can be simply reversed without prejudging its thematic properties.

[9] This analysis is confirmed by the occurrence of "pseudo-clefts" like

> What the paper is after, it wants to publish your story.
> What I'd like, I'd like to tell you to go somewhere and scratch your ass with your elbow.

Here the complement of the cleft is not syntactically fit to replace the question phrase of the subject; still it answers the subject question all right. (The examples are from Rex Stout's novel *Plot it yourself*.)

[10] Yet another peculiarity of clefts is the treatment of anaphora across the subject and complement. To put the point simply, anaphora in a cleft like (27) is determined by reference to the full answer (30) implicit in it.

[11] For more examples of this character, see Jespersen [356], §4.68.

CHAPTER 5

[1] For instance, Halliday [562] has been criticized for "defining theme as the first element of a sentence". Actually, Halliday's functional definition of theme is "what I am talking about (now)". What is taken exception to is his assertion that theme is always sentence initial.

[2] Firbas [552], p. 12.

[3] This distinction is contrasted with the topic-comment distinction in Chomsky [434], n. 32. For the latter distinction, see Chomsky [544], p. 221.

[4] Jespersen [569], p. 146. Jespersen is actually criticizing the traditional definition of subject as what a sentence talks about.

[5] The term 'topic' is already reserved for the topical question of a dialogue. Cf. Section 5 below. My usage here conforms with that of Chafe [543].

[6] In other words, the object position of *about* exhibits the same range of intensional (*de dicto — de re*) ambiguities as other propositional attitude contexts. For discussion, see Heny [564] (esp. papers by E. Saarinen and D. Smith), Donnellan [548–9] and Kripke [575].

[7] Conversely, objects of *about* phrases serve to indicate dialogue subjects. For instance, John is the subject of discussion in *What about John?*

[8] Lewis Carroll, *Through the looking-glass*, Ch. IV.

[9] Keenan-Ochs and Schieffelin [573] definition of topic as a "question of immediate concern" resembles mine.

[10] See Grimshaw [558], Richards [588], and Ross [591].

[11] See Hintikka [565], [127–8] and his paper 'Knowledge by Acquaintance – Individuation by Acquaintance' in D. Pears (ed.) *Bertrand Russell: A Collection of Critical Essays*, Doubleday, Garden City, N.J. 1971 (reprinted in Hintikka [70]).

[12] Mathesius [582], p. 61, anticipates (D.subject) in his observation that

. . . Modern English shows a characteristic tendency for the thematical conception of the subject. In English sentences, accordingly, the theme of the enunciation is expressed as a rule by the grammatical subject . . .

(He adds in a footnote that his "theme" here is what is usually called the psychological subject.)

[13] Chafe [543], p. 43.

[14] See Kuno and Kaburaki [576].

[15] Cf. Chafe [543] for observations to the same effect. For further discussion of ambiguous anaphora, see Lakoff [577–579], Akmajian [539], Akmajian and Jackendoff [540], Gundel [560], Clark and Haviland [437]. On the role of subject in paragraph organization, see Young et al. [388], Chapter 15.

[16] For the relevant constraints, see e.g., Chomsky [435] and references therein.

[17] See last paragraph of this Chapter, §4.

[18] Note that dislocations cannot be analyzed as movements in terms of our functional definitions in Chapter 3.3 on account of the anaphoric copy in the main clause.

[19] As Gundel [453], Chapter 3.3.1. observes, indefinite noun phrases can be dislocated when they are generic (refer to a kind):

A bottle of Scotch, I have not been able to find one.

On left dislocation, see also Gundel [559], Keenan-Ochs and Schieffelin [573–574], Ochs [583], and Rodman [589].

[20] Gundel [453], p. 121.

[21] Cf. Kuno (class notes, Harvard 1980): "(In right dislocation), the speaker assumes that the hearer can determine the referent of the pronoun from the left context, but adds the full-fledged noun for confirmation/clarification."

[22] Vygotsky, L., *Thought and Language*, MIT Press, Cambridge, Mass. 1962, p. 139.

BIBLIOGRAPHY

INTRODUCTION

[1]   Andersson, E., 'Style, optional rules, and contextual conditioning', in H. Ringbom et al. (ed.), *Style and Text: Studies Presented to Nils-Erik Enkvist*, Skriptor, Stockholm 1975, pp. 15–26.

[2]   Aristotle, *The Art of Rhetoric*, with an English translation by J. Freese, Loeb Classical Library, Harvard University Press, Cambridge, Ma. 1926.

[3]   Carlson, L., 'Language games and speech acts', in *Papers from the III Scandinavian Conference of Linguistics*, ed. F. Karlsson, Turku 1976, pp. 95–107.

[4]   Carlson, L., 'Focus and dialogue games', in L. Vaina and J. Hintikka (ed.), *Cognitive Constraints on Communication*, D. Reidel, Dordrecht forthcoming.

[5]   Carnap, R., *Introduction to Semantics*, Harvard University Press, Cambridge, Ma. 1942.

[6]   Coulthard, M., *An Introduction to Discourse Analysis*, Longman, London 1977.

[7]   Dressler, W. (ed.), *Current Trends in Textlinguistics*, Walter de Gruyter, Berlin 1978.

[8]   Enkvist, N., *Linguistic Stylistics*, Mouton, The Hague 1973.

[9]   Enkvist, N., 'Style and types of context', in N. Enkvist (ed.), *Reports on Text Linguistics: Four Papers on Text, Style and Syntax*, Publications of the research institute of the Åbo Akademi Foundation, No. 1, Åbo 1974, pp. 30–75.

[10] Grice, P., 'Logic and conversation', William James Lectures, Harvard 1967. Published in part in P. Cole and J. Morgan (eds.), *Syntax and Semantics 3: Speech Acts*, Academic Press, New York 1975, pp. 43–58, and in D. Davidson and G. Harman (eds.), *The Logic of Grammar*, Dickenson, California 1975, pp. 64–75.

[11] Harrah, D., *Communication: A Logical Model*, MIT Press, Cambridge, Ma. 1963.

[12] Harris, Z. 'Discourse Analysis', *Language* 28 (1952), 1–30.

[13] Hendricks, W., 'Current trends in discourse analysis', in B. Kachru and H. Stalker (eds.), *Current Trends in Stylistics*, Linguistic Research Inc., Edmonton, Alberta 1971.

[14] Hendricks, W., *Grammars of Style and Styles of Grammar*, North-Holland, Amsterdam 1976.

[15] Hintikka, J., *Logic, Language-Games, and Information*, Clarendon Press, Oxford 1973.

[16] Hintikka, J., 'Toward an interrogative model of scientific inquiry', in W. Callebaut et al. (eds.), *Theory of Knowledge and Science Policy*, Communication and Cognition, Ghent 1979, pp. 208–220.

[17] Hintikka, J., 'Information-seeking dialogues: some of their logical properties', *Studia Logica* 32 (1979), 355–363.

284

[18] Hintikka, J., 'The logic of information-seeking dialogues: A model' in W. Becker and W. Essler (eds.), *Konzepte der Dialektik*, Vittorio Klostermann, Frankfurt am Main, 1981.

[19] Hintikka, J., 'On the logic of an interrogative model of scientific inquiry', *Synthese* **47** (1981), 69–83.

[20] Hintikka, J., 'Sherlock Holmes formalized', to appear in a *Festschrift for Alwin Diemer*.

[21] Hintikka, J. and M. Hintikka, 'Sherlock Holmes confronts modern logic', in E. Barth (ed.), *Theory of Argumentation*, Benjamins, Amsterdam 1981.

[22] Labov, W., 'The study of language in its social context', *Studium Generale* **23** (1970), 30–87. Reprinted in P. Giglioli (ed.), *Language and Social Context*, Penguin Press 1972, pp. 283–308, and in J. Pride and J. Holmes (ed.), *Sociolinguistics*, Penguin Books 1972.

[23] Labov, W., *Sociolinguistic Patterns*, Philadelphia 1972.

[24] Labov, W., 'Rules for ritual insults', in D. Sudnov (ed.), *Studies in Social Interaction*, Free Press, New York 1972, p. 120–169.

[25] Luce, D. and H. Raiffa, *Games and Decisions*, John Wiley and Sons, New York 1957.

[26] McGee, D., 'Fun, games and natural language', *Australasian Journal of Philosophy* **42** (1964), 335–344.

[27] Montague, R., 'Pragmatics', in R. Klibansky (ed.), *Contemporary Philosophy – La Philosophie Contemporaine*, Vol. 1, La Nuova Italia Editrice, Florence 1968, pp. 102–122.

[28] Morris, C. *Foundations of the Theory of Signs*, International Encyclopedia of Unified Science, Vol. 1, Chicago University Press, Chicago 1938.

[29] Morris, C. *Signs, Language and Behavior*, Prentice-Hall, New York 1946.

[30] von Neumann, J. and O. Morgenstern, *Theory of Games and Economic Behavior*, John Wiley & Sons, New York 1944.

[31] Saarinen, E., 'Game-theoretical semantics', *Monist* **60** (1977), 406–418.

[32] Saarinen, E. (ed.), *Game-theoretical Semantics*, D. Reidel, Dordrecht 1979.

[33] Stalnaker, R., 'Pragmatics', *Synthese* **22**/1 (1970), 272–289.

[34] Stalnaker, R., 'Assertion', in P. Cole (ed.), *Syntax and Semantics 9: Pragmatics*, Academic Press, New York 1975, pp. 315–332.

[35] Stenius, E. 'Mood and language-game', *Synthese* **17** (1967), 254–274.

[36] Tarski, A., 'The semantic conception of truth', *Philosophy and Phenomenological Research* **4** (1944).

[37] Wittgenstein, L. *Philosophische Untersuchungen/Philosophical Investigations*, Basil Blackwell, Oxford 1953.

[38] Wittgenstein, L., *Philosophical Grammar*, Basil Blackwell, Oxford 1974.

PART I
CHAPTER 1

[39] Chomsky, N., *Reflections on Language*, Parthenon Press, New York 1975.

[40] Cohen, L. and M. Hesse (eds.), *Applications of Inductive Logic*, Clarendon Press, Oxford 1980.

[41] Gale, S., 'A prolegomenon to an interrogative theory of scientific inquiry', in Hiż, H. (ed.), *Questions*, D. Reidel, Dordrecht 1977, pp. 319–345.

[42] Hilpinen, R., *Rules of Acceptance and Inductive Logic*, Acta Philosophica Fennica 22, North-Holland, Amsterdam 1968.

[43] Hilpinen, R., 'Scientific rationality and the ethics of belief', in Hilpinen, R. (ed.), *Rationality in Science*, D. Reidel, Dordrecht 1980.

[44] Hintikka, J., 'Rules, utilities, and strategies in dialogical games', MS, Dept. of Philosophy, Florida State University 1981.

[45] Hintikka, J., and P. Suppes (ed.), *Information and Inference*, D. Reidel, Dordrecht 1970.

[46] Levi, I., *Gambling with Truth, An Essay on Induction and the Aims of Science*, MIT Press, Cambridge, Ma. 1967.

[47] Schiffer, S., *Meaning*, Clarendon Press, Oxford 1972.

[48] Swain, M. (ed.), *Induction, Acceptance, and Rational Belief*, D. Reidel, Dordrecht 1970.

CHAPTER 2

[49] Ackermann, R., 'Opacity in belief structures', *Journal of Philosophy* 69 (1972), 55–67.

[50] Bell, J., 'What is referential opacity?', *Journal of Philosophical Logic* 2 (1973), 155–180.

[51] Bigelow, J., 'Believing in semantics', *Linguistics and Philosophy* 2 (1978), 101–144.

[52] Carnap, R., *Meaning and Necessity*, Chicago 1947.

[53] Chisholm, R., 'The logic of knowing', *Journal of Philosophy* 60 (1963).

[54] Chisholm, R., 'Identity through possible worlds', *Noûs* 1 (1967), 1–8.

[55] Chomsky, N., 'Logical syntax and semantics: Their linguistic relevance', *Language* 30 (1954), 36–45.

[56] Cresswell, M., *Logics and Languages*, Methuen & Co., London 1973.

[57] Cresswell, M., 'Hyperintensional logic', *Studia Logica* 34 (1975), 25–38.

[58] Eberle, R., 'A logic of believing, knowing, and inferring', *Synthese* 26 (1974), 356–382.

[59] Frege, G., 'On sense and reference', German original in *Zeitschrift für Philosophie und philosophische Kritik* 100 (1892), 25–50; English translation in P. Geach and M. Black (eds.), *Translations from the Philosophical Writings of Gottlob Frege*, Oxford 1960.

[60] Goddard, L. and R. Routley, *The Logic of Significance and Context*, Vol. I, John Wiley and Sons, New York 1973.

[61] Hintikka, J., 'Modality as referential multiplicity', *Ajatus* 20 (1957), 49–64.

[62] Hintikka, J., 'Modality and quantification', *Theoria* 27 (1961), 119–129.

[63] Hintikka, J., *Knowledge and Belief*, Cornell University Press, Ithaca, N.Y. 1962.

[64] Hintikka, J., 'Individuals, possible worlds, and epistemic logic', *Noûs* 1 (1967), 33–62.

[65] Hintikka, J., 'Semantics for propositional attitudes', in J. Davis, D. Hockney and W. Wilson (eds.), *Philosophical Logic*, D. Reidel, Dordrecht 1968.

[66] Hintikka, J., *Models for Modalities*, D. Reidel, Dordrecht 1969.
[67] Hintikka, J., 'The semantics of modal notions and the indeterminacy of ontology', *Synthese* **21** (1970), 408–424.
[68] Hintikka, J., 'Existential presuppositions and uniqueness presuppositions', in K. Lambert (ed.), *Philosophical Problems in Logic*, D. Reidel, Dordrecht 1970, pp. 20–55.
[69] Hintikka, J., 'Knowledge, belief, and logical consequence', *Ajatus* **32** (1970), 32–47.
[70] Hintikka, J., *Knowledge and the Known*, D. Reidel, Dordrecht 1974.
[71] Hintikka, J., 'Impossible possible worlds vindicated', *Journal of Philosophical Logic* **4** (1975), 475–484.
[72] Hintikka, J., *The Intentions of Intentionality and Other New Models for Modalities*, D. Reidel, Dordrecht 1975.
[73] Jackendoff, R., 'On Belief-Contexts', *Linguistic Inquiry* **6** (1975), 53–93.
[74] Jackendoff, R., 'Belief-contexts revisited', *Linguistic Inquiry* **11** (1980), 395–413.
[75] Kanger, S., 'The Morning Star paradox', *Theoria* **23** (1957), 1–11.
[76] Kaplan, D., 'Quantifying in', in D. Davidson and J. Hintikka (eds.), *Words and Objections*, D. Reidel, Dordrecht 1969.
[77] Kripke, S., 'A completeness theorem in modal logic', *Journal of Symbolic Logic* **24** (1959), 1–14.
[78] Kripke, S., 'Semantical considerations on modal logic', *Acta Philosophica Fennica* **16** (1963), 83–94.
[79] Kripke, S., 'Identity and necessity', in M. Munitz (ed.), *Identity and Individuation*, New York University Press, New York 1971.
[80] Kripke, S., 'Naming and necessity', in D. Davidson and G. Harman (eds.), *Semantics of Natural Language*, D. Reidel, Dordrecht 1972.
[81] Lewis, D., 'Counterpart theory and quantified modal logic', *Journal of Philosophy* **65** (1968), 113–126.
[82] Linsky, L., 'Interpreting doxastic logic', *Journal of Philosophy* **65** (1968), 500–502.
[83] Montague, R., 'Pragmatics and intensional logic', *Synthese* **21** (1970), 68–94.
[84] Montague, R. and D. Kalish, 'That', *Philosophical Studies* **10** (1959), 54–61.
[85] Nelson, R., 'On machine expectation', *Synthese* **31** (1975), 129–139.
[86] Nelson, R., 'Objects of occasion beliefs', *Synthese* **39** (1978), 105–139.
[87] Parsons, T., 'Essentialism and quantified modal logic', in L. Linsky (ed.), *Reference and Modality*, Oxford University Press, Oxford 1971.
[88] Partee, B., 'The semantics of belief sentences', in J. Hintikka, J. Moravcsik, and P. Suppes (eds.), *Approaches to Natural Language*, D. Reidel, Dordrecht 1973, pp. 309–336.
[89] Partee, P., 'Possible worlds semantics and linguistic theory', *The Monist* **60** (1977), 303–326.
[90] Purtill, R., 'Believing the impossible', *Ajatus* **32** (1970), 18–24.
[91] Putnam, H., 'Synonymity and the analysis of belief sentences', *Analysis* **14** (1954), 114–122.
[92] Quine, W., 'Quantifiers and propositional attitudes', *Journal of Philosophy* **53** (1956), 177–187.

[93]   Rantala, V., 'Urn models', *Journal of Philosophical Logic* 4 (1975), 455–474.
[94]   Rescher, N. and R. Brandon, *The Logic of Inconsistency: A Study in Non-Standard Possible-world Semantics and Ontology*, Rowman and Littlefield, Totowa, N.J. 1979.
[95]   Routley, R. and V. Routley, 'The role of inconsistent and incomplete theories in the logic of belief', *Communication and Cognition* 8 (1975), 185–235.
[96]   Saarinen, E., 'Continuity and similarity in cross-identification', in E. Saarinen et al. (eds.), *Essays in Honour of Jaakko Hintikka*, D. Reidel 1979, pp. 189–215.
[97]   Scott, D., 'Advice on modal logic', in K. Lambert (ed.), *Philosophical Problems in Logic*, D. Reidel, Dordrecht 1969, pp. 143–173.
[98]   Segerberg, K., *An Essay in Classical Modal Logic*, Filosofiska Studier 13, Uppsala 1971.
[99]   Sellars, W., 'Some problems about belief', *Synthese* 19 (1968–9), 158–177.
[100] Sleigh, R., 'On quantifying into epistemic contexts', *Noûs* 1 (1967), 23–32.
[101] Sleigh, R., 'Restricted range in epistemic logic', *Journal of Philosophy* 69 (1972), 67–77.
[102] Sosa, E., 'Propositional attitudes "de dicto" and "de re"', *Journal of Philosophy* 57 (1970), 883–896.
[103] Stine, G., 'Hintikka on quantification and belief', *Noûs* 3 (1969), 339–408.
[104] Tennant, N., 'Recursive semantics for knowledge and belief', *The Monist* 60 (1977), 419.
[105] Thomason, R., 'A model theory for propositional attitudes', MS, Dept. of Philosophy, University of Pittsburgh, Nov. 1977.
[106] Wallace, J., 'Belief and satisfaction', *Noûs* 6 (1972), 85–95.

CHAPTER 3

[107] Åqvist, L., *A New Approach to the Logical Theory of Interrogatives*, Filosofiska Föreningen, Uppsala 1965.
[108] Åqvist, L., 'Revised foundations for imperative, epistemic, and interrogative logic', *Theoria* 37 (1971), 33–73.
[109] Bach, E., 'Questions', *Linguistic Inquiry* 2/2 (1971).
[110] Baker, C., 'Notes on the description of English questions: The role of a Q morpheme', *Foundations of Language* 6 (1970), 197–219.
[111] Belnap, N., 'Questions, answers, and presuppositions', *Journal of Philosophy* 63 (1966), 609–611.
[112] Belnap, N., 'Questions: Their presuppositions and how they can fail to arise', in K. Lambert (ed.), *The Logical Way of Doing Things*, Yale University Press, New Haven and London, 1969.
[113] Belnap, N. and T. Steel, *The Logic of Questions and Answers*, Yale University Press, New Haven and London, 1976.
[114] Bennett, M., *Questions in Montague Grammar*, Indiana University Linguistics Club, Bloomington, Indiana 1979.
[115] Boër, S., '*Who* and *whether*: towards a theory of indirect question clauses', *Linguistics and Philosophy* 2 (1978), 307–345.

[116] Boër, S. and W. Lycan, 'Knowing who', *Philosophical Studies* **28** (1975), 299–344.

[117] Bolinger, D., *Interrogative Structures of American English: The Direct Question*, Publication no. 28 of the American Dialect Society, University of Alabama, 1957.

[118] Bromberger, S., 'Questions', *Journal of Philosophy* **63** (1966), 597–606.

[119] Cohen, F., 'What is a question', *The Monist* **39** (1929), 350–364.

[120] Cresswell, M., 'The logic of interrogatives', in J. Crossley and M. Dummett (eds.), *Formal Systems and Recursive Functions*, North-Holland, Amsterdam 1965, pp. 7–11.

[121] Hamblin, C., 'Questions', *Australasian Journal of Philosophy* **36** (1958), 159–168.

[122] Hamblin, C., 'Questions aren't statements', *Philosophy of Science* **30** (1963), 62–63.

[123] Hamblin, C., 'Questions in Montague English", *Foundations of Language* **10** (1973), 41–53.

[124] Harrah, D., 'A logic of questions and answers', *Philosophy of Science* **28** (1961), 40–46.

[125] Harrah, D., 'Erotetic logistics', in K. Lambert (ed.), *The Logical Way of Doing Things*, Yale University Press, New Haven 1969, pp. 3–21.

[126] Harrah, D., 'Completeness in the logic of questions', *American Philosophical Quarterly* **6** (1969), 158–164.

[127] Hintikka, J., 'On the logic of perception', in N. Care and R. Grimm (eds.), *Perception and Personal Identity*, Press of Case Western Reserve University 1969, pp. 140–170.

[128] Hintikka, J., 'Objects of knowledge and belief: Acquaintances and public figures' *Journal of Philosophy* **67** (1970), 869–883.

[129] Hintikka, J., 'Questions about questions', in M. Munitz and P. Unger (eds.), *Semantics and Philosophy*, New York University Press, New York 1974.

[130] Hintikka, J., *The Semantics of Questions and the Questions of Semantics*, *Acta Philosophica Fennica* **28**/4, North-Holland, Amsterdam 1976.

[131] Hintikka, J., 'The Ross paradox as evidence for the reality of semantical games", *The Monist* **60** (1977), 370–379.

[132] Hintikka, J., 'Answers to Questions', in J. Hintikka, *Intentions of Intentionality*, D. Reidel, Dordrecht 1975, pp. 137–158.

[133] Hintikka, J., 'New foundations for a theory of questions and answers', forthcoming in the proceedings of the 1980 symposium on questions and answers, Visegrad, Hungary.

[134] Hiż, H., 'Questions and answers', *Journal of Philosophy* **59** (1962), 253–265.

[135] Hiż, H. (ed.), *Questions*, D. Reidel, Dordrecht 1978.

[136] Hudson, R., 'The meaning of questions', *Language* **51** (1975), 1–31.

[137] Kamp, H., 'Free choice permission', *Proceedings of the Aristotelian Society*, 1973.

[138] Kamp, H., 'Semantics vs. pragmatics', in F. Guenthner and S. Smith (eds.), *Formal Semantics and Pragmatics for Natural Languages*, D. Reidel, Dordrecht 1978, pp. 255–287.

[139] Karttunen, L., 'Syntax and semantics of questions', *Linguistics and Philosophy* **1** (1977), 3–44.

[140]   Karttunen, L. and S. Peters, 'What indirect questions conventionally implicate', *CLS* 12 (1976), Chicago Linguistic Society, Chicago.

[141]   Katz, J., 'The logic of questions', in B. van Rootselar and J. Staal (eds.), *Logic, Methodology, and Philosophy of Science III*, North-Holland, Amsterdam 1968, pp. 463–493.

[142]   Katz, J. and P. Postal, *An Integrated Theory of Linguistic Descriptions*, MIT Press, Cambridge, Ma. 1964.

[143]   Keenan, E. and R. Hull, 'The logical presuppositions of questions and answers', in J. Petöfi and D. Frank (eds.), *Präsuppositionen in Philosophie und Linguistik*, Athenäum, Frankfurt am Main 1973.

[144]   Kuno, S., and J. Robinson, 'Multiple wh questions', *Linguistic Inquiry* 3 (1972), 463–487.

[145]   Lang, R., 'Questions as epistemic requests", in H. Hiż (ed.), *Questions*, D. Reidel, Dordrecht 1978, pp. 301–318.

[146]   Langacker, R., 'The question of Q', *Foundations of Language* 11 (1974), 1–37.

[147]   Lewis, D., 'A problem about permission', in E. Saarinen et al. (eds.), *Essays in Honour of Jaakko Hintikka*, D. Reidel, Dordrecht 1979, pp. 136–175.

[148]   Llewelyn, J., 'What is a question?', *Australasian Journal of Philosophy* 42 (1964), 67–85.

[149]   Prior, M. and A. Prior, 'Erotetic Logic', *Philosophical Review* 64 (1955), 43–59.

[150]   Rorty, A. (ed.), *The Identities of Persons*, University of California Press, California 1976.

CHAPTER 4

[151]   Adams, E., 'The logic of conditionals', *Inquiry* 8 (1965), 166–197.

[152]   Adams, E., 'Subjunctive and indicative conditionals', *Foundations of Language* 6 (1970), 89–94.

[153]   Adams, E., *The Logic of Conditionals*, D. Reidel, Dordrecht 1975.

[154]   Ayers, M., 'Counterfactuals and subjunctive conditionals', *Mind* 74 (1965), 347–364.

[155]   Belnap, N., 'Conditional assertion and restricted quantification', *Noûs* 4 (1970).

[156]   Braine, M., 'On some claims about if-then', *Linguistics and Philosophy* 3 (1979), 35–47.

[157]   Butterworth, B., 'Maxims for studying conversations', *Semiotica* 24 (1978), 317–339.

[158]   Chisholm, R., 'The contrary-to-fact conditional', *Mind* 55 (1946), 289–307.

[159]   Dascal, M., 'Conversational relevance', *Journal of Pragmatics* 1 (1977), 309–328.

[160]   van Dijk, T., 'Relevance assignment in discourse comprehension', *Discourse Processes* 2 (1979), 113–126.

[161]   Gärdenfors, P., 'On the logic of relevance', *Synthese* 37 (1978), 351–367.

[162]   Goffman, E., 'Replies and responses', *Language in Society* 5 (1976), 257–313.

[163]   Goodman, N., 'The problems of counterfactual conditionals', *Journal of Philosophy* 44 (1947), 113–128.

[164]   Harper, W., R. Stalnaker and G. Pearce (eds.), *Ifs*, D. Reidel, Dordrecht 1981.
[165]   Karttunen, L., 'Counterfactual conditionals', *Linguistic Inquiry* 2 (1971), 566–569.
[166]   von Kutschera, F., 'Indicative conditionals', *Theoretical Linguistics* 1 (1974), 257–269.
[167]   Lewis, D., *Convention: A Philosophical Study*, Harvard University Press, Cambridge, Ma. 1969.
[168]   Lewis, D., *Counterfactuals*, Harvard University Press, Cambridge, Ma. 1973.
[169]   Morgan, J., 'Two types of convention in indirect speech acts' in P. Cole (ed.), *Syntax and Semantics, Vol. 9: Pragmatics*, Academic Press 1978, pp. 261–280.
[170]   Pollock, J., *Subjunctive Reasoning*, D. Reidel, Dordrecht 1975.
[171]   Poythress, V., 'A formalism for describing rules of conversation', *Semiotica* 7 (1973), 285–299.
[172]   Rescher, N., 'Belief-contravening suppositions and the problem of contrary-to-fact conditionals', *Philosophical Review* 60 (1961), 176–196.
[173]   Rescher, N., *Hypothetical Reasoning*, North-Holland, Amsterdam 1964.
[174]   Sadock, J., 'Queclaratives', *CLS* 7, Chicago Linguistics Society, 1971, 223–232.
[175]   Sadock, J., *Toward a Linguistic Theory of Speech Acts*, Academic Press, New York 1974.
[176]   Sperber, D., and D. Wilson, 'Language and relevance', forthcoming.
[177]   Stalnaker, R., 'A theory of conditionals', in N. Rescher (ed.), *Studies in Logical Theory*, Blackwell, Oxford 1968.
[178]   Strawson, P., 'Intention and convention in speech acts', *Philosophical Review* 73 (1964), 439–460.
[179]   Tichy, P., 'A new theory of subjunctive conditionals', *Synthese* 37 (1978), 433–458.
[180]   Weiner, S. and D. Goodenough, 'A move toward a psychology of conversation', in R. Freedle (ed.), *Discourse Production and Comprehension*, Ablex, Norwood, N.J., 1977, pp. 213–225.
[181]   Werth, P., 'The concept of relevance in conversational analysis', in P. Werth (ed.), *Conversation, Speech, and Discourse*, Croom Helm, 1981.
[182]   Wilson, D., and D. Sperber, 'On defining "relevance"', to appear in R. Grandy (ed.), *Festschrift for Paul Grice*.

CHAPTER 5

[183]   Christensen, F., 'A generative rhetoric of the paragraph', *College Composition and Communication* 16 (1965).
[184]   Clements, P., 'The effects of staging on recall from prose', in R. Freedle (ed.), *New Directions in Discourse Processing*, Ablex, N.J. 1979, pp. 287–330.
[185]   Covelli, L. and S. Murray, 'Accomplishing topic change', *Anthropological Linguistics* 22/9 (1980).
[186]   Donaldson, S., 'One kind of speech act: how do we know when we're conversing?' *Semiotica* 28 (1979), 259–299.
[187]   Dressler, W., 'Towards a semantic deep structure of discourse grammar', *CLS* 6, Chicago Linguistic Society 1970, 202–209.

[188]   Duncan, S., 'Some signals and rules for taking speaking turns in conversation',
        Journal of Personality and Social Psychology **23** (1972), 283–292.
[189]   Duncan, S., 'Toward a grammar for dyadic conversation', *Semiotica* **9** (1973),
        29–45.
[190]   Duncan, S., 'On the structure of speaker-auditor interaction during speaking
        turns', *Language and Society* **3** (1974), 161–180.
[191]   Duncan, S., and Niederehe, G., 'On signaling that it's your turn to speak',
        Journal of Experimental Social Psychology **10** (1974), 234–247.
[192]   Ervin-Tripp, S., 'An analysis of the interaction of language, topic, and listeners',
        American Anthropologist **66** (1964), 86–102.
[193]   Fodor, J., *The Language of Thought*, Crowell, New York 1975.
[194]   Freedle, R., 'Dialogue and inquiring systems: the development of a social
        logic', *Human Development* **18** (1975), 97–118.
[195]   Garfinkel, H. *Studies in Ethnomethodology*, Prentice-Hall, Englewood Cliffs,
        N.J. 1967.
[196]   Good, C., 'Language as social activity: Negotiating conversation', *Journal of
        Pragmatics* **3** (1979), 151–167.
[197]   Hamblin, C., 'Mathematical models of dialogue', *Theoria* **37** (1971), 130–
        155.
[198]   Heritage, J. and D. Watson, 'Aspects of the properties of formulations in natural
        conversations: some instances analyzed', *Semiotica* **30** (1980), 245–262.
[199]   Hurtig, R., 'Toward a functional theory of discourse', in R. Freedle (ed.),
        Discourse Production and Comprehension, Ablex, Norwood, N.J. 1977, pp.
        89–106.
[200]   Jefferson, G., 'Side sequences', in D. Sudnow (eds.), *Studies in Social Interac-
        tion*, Free Press, New York 1972, pp. 294–338.
[201]   Keller, E., 'Gambits: Conversational strategy signals', *Journal of Pragmatics* **3**
        (1979), 219–238.
[202]   Kendon, A., 'Some functions of gaze direction in social interaction', *Acta
        Psychologica* **26** (1967), 22–63.
[203]   Klammer, T., 'Foundations for a theory of dialogue structure', *Poetics* **9** (1973),
        27–64.
[204]   Kummer, W., 'Outlines of a model for a grammar of discourse', *Poetics* **3** (1972),
        29–56.
[205]   Maynard, D. 'Placement of topic changes in conversation', *Semiotica* **30** (1980),
        263–290.
[206]   Meritt, M., 'On questions following questions in service encounters', *Language in
        Society* **5** (1976), 315–357.
[207]   Mohan, B., 'Do sequencing rules exist?', *Semiotica* **12** (1974), 74–96.
[208]   Nowakowska, M., 'Towards a formal theory of dialogues', *Semiotica* **17** (1976),
        291–313.
[209]   Ochs, E., 'Planned and unplanned discourse', in T. Givon (ed.), *Syntax and
        Semantics 14: Discourse Analysis*, Academic Press, New York 1979.
[210]   Paun, G., 'A generative model of conversation', *Semiotica* **17** (1976), 21–
        33.
[211]   Plato, *Theaetetus, Sophist*, with English translation, ed. H. Fowler, Loeb Clas-
        sical Library, Harvard University Press 1921.

[212] Posner, R., 'Types of dialogue – the use of microstructures for the classification of texts', in R. Hilpinen (ed.), *Rationality in Science*, D. Reidel, Dordrecht 1980, pp. 111–135.

[213] Poyatos, F., 'Interactive functions and limitations of verbal and nonverbal behavior in natural conversation', *Semiotica* 30 (1980), 211–244.

[214] Ritchie, G. *Computational Grammar: An Artificial Intelligence Approach to Linguistic Description*, The Harvester Press, Sussex 1980.

[215] Sacks, H., E. Schegloff, and G. Jefferson, 'A simplest systematics for the organization of turn-taking in conversation', *Language* 50 (1974), 696–735.

[216] Schank, R., and R. Abelson, *Scripts, Plans, Goals and Understanding: An Inquiry into Human Knowledge Structures*, Lawrence Erlbaum Associates, Hillsdale, N.J., 1977.

[217] Schegloff, E., 'Sequencing in conversational openings', *American Anthropologist* 70 (1968), 1075–1095.

[218] Schegloff, E., 'Notes on a conversational practice: formulating place', in D. Sudnow (eds.), *Studies in Social Interaction*, Free Press, New York 1972, pp. 75–119.

[219] Schegloff, E. and H. Sacks, 'Opening up closings', *Semiotica* 8 (1973), 289–327.

[220] Schegloff, E., G. Jefferson and H. Sacks, 'The preference of self-correction in the connection of the organization of repair conversation', *Language* 53 (1977), 361–382.

[221] Schenkein, J., 'Towards an analysis of natural conversations and the sense of *heheh*', *Semiotica* 6 (1972), 344–377.

[222] Schenkein, J., 'An introduction to the study of "socialization" through analyses of conversational interaction', *Semiotica* 24 (1978), 277–304.

[223] Schenkein, J., *Studies in the Organization of Conversational Interaction*, Academic Press, New York 1978.

[224] Schlesinger, I., 'Towards a structural analysis of discussions', *Semiotica* 11 (1974), 109–122.

[225] Sudnow, D. (ed.), *Studies in Social Interaction*, Free Press, New York 1972.

[226] Turner, R., 'Utterance positioning as an interactional resource', *Semiotica* 17 (1976), 233–254.

[227] Ventola, E., 'The structure of casual conversation in English', *Journal of Pragmatics* 3 (1979), 267–298.

[228] Vuchinich, S., 'Elements of cohesion between turns in ordinary conversation', *Semiotica* 20 (1977), 229–257.

[229] Weizenbaum, J., 'ELIZA – a computer program for the study of natural language communication between man and machine', *Communications of the Association for Computing Machinery* 9 (1966), 36–45.

[230] Weizenbaum, J., 'Contextual understanding by computers', *Communications of the Association for Computing Machinery* 10 (1967), 474–480.

[231] Winograd, T., *Procedures as a Representation for Data in a Computer Program for Understanding Natural Language*, Artificial Intelligence Laboratory Report AI TR–17, MIT, Cambridge 1971.

[232] Winograd, T., 'Understanding natural language', *Cognitive Psychology* 3 (1972), 1–191.

CHAPTER 6

[233]   Bennett, M., 'A response to Karttunen on questions', *Linguistics and Philosophy* 1 (1977), 279–300.

[234]   Beth, E., 'Semantic entailment and formal derivability', *Mededelingen van de Koninklijke Nederlandse Akademie van Wetenschappen*, Afd. Letterkunde, N.R., Vol. 18, No. 13, Amsterdam 1955, pp. 309–342. Reprinted in J. Hintikka (ed.), *Philosophy of Mathematics*, Oxford University Press, Oxford 1969, pp. 9–41.

[235]   Beth, E., *Aspects of Modern Logic*, D. Reidel, Dordrecht 1970.

[236]   Carlson, L., 'Plural quantification', in preparation, to appear in *Acta Philosophica Fennica*.

[237]   Chang, C., and H. Keisler, *Model Theory*, North-Holland, Amsterdam 1973.

[238]   Fitch, F., 'Natural deduction rules for English', *Philosophical Studies* 24 (1973), 89–104.

[239]   Günther, A., *Dialogkonstruktionen auf der Basis logischer Ableitungen*, Ph.D. dissertation, Bonn 1977.

[240]   Higginbotham, J., and R. May, 'Questions, Quantifiers, and crossing', *The Linguistic Review* 1 (1981), 41–80.

[241]   Hirschbühler, P., *The Syntax and Semantics of Wh-constructions*, Indiana University Linguistics Club, Bloomington, Indiana 1979.

[242]   Jeffrey, R., *Formal Logic: Its Scope and Limits*, McGraw-Hill, New York 1967.

[243]   Karttunen, L., 'Questions revisited', to appear in the proceedings of the Albany conference on Montague Grammar, philosophy, and linguistics.

[244]   Lorenz, K., 'Dialogspiele als semantische Grundlage von Logik-kalkülen', *Archiv für mathematische Logik und Grundlagen-forschung* 11 (1968), 32–55, 73–100.

[245]   Lorenzen, P., *Normative Logic and Ethics*, Mannheim 1969.

[246]   Lorenzen, P., *Konstruktive Logik, Ethik und Wissenschaftstheorie*, Bibliographisches Institut, Mannheim 1975.

[247]   Saarinen, E., 'Dialogue semantics vs. game-theoretical semantics', in P. Asquith and I. Hacking (eds.), *PSA 1978*, Vol. 2, East Lansing, Michigan (in press).

CHAPTER 7

[248]   Boër, S. and W. Lycan, 'Invited inferences and other unwelcome guests', *Papers in Linguistics* 6 (1973), 483–505.

[249]   Castañeda, H., 'On the logic of self-knowledge', *Noûs* 1 (1967), 9–21.

[250]   Castañeda, H., 'On the logic of attributing self-knowledge to others', *Journal of Philosophy* 65 (1968), 439–456.

[251]   Castañeda, H., 'On knowing (or believing) that one knows (or believes)', *Synthese* 21 (1970), 187–203.

[252]   Collins, A., 'Unconscious belief', *Journal of Philosophy* 66 (1969), 667–680.

[253]   Geach, P., 'On beliefs about oneself', *Analysis* 18 (1957), 23–24.

[254]   Geis, M., and A. Zwicky, 'On invited inferences', *Linguistic Inquiry* 2/4 (1971).

[255] Ginet, C., 'What must be added to knowing to obtain knowing that one knows', *Synthese* 21 (1970), 113–186.

[256] Gordon, D. and G. Lakoff, 'Conversational postulates', *CLS* 7, Chicago Linguistic Society, Chicago 1971, 63–84.

[257] Grice, P., 'Further notes on logic and conversation', in P. Cole (ed.), *Syntax and Semantics, Vol. 9: Pragmatics*, Academic Press, New York 1978, pp. 113–127.

[258] Harnish, R., 'Logical form and implicature', in T. Bever, J. Katz and D. Langendoen (eds.), *An Integrated Theory of Linguistic Ability*, Harvester Press, Sussex 1977.

[259] Hilpinen, R., 'Knowing that one knows and the classical definition of knowledge', *Synthese* 21 (1970), 109–132.

[260] Hintikka, J., 'Knowing oneself and other problems of epistemic logic', *Theoria* 32 (1966), 1–13.

[261] Hintikka, J., 'On attributions of "self-knowledge"', *Journal of Philosophy* 67 (1970), 73–87.

[262] Hintikka, J., 'Knowing that one knows reviewed', *Synthese* 21 (1970), 141–161.

[263] Horn, L., 'Greek Grice: A brief survey of protoconversational rules in the history of logic', *CLS* 9, Chicago Linguistic Society, 1973, 205–214.

[264] Hungerland, I., 'Contextual implication', *Inquiry* 3 (1960), 211–258.

[265] Johnson-Laird, P. and M. Steedman, 'The psychology of syllogisms', *Cognitive Psychology* 10 (1978), 64–99.

[266] Johnson-Laird, P., 'Models of deduction', in R. Falmagne (ed.), *Reasoning: Representations and Processes in Adults and Children*, Erlbaum, Hillsdale N.J.

[267] Karttunen, L., and S. Peters, 'Conventional implicature', in C. Oh and D. Dinneen (eds.), *Syntax and Semantics, Vol. 11: Presupposition*, Academic Press, New York 1979, pp. 1–56.

[268] Kummer, W., 'Aspects of a theory of argumentation', in E. Gülich and W. Raible (eds.), *Textsorten*, Athenäum, Frankfurt 1972, pp. 25–50.

[269] Kummer, W., 'Pragmatic implication', in J. Petöfi and H. Rieser (eds.), *Studies in Text Grammar*, D. Reidel, Dordrecht 1973, pp. 96–112.

[270] Lakoff, G., 'Pragmatics and natural logic', in E. Keenan (ed.), *Formal Semantics of Natural Languages*, Cambridge University Press, Cambridge 1975.

[271] Lehrer, K., 'Believing that one knows', *Synthese* 21 (1970), 133–140.

[272] Morgan, J., 'Conversational postulates revisited', *Language* 53 (1977), 277–284.

[273] Ochs Keenan, E., 'The universality of conversational postulates', *Language in Society* 5 (1976), 67–80.

[274] Pailthorp, C., 'Hintikka and knowing that one knows', *Journal of Philosophy* 64 (1967), 487–500.

[275] Sadock, J., 'Modus brevis: The truncated argument', *CLS* 13, Chicago Linguistic Society, Chicago, Ill. 1977, 545–554.

[276] Sadock, J., 'On testing for conversational implicature', in P. Cole (ed.), *Syntax and Semantics, Vol. 9: Pragmatics*, Academic Press, New York 1978, pp. 281–297.

[277] de Sousa, R., 'Knowledge, consistent belief, and self-consciousness', *Journal of Philosophy* 67 (1970), 66–73.

[278]   Walker, R., 'Conversational implicatures', in S. Blackburn (ed.), *Meaning, Reference and Necessity*, Cambridge University Press, Cambridge 1975, 133–181.

[279]   Wiggins, D., 'On knowing, knowing that one knows and consciousness', in E. Saarinen et al. (eds.), *Essays in Honour of Jaakko Hintikka*, D. Reidel, Dordrecht 1979, pp. 237–248.

[280]   Wilson, D., and D. Sperber, 'On Grice's theory of conversation', in P. Werth (ed.), *Conversation, Speech and Discourse*, Croom Helm 1981.

CHAPTER 8

[281]   Arbini, R., 'Tag-questions and tag-imperatives in English', *Journal of Linguistics* 5 (1969), 205–214.

[282]   Austin, H. *How to do Things with Words*, Clarendon Press, Oxford 1962.

[283]   van der Auwera, J., *Indirect Speech Acts Revisited*, Indiana University Linguistics Club, Bloomington, Indiana 1980.

[284]   Bach, K. and R. Harnish, *Linguistic Communication and Speech Acts*, MIT Press, Cambridge, Ma. 1979.

[285]   Bell, M., 'Questioning', *The Philosophical Quarterly* 25 (1975), 193–212.

[286]   Bolinger, D., 'Yes-no questions are not alternative questions', in H. Hiż (ed.), *Questions*, D. Reidel, Dordrecht 1978.

[287]   Bolinger, D., 'Asking more than one thing at a time', in H. Hiż (ed.), *Questions*, D. Reidel, Dordrecht 1978.

[288]   Brown, P. and S. Levinson, 'Universals in language use: Politeness phenomena', in E. Goody (ed.), *Questions and Politeness: Strategies in Social Interaction*, Cambridge University Press, Cambridge 1978, pp. 56–310.

[289]   Cattell, R., 'Negative transportation and tag questions', *Language* 49 (1973), 612–639.

[290]   Cohen, L., 'Speech acts', in T. Sebeok (ed.), *Current Trends in Linguistics*, Mouton, The Hague 1974.

[291]   Cole, P. and J. Morgan (ed.), *Syntax and Semantics, Vol. 3: Speech Acts*, Academic Press, New York 1975.

[292]   Culicover, P., *Syntactic and Semantic Investigations*, Ph.D. diss., MIT 1970.

[293]   Culicover, P., 'On the coherence of syntactic descriptions', *Journal of Linguistics* 9 (1973), 35–51.

[294]   Ferrara, A., 'An extended theory of speech acts: appropriateness conditions for subordinate speech acts in sequences', *Journal of Pragmatics* 4 (1980), 233–252.

[295]   Ferrara, A., 'Appropriateness conditions for entire sequences of speech acts', *Journal of Pragmatics* 4 (1980), 321–240.

[296]   Fraser, B., 'On accounting for illocutionary forces', in S. Anderson and P. Kiparsky (eds.), *A Festschrift for Morris Halle*, Holt, Rinehart and Winston, New York 1973, pp. 287–307.

[297]   Fraser, B., 'The concept of politeness', in the proceedings of the colloquium on new ways of analyzing variation in English, Georgetown University Press, Washington D.C.

[298] Horn, L., 'Remarks on neg-raising', in P. Cole (ed.), *Syntax and Semantics Vol. 9: Pragmatics*, Academic Press, New York 1978, pp. 129–220.

[299] Huddleston, R., 'Two approaches to the analysis of tags', *Journal of Linguistics* 6 (1970), 215–222.

[300] Katz, J., *Propositional Structure and Illocutionary Meaning*, Crowell, New York 1977.

[301] Kiefer, F., 'Yes-no questions as wh-questions', in J. Searle, F. Kiefer and M. Bierwisch (eds.), *Speech Act Theory and Pragmatics*, D. Reidel, Dordrecht 1980, pp. 97–119.

[302] Klima, E., 'Negation in English', in J. Fodor and J. Katz (eds.), *The Structure of Language*, Prentice-Hall, Englewood Cliffs, N.J. 1964.

[303] Lakoff, R., 'A syntactic argument for negative transportation', *CLS 5*, Chicago Linguistic Society 1969.

[304] Lakoff, R., 'Questionable answers and answerable questions', in B. Kachru, R. Lees, Y. Malkiel, A. Pietrangeli, and S. Saporta (eds.), *Issues in Linguistics: Papers in Honor of Henry and Renée Kahane*, University of Illinois Press, Urbana, Ill. 1973, pp. 453–467.

[305] Lakoff, R., 'The logic of politeness: on minding your P's and Q's', *CLS* 9, Chicago Linguistic Society, 1973, 292–305.

[306] Malone, J., 'A transformational re-examination of English questions', *Language* 43 (1967), 686–702.

[307] McCarthy, J., 'Formalization of two puzzles involving knowledge', MS., Artificial Intelligence Laboratory, Computer Science Dept., Stanford University, Stanford, Ca. 1978.

[308] Morin, Y., 'Tag questions in French', *Linguistic Inquiry* 4 (1973), 97–100.

[309] Pollack, J., 'A problem for neg-raising', in E. Fox et al. (eds.), *CLS Book of Squibs*, Chicago Linguistic Society, Chicago 1977, pp. 72–73.

[310] Pope, E., *Questions and Answers in English*, Mouton, the Hague 1976.

[311] Ross, J., 'Where to do things with words', in P. Cole and J. Morgan (eds.), *Syntax and Semantics, Vol. 3: Speech Acts*, Academic Press, 1975, pp. 253–256.

[312] Sarles, H., 'An examination of the question-response system in language', *Semiotica* 2 (1970), 79–101.

[313] Schmidt-Radefelt, J., 'On so-called rhetorical questions', *Journal of Pragmatics* 1 (1977), 375–392.

[314] Searle, J. *Speech Acts: an Essay in the Philosophy of Language*, Cambridge University Press, Cambridge 1969.

[315] Searle, J., 'Indirect speech acts', in P. Cole and J. Morgan (eds.), *Syntax and Semantics, Vol. 3: Speech Acts*, Academic Press 1975, pp. 59–82.

[316] Searle, J., 'A classification of illocutionary acts', *Language and Society* 5 (1976), 1–23.

[317] Searle, J., *Expression and Meaning: Studies in the Theory of Speech Acts*, Cambridge University Press, Cambridge 1979.

[318] Searle, J., F. Kiefer, and M. Bierwisch (eds.), *Speech Act Theory and Pragmatics*, D. Reidel, Dordrecht 1980.

[319] Seuren, P., 'Negative's travels', in P. Seuren (ed.), *Semantic Syntax*, Oxford University Press, Oxford 1974, pp. 183–208.

[320]   Wunderlich, D., *Studien zur Sprechakttheorie*, Suhrkamp, Frankfurt am Main 1976.

[321]   Wunderlich, D., 'On problems of speech act theory', in R. Butts and J. Hintikka (eds.), *Basic Problems in Methodology and Linguistics*, D. Reidel, Dordrecht 1977, pp. 243–258.

[322]   Wunderlich, D., *Foundations of Linguistics*, Cambridge University Press, Cambridge 1979.

[323]   Wunderlich, D., 'Methodological remarks on speech act theory', in J. Searle et al. (eds.), *Speech Act Theory and Pragmatics*, D. Reidel, Dordrecht 1980, pp. 291–312.

PART II
CHAPTER 1

[324]   de Beaugrande, R., *Text, Discourse and Process: Toward a Multidisciplinary Science of Texts*, Ablex, Norwood N.J. 1980.

[325]   de Beaugrande, R., 'The pragmatics of discourse planning', *Journal of Pragmatics* 4 (1980), 15–42.

[326]   Bellert, I., 'On a condition of the coherence of texts', *Semiotica* 2 (1970), 335–363.

[327]   Bolinger, D., 'Judgments of grammaticality', *Lingua* 21 (1968), 34–40.

[328]   Behre, P., 'On the principle of connecting elements of speech in contemporary English', in G. A. Bonnard (ed.), *English Studies Today*, Francke Verlag, Bern 1961.

[329]   Christensen, F., 'A generative rhetoric of the sentence', *College Composition and Communication* 14 (1963).

[330]   Crothers, E., *Paragraph Structure Inference*, Ablex, Norwood, N.J. 1979.

[331]   Curme, G., *A Grammar of the English Language, Vol II: Syntax*, D.C. Heath & Co., 1931.

[332]   Dascal, M., 'Digression: A study in conversational coherence', MS., Tel Aviv University, 1979.

[333]   Dascal, M. and A. Margalit, 'A new "revolution" in linguistics – "text grammars" vs. sentence grammars', *Theoretical linguistics* 1 (1974), 195–213.

[334]   van Dijk, T., *Text and Context: Explorations in the Semantics and Pragmatics of Discourse*, Longman, London 1977.

[335]   Dik, S., *Functional Grammar*, North-Holland, Amsterdam 1978.

[336]   Dinsmore, J., *Pragmatics, Formal Theory, and the Analysis of Supposition*, Indiana University Linguistics Club, Bloomington, Indiana 1981.

[337]   Enkvist, N., 'Coherence, pseudo-coherence, and non-coherence', in J. Östman (ed.), *Cohesion and Semantics*, Publications of the Research Institute of the Åbo Academic Foundation 41, Åbo 1978.

[338]   Freedle, R. (ed.), *Discourse Production and Comprehension*, Ablex, Norwood, N.J. 1977.

[339]   Freedle, R. (ed.), *New Directions in Discourse Processing*, Ablex, Norwood, N.J. 1979.

[340]   Gazdar, G., *Formal Pragmatics for Natural Language*, Academic Press, London and New York 1978.

[341] Givon, T. (ed.), *Syntax and Semantics, Vol. 12: Discourse and Syntax*, Academic Press, New York.

[342] Gleason, H., 'Contrastive analysis in discourse structure', *Monograph Series on Languages and Linguistics* 21, Georgetown University Press, Washington, D.C. 1968.

[343] Gray, B., 'From discourse to dialog', *Journal of Pragmatics* 1 (1977), 283–298.

[344] Gray, B., *The Grammatical Foundations of Rhetoric: Discourse Analysis*, Mouton, the Hague 1977.

[345] Grimes, J., *The Thread of Discourse*, Mouton, the Hague 1975.

[346] Gulstad, D., 'A generative discourse model', *Linguistics* 99 (1973), 5–70.

[347] Gunter, R., *Sentences in Dialog*, Hornbeam Press, Columbia, S. C. 1974.

[348] Gutwinski, W., *Cohesion in Literary Texts: A Study of Some Grammatical and Lexical Features of English Discourse*, Mouton, the Hague 1976.

[349] Halliday, M., 'Descriptive linguistics and literary studies', in G. Duthie (ed.), *English Studies Today*, Edinburgh 1964, pp. 25–39.

[350] Halliday, M., 'The linguistic study of literary texts', in H. Lunt (ed.), *Proceedings of the IXth International Congress of Linguists*, The Hague 1968, pp. 302–307.

[351] Halliday, M. and R. Hasan, *Cohesion in English*, Longman, London 1976.

[352] Hasan, R., *Grammatical Cohesion in Spoken and Written English*, Longman, London 1968.

[353] Henne, H., *Sprachpragmatik*, Niemeyer, Tübingen 1975.

[354] Householder, F., 'On arguments from asterisks', *Foundations of Language* 10 (1973), 365–376.

[355] Jackendoff, R., *Semantic Interpretation in Generative Grammar*, MIT Press, Cambridge, Ma. 1972.

[356] Jespersen, O., *A Modern English Grammar on Historical Principles, Part VII: Syntax*, completed and edited by Niels Haislund, George Allen and Unwin Ltd., London 1949.

[357] Jespersen, O., *Essentials of English Grammar*, University of Alabama Press, Alabama 1964.

[358] Joshi, A., B. Webber and I. Sag (ed.), *Discourse Structure and Discourse Setting*, Cambridge University Press, Cambridge (to appear).

[359] Kinnleavy, J., *A Theory of Discourse*, Norton, New York 1971.

[360] Kinnleavy, J., J. Cope and J. Campbell, *The Design of Discourse*, Prentice-Hall, Englewood Cliffs, N.J. 1969.

[361] Kruisinga, E., and P. Erades, *An English Grammar, Vol. I*, Groningen 1953.

[362] Kummer, W., *Grundlagen der Texttheorie*, Rowohlt, Reinbek 1975.

[363] Morgan, J., *English Structures above the Sentence Level*, Monograph series on language and linguistics 20, Georgetown University Press, Washington, D.C. 1967.

[364] Onions, C., *Advanced English Syntax*, Routledge and Kegan Paul, London 1904.

[365] Östman, J. (ed.), *Cohesion and Semantics*, Publications of the Research Institute of the Åbo Akademi Foundation 41, Åbo 1978.

[366] Petöfi, J. and H. Rieser (ed.), *Studies in Text Grammar*, D. Reidel, Dordrecht 1973.

[367] Pierrehumbert, J., Review of T. van Dijk, Text and Context, *Journal of Linguistics* **16** (1980).

[368] Polanyi, L., 'So what's the point?', *Semiotica* **25** (1979), 207–241.

[369] Poutsma, H., *A Grammar of Late Modern English, Part I: The Sentence*, P. Noordhoff, Groningen 1928.

[370] Pratt, M., *Toward a Speech Act Theory of Literary Discourse*, Indiana University Press, Bloomington, Indiana 1977.

[371] Quirk, R., S. Greenbaum, G. Leech and J. Svartvik, *A Grammar of Contemporary English*, Longman, London 1972.

[372] Reinhart, T., 'Conditions on text coherence', *Poetics Today* 1/3 (1979).

[373] Rosengren, I. (ed.), *Sprache und Pragmatik: Lunder Symposium 1978*, CWK Gleerup, Malmö 1979.

[374] Ruhl, C., 'Prerequisites for a linguistic description of coherence', *Language Sciences* **25** (1973).

[375] Saloni, Z., and A. Trybulec, 'Coherence of a text and its topology', *Semiotica* **11** (1974), 101–108.

[376] Scherzer, D., 'Dialogic incongruities in the theater of the absurd', *Semiotica* **22** (1978), 269–285.

[377] Schlieben-Lange, B., *Linguistische Pragmatik*, Kohlhammer, Stuttgart 1975.

[378] Schmidt, J., *Texttheorie: Probleme einer Linguistik der sprachlichen Kommunikation*, Fink, München 1973.

[379] Sinclair, J., and R. Coulthard, *Towards an Analysis of Discourse*, Oxford University Press, London 1975.

[380] Smith, C., 'Sentences in discourse: An analysis of a discourse by Bertrand Russell', *Journal of Linguistics* 7 (1971).

[381] de Sola Pool, I., *Trends in Content Analysis*, New York 1959.

[382] Steinmann, M. (ed.), *New Rhetorics*, Charles Scribner's Sons, New York 1967.

[383] Stockwell, R., P. Schachter, and B. Partee, *Integration of Transformational Theories of Syntax, Vol. 2*, Electronic Systems Division, University of California 1968.

[384] Sweet, H., *A New English Grammar: Logical and Historical, Part II: Syntax*, Clarendon Press, Oxford 1898.

[385] Warren, W., D. Nicholas, and T. Trabasso, 'Event chains and inferences in understanding narratives', in R. Freedle (ed.), *New Directions in Discourse Processing*, Ablex, Norwood, N.J. 1979, pp. 23–52.

[386] Williams, E., 'Discourse and logical form', *Linguistic Inquiry* 8 (1977), 101–139.

[387] Winterowd, R., 'The grammar of coherence', *College English* **31** (1969), 828–835.

[388] Young, R., A. Becker, and K. Pike, *Rhetoric: Discovery and Change*, Harcourt, Brace and World, New York 1970.

[389] Ziv, Y., 'On the relevance of context to the form-function correlation', *Papers from the Parasession on Functionalism*, Chicago Linguistic Society, Chicago 1975, pp. 568–579.

CHAPTER 2

[390]   Abraham, W., 'Some semantic properties of some conjunctions', in S. Corder and E. Roulet (eds.), *Some Implications of Linguistic Theory for Applied Linguistics*, Aimav & Didier, Brussels and Paris 1975, pp. 7–31.

[391]   Akademija Nauk SSSR, Institut russkogo jazyka, *Slovar' sovremennogo russkogo jazyka, Tom I*, A–B, Izdatel'stvo Akademii Nauk SSSR, Moskva and Leningrad 1950.

[392]   Akademija Nauk SSSR, Institut russkogo jazyka, *Grammatika russkogo jazyka, Tom II*: Sintaksis, Čast' vtoraja. Izdatel'stvo Akademii Nauk SSSR, Moskva 1960.

[393]   Aristotle, *Topics*, translated by E. S. Forster, Loeb Classical Library No. 391, Heinemann, London; Harvard University Press, Cambridge, Ma. 1960.

[394]   Bellert, I., 'On certain syntactical properties of the English connectives *and* and *but*', *Transformations and Discourse Analysis Papers* 64, University of Pennsylvania, Dept. of Linguistics 1966.

[395]   Carden, G., 'Modus brevis and the Easter bunny', *CLS Book of Squibs*, Chicago Linguistic Society, Chicago 1977, pp. 24–25.

[396]   Chatman, S., 'English sentence connectives', in *Studies in Languages and Linguistics in Honor of Charles C. Fries*, Ann Arbor, Michigan 1964.

[397]   Crockett, D., 'More on conjunction reduction', *CLS* 8, Chicago Linguistic Society, Chicago 1972, 52–61.

[398]   Dascal, M. and T. Katriel, 'Between semantics and pragmatics: the two types of "but" – Hebrew "aval" and "ela"', *Theoretical Linguistics* 4 (1977), 143–172.

[399]   van Dijk, T., 'Pragmatic connectives', *Journal of Pragmatics* 3 (1979), 447–456.

[400]   Dik, S., *Co-ordination: Its Implications for the Theory of General Linguistics*, North-Holland, Amsterdam 1968.

[401]   Dougherty, R., 'A grammar of coordinate conjoined structures I', *Language* 46 (1970), 850–898.

[402]   Dougherty, R., 'A grammar of coordinate conjoined structues II', *Language* 47 (1971), 298–339.

[403]   Fraser, B., 'An examination of the performative analysis', *Papers in Linguistics* 7 (1974), 1–40.

[404]   Fretheim, T., 'Conjunction and pragmatics', in *Proceedings of the Scandinavian Seminar on Philosophy of Language*, Vol. 2, Uppsala 1974, pp. 19–46.

[405]   Fretheim, T., 'Exclusive and non-exclusive coordination', *Working Papers in Linguistics* 6 (1974), University of Oslo.

[406]   Gazdar, G. and G. Pullum, 'Truth-functional connectives in natural language', *CLS* 12, Chicago Linguistic Society, Chicago 1976, 220–234.

[407]   Gazdar, G., 'Univocal "or"', *CLS Book of Squibs*, Chicago Linguistic Society, Chicago 1977, pp. 44–45.

[408]   Gleitman, L., 'Coordinating conjunctions in English', *Language* 41 (1965), 260–293.

[409]   Goddard, C., *On the Semantics of Conjunctions*, B.A. honours thesis, Australian National University, November 1976.

[410]   Green, G., 'The expressions of emphatic conjunctions in natural language',
        Foundations of Language **10** (1973), 197–248.
[411]   Lakoff, R., 'Ifs, ands, and buts about conjunction', in C. Fillmore and D.
        Langendoen (eds.), *Studies in Linguistic Semantics*, Holt, Rinehart and Winston,
        New York 1971, pp. 115–150.
[412]   Lang, E., *Studien zur Semantik der koordinativen Verknüpfung*, Ph.D. diss.,
        Akademie der Wissenschaften der DDR, Berlin.
[413]   Leibniz, G., *New Essays Concerning Human Understanding*, Cambridge Univer-
        sity Press, Cambridge 1981.
[414]   Levin, J., 'Über eine Gruppe von Konjunktionen im Russischen', *Studien zur
        Grammatik des Deutschen* **2**.
[415]   Locke, J., *An Essay Concerning Human Understanding*, London 1775.
[416]   McCawley, J., 'A program for logic', in D. Davidson and G. Harman (eds.),
        Semantics of Natural Language, D. Reidel, Dordrecht 1972, pp. 498–544.
[417]   Naess, A., 'A study of "or" ', *Synthese* **13** (1961), 49–60.
[418]   Pelletier, F., 'Or', *Theoretical Linguistics* **4** (1977), 60–74.
[419]   Piaget, J., *Judgment and Reasoning in the Child*, Routledge and Kegan Paul,
        London 1951.
[420]   Piaget, J., *Thought and Judgment in the Child*, Routledge and Kegan Paul,
        London 1952.
[421]   Posner, R., 'Semantics and pragmatics of sentence connectives in natural lan-
        guage', in J. Searle, F. Kiefer and M. Bierwisch (eds.), *Speech Act Theory and
        Pragmatics*, D. Reidel, Dordrecht 1980, pp. 169–203.
[422]   Reis, M., 'Further ands and buts about conjunction', *CLS* **10**, Chicago Linguistic
        Society, Chicago 1974, 539–550.
[423]   Robinson, R., 'Begging the question, 1971', *Analysis* **31** (1971), 113–117.
[424]   Ross, J., 'On declarative sentences', in R. Jacobs and P. Rosenbaum (eds.),
        Readings in English Transformational Grammar, Ginn, Waltham, Ma. 1970,
        pp. 222–272.
[425]   Schmerling, S., 'Asymmetric conjunction and rules of conversation', in P. Cole
        and J. Morgan (eds.), *Syntax and Semantics* **3**, Academic Press, New York 1975,
        pp. 211–232.
[426]   Staal, J., 'And', *Journal of Linguistics* **4** (1968), 79–81.

                                    CHAPTER 3

[427]   Adamec, P., *Porjadok slov v sovremennom russkom jazyke*, Prague 1966.
[428]   Akmajian, A., S. Steele and T. Wasow, 'The category AUX in universal grammar',
        Linguistic Inquiry **10** (1979), 1–64.
[429]   Allerton, D., 'The notion of "givenness" and its relations to presupposition and
        to theme', *Lingua* **44** (1978), 133–168.
[430]   Blinkenberg, A., 'L'ordre des mots en français moderne', in *Det Kgl. Danske
        Videnskabernes Selskab, Historiskfilologiske meddelerser* **20**, 1, Copenhagen
        1933.
[431]   Bolinger, D., 'Linear modification', *Publications of the Modern Language
        Association*, 1952, pp. 1117–1144.

[432] Chafe, W., *Meaning and the Structure of Language*, University of Chicago Press, Chicago, Ill. 1970.

[433] Chomsky, N., *Syntactic Structures*, Mouton, The Hague 1957.

[434] Chomsky, N., 'Deep structure, surface structure, and semantic interpretation', in R. Jakobson and S. Kawamoto (eds.), *Studies in General and Oriental Linguistics presented to Shiro Hattori on the Occasion of His Sixtieth Birthday*, TEC Co. Ltd., Tokyo 1970.

[435] Chomsky, N., *Lectures on Government and Binding*, Foris Publications, Dordrecht 1981.

[436] Chomsky, N., and H. Lasnik, 'Filters and control', *Linguistic Inquiry* 8 (1977).

[437] Clark, H. and S. Haviland, 'Comprehension and the given-new contract', in R. Freedle (ed.), *Discourse Production and Comprehension*, Ablex, Norwood, N.J., 1977, pp. 1–40.

[438] Contreras, H., *A Theory of Word Order with Special Reference to Spanish*, North-Holland, Amsterdam 1976.

[439] Dahl, Ö., 'What is new information?', in N. Enkvist and V. Kohonen (eds.), *Reports on Text Linguistics: Approaches to Word Order*, Åbo Akademi, Åbo 1976, pp. 37–50.

[440] Dahl, Ö. (ed.), *Topic and Comment, Contextual Boundness, and Focus*, Helmut Buske Verlag, Hamburg 1974.

[441] Daneš, F., 'A three-level approach to syntax', *Travaux Linguistiques de Prague* 1 (1966), 225–240.

[442] Daneš, F., 'Order of elements and sentence intonation', in *To Honor Roman Jakobson: Essays on the Occasion of His Seventieth Birthday*, Mouton, The Hague 1967, p. 499–512.

[443] Daneš, F., 'Zur linguistischen Analyse der Textstrukturen', *Folia Linguistica* 4 (1969).

[444] Daneš, F. (ed.), *Papers on Functional Sentence Perspective*, Mouton, The Hague 1974.

[445] Daneš, F., et al., 'Zur Terminologie der FSP', in F. Daneš (ed.), *Papers on Functional Sentence Perspective*, Mouton, The Hague 1974, p. 217–222.

[446] Emonds, J., *A Transformational Approach to Syntax: Root, Structure-preserving and Local Transformations*, Academic Press, New York 1976.

[447] Enkvist, N. and V. Kohonen (ed.), *Reports on Text Linguistics: Approaches to Word Order*, Åbo Akademi, Åbo 1976.

[448] Firbas, J., 'From comparative word-order studies', *Brno Studies in English* 4 (1964), 111–128.

[449] Firbas, J., 'A functional view on ordo naturalis', *Brno Studies in English* 13 (1979), p. 29–59.

[450] Fries, C., 'On the development of the structural use of word order in Old English and Modern English', *Language* 16 (1940), 199–208.

[451] Garvin, P. (ed.), *A Prague School Reader on Aesthetics, Library Structure, and Style*, Georgetown University Press, Washington, D.C. 1964.

[452] Green, G., *Semantics and Syntactic Regularity*, Indiana University Press, Bloomington and London 1974.

[453] Gundel, J., *The Role of Topic and Comment in Linguistic Theory*, Indiana University Linguistics Club, Bloomington, Indiana 1977.

[454] Hakulinen, A., 'On some movement rules in Finnish', in Ö. Dahl (ed.), *Papers from the 1st Scandinavian Conference on Linguistics*, Göteborg University, Goteborg 1974, pp. 149–162.

[455] Hakulinen, A., 'Suomen sanajärjestyksen kieliopillisista ja temaattisista tehtävistä (Functions of word order in Finnish)', *Reports on Text Linguistics: Suomen kielen generatiivista lauseoppia* 2, Åbo Akademi, Åbo 1976.

[456] Heinämäki, O., 'Problems of basic word order', in N. Enkvist and V. Kohonen (eds.), *Reports on Text Linguistics: Approaches to Word Order*, Åbo Akademi, Åbo 1976, pp. 95–106.

[457] Isačenko, A., 'O gramatičeskom porjadke slov', *Voprosy Jazykoznanija* 15 (1966), 27–34.

[458] Isačenko, A., 'Frazovoje udarenie i porjadok slov', in *To Honor Roman Jakobson*, Mouton, The Hague and Paris 1967, pp. 967–976.

[459] Janoš, J., 'Some problems of functional sentence perspective in modern Japanese', *Journal of Pragmatics* 2 (1978), 247–260.

[460] Karttunen, F., 'Functional constraints in Finnish syntax', in *Papers from the Parasession on Functionalism*, Chicago Linguistic Society, Chicago 1975, pp. 232–243.

[461] Kiefer, F., *On Emphasis and Word Order in Hungarian*, Mouton, The Hague 1967.

[462] Kiefer, F., 'On the problem of word order', in M. Bierwisch and K. Heidolph (eds.), *Progress in Linguistics*, Mouton, The Hague 1970.

[463] Kirkwood, H., 'Aspects of word order and its communicative function in English and German', *Journal of Linguistics* 5 (1969), 85–107.

[464] Kiss, K., 'Topic and focus in Hungarian syntax', *Montreal Working Papers in Linguistics* 8 (1977), 1–42.

[465] Kiss, K., 'Structural relations in Hungarian, a "free" word order language', *Linguistic Inquiry* 12 (1981), 185–213.

[466] Kučera, H. and E. Cowper, 'Functional sentence perspective revisited', in L. Metejka (ed.), *Sound, Sign, and Meaning*, Michigan Slavic Contributions 6, Ann Arbor, Michigan, pp. 191–230.

[467] Kuno, S., 'The position of locatives in existential sentences', *Linguistic Inquiry* 2 (1971).

[468] Kuno, S., 'Functional sentence perspective', *Linguistic Inquiry* 3 (1972), 269–320.

[469] Kuno, S., *The Structure of the Japanese Language*, MIT Press, Cambridge, Ma. 1973.

[470] Kuno, S., 'Three perspectives in the functional approach to syntax', *Papers from the Parasession on Functionalism*, Chicago Linguistic Society, Chicago 1975, pp. 276–336.

[471] Kuroda, S., 'The categorial and the thetic judgment: evidence from Japanese syntax', *Foundations of Language* 9 (1973), pp. 153–185.

[472] Langacker, R., 'Movement rules in functional perspective', *Language* 50 (1974), 629–664.

[473] Li, C. (ed.), *Word Order and Word Order Change*, University of Texas Press, Austin and London 1973.

[474] Meisel, J. and M. Pam (eds.), *Linear Order and Generative Theory*, John Benjamins, Amsterdam 1979.

[475] Oehrle, R., *The Grammatical Status of the English Dative Alternation*, Ph.D. diss., MIT 1976.

[476] Oh, C., 'Topicalization: *nin* vs. *ka* (comparable to Japanese *wa* vs. *ga*)', *Papers in Linguistics* 5 (1972), 624–655.

[477] Ostler, N., *A Theory of Case Linking and Agreement*, Indiana University Linguistics Club, Bloomington, Indiana 1980.

[478] Prince, E., 'On the given/new distinction', *CLS* 15, Chicago Linguistic Society, Chicago, Ill. 1979.

[479] Rivero, M., 'On topicalization and wh-movement in Spanish', *Linguistic Inquiry* 9 (1977), 513–517.

[480] Rivero, M., 'On left dislocation and topicalization in Spanish', *Linguistic Inquiry* 11 (1980), 363–393.

[481] Rochemont, M., *A Theory of Stylistic Rules in English*, Ph.D. diss., University of Massachusetts at Amherst, 1978.

[482] Schubiger, M., 'The interplay and cooperation of word order and intonation in English', in P. Abercrombie, D. Fry, P. McCarthy, N. Scott and J. Trim (eds.), *In Honour of Daniel Jones*, Longmans, London 1964.

[483] Seiler, H., 'On the syntactic role of word order and prosodic features', *Word* 18 (1962), 121–131.

[484] Sgall, P., 'Focus and contextual boundness', in Ö. Dahl (ed.), *Topic and Comment, Contextual Boundness and Focus*, Helmut Buske Verlag, Hamburg 1974, pp. 25–52.

[485] Smyth, R., Prideaux, G., and Hogan, J., 'The effect of context on dative position', *Lingua* 47 (1979), 24–72.

[486] Spencer, A., *Functional Sentence Perspective and Contrastivity*, Ph.D. diss., University of Essex 1980.

[487] Staal, J., 'Word order in Sanskrit and universal grammar', *Foundations of Language*, Supplementary Series 5, D. Reidel, Dordrecht 1967.

CHAPTER 4

[488] Akmajian, A., 'On deriving cleft sentences from pseudo-cleft sentences', *Linguistic Inquiry* 1 (1970), 149–168.

[489] Akmajian, A., *Aspects of the Grammar of Focus in English*, Ph.D. dissertation, MIT 1970.

[490] Baltin, M., 'Some aspects of cleft sentences in English', MS., MIT 1977.

[491] Bickerton, D., 'Where do presuppositions come from', in C. Oh and D. Dinneen (eds.), *Syntax and Semantics 11: Presupposition*, pp. 235–248.

[492] Boër, S., and W. Lycan, *The Myth of Semantic Supposition*, Indiana University Linguistics Club, Bloomington, Indiana 1976.

[493] Bolinger, D., 'A look at equations and cleft sentences', in E. Fircher (ed.), *Studies for Einar Haugen*, Mouton, The Hague 1972, pp. 96–114.

[494] Bolinger, D., 'Gradience in entailment', *Language Sciences* 4 (1976), 1–13.

[495] Bolinger, D., 'Another glance at main clause phenomena', *Language* 53 (1977), 511–519.

[496] Bolinger, D., *Meaning and Form*, Longmans, London 1977.

[497]   Cantrall, W., *Viewpoint, Reflexives, and the Nature of Noun Phrases*, Mouton,
        The Hague 1974.
[498]   Carter, R., 'A class of emphatic sentences in English', *Papers in Linguistics* 5
        (1972), 402–420.
[499]   Chafe, W., 'Discourse structure and human knowledge', in R. Freedle and J.
        Carroll (eds.), *Language Comprehension and the Acquisition of Knowledge*,
        Winston, New York 1972, p. 41–69.
[500]   Chafe, W., 'Language and consciousness', *Language* 50 (1974), 111–113.
[501]   van Fraassen, B., 'Presuppositions, supervaluations, and free logic', in K. Lambert
        (ed.), *The Logical Way of Doing Things*, Yale University Press, New Haven
        1969.
[502]   Faraci, R., 'On the deep question of pseudo-clefts', MS., MIT 1970.
[503]   Garner, R., '"Presupposition" in philosophy and linguistics', in C. Fillmore and
        D. Langendoen (eds.), *Studies in Linguistic Semantics*, Holt, Rinehart and
        Winston, New York 1971.
[504]   Green, G., 'Main clause phenomena in subordinate clauses', *Language* 52 (1976),
        382–397.
[505]   Gundel, J., 'Where do cleft sentences come from?', *Language* 53 (1977), 543–
        559.
[506]   Hajičova, E., 'Meaning, presupposition and allegation', *Philologica Praguensia*
        56 (1974), 18–25.
[507]   Harries, H., 'The role of cleft sentences in the formation of questions and
        answers: Some evidence from German', *CLS* 8, Chicago Linguistic Society,
        Chicago, Ill. 1972, 124–138.
[508]   Hatcher, A., 'Syntax and the sentence', *Word* 12 (1956), 234–250.
[509]   Hatcher, A., 'Theme and underlying question: Two studies in Spanish word
        order', *Word* 12, Supplement 3, 1956.
[510]   Higgins, F., *The Pseudo-cleft Construction in English*, Ph.D. diss., MIT 1973.
[511]   Horn, L., 'The role of topic-comment in the recall of cleft and pseudo-cleft
        sentences', *CLS* 7, Chicago Linguistic Society, Chicago 1971, 445–453.
[512]   Karttunen, L., 'The semantics of complement sentences', *CLS* 5, Chicago
        Linguistic Society, Chicago, Ill. 1970.
[513]   Karttunen, L., 'Some observations on factivity', *Papers in Linguistics* 4 (1971).
[514]   Karttunen, L., 'Implicative verbs', *Language* 47 (1971), 340–358.
[515]   Karttunen, L., 'Presuppositions of compound sentences', *Linguistic Inquiry*
        2 (1973), 566–569.
[516]   Karttunen, L., 'Presupposition and linguistic context', *Theoretical Linguistics*
        1 (1974), 181–194.
[517]   Karttunen, L. and S. Peters, 'A requiem for presupposition', *BLS* 3, Berkeley
        Linguistic Society, Berkeley, Ca. 1977.
[518]   Keenan, E., 'Two kinds of presupposition in natural language', in C. Fillmore
        and D. Langendoen (eds.), *Studies in Linguistic Semantics*, Holt, Rinehart and
        Winston 1971, pp. 45–42.
[519]   Kempson, R., *Presupposition and the Delimitation of Semantics*, Cambridge
        University Press, Cambridge 1975.
[520]   Kiparsky, P. and C. Kiparsky, 'Fact', in M. Bierwisch and K. Heidolph (eds.),
        Progress in Linguistics, Mouton, The Hague 1970.

[521] Langendoen, D. and H. Savin, 'The projection problem for presuppositions', in C. Fillmore and D. Langendoen (eds.), *Studies in Linguistics Semantics*, Holt, Rinehart and Winston, New York 1971, pp. 55–60.

[522] McCawley, J., 'Presupposition and discourse structure', in C. Oh and D. Dinneen (eds.), *Syntax and Semantics, Vol. 11: Presupposition*, Academic Press, New York 1979.

[523] Morgan, J., 'On the treatment of presupposition in transformational grammar', *CLS* 5, Chicago Linguistic Society, Chicago, Ill. 1969.

[524] Muraki, M., 'Presupposition and pseudo-clefts', *CLS* 6, Chicago Linguistic Society, Chicago, Ill. 1970, 390–399.

[525] Muraki, M., 'Discourse presupposition', *Papers in Linguistics* 5 (1972), 300–320.

[526] Oh, C., 'More on degree of factivity', *CLS* 10, Chicago Linguistic Society, Chicago, Ill. 1974, 517–527.

[527] Oh, C. and D. Dinneen (eds.), *Syntax and Semantics, Vol. 11: Presupposition*, Academic Press, New York 1979.

[528] Permesly, S., *Some Aspects of Presupposition in Generative Grammar*, Ph. D. dissertation, MIT 1973.

[529] Peters, S., 'Presuppositions and conversation', *Texas Linguistic Forum* 2 (1975), 122–133.

[530] Petöfi, J. and D. Franck, *Präsuppositionen in Philosophie und Linguistik*, Athenäum, Frankfurt am Main 1973.

[531] Prince, E., 'A comparison of wh-clefts and it-clefts in discourse', *Language* 54 (1978), 883–906.

[532] Ross, J., 'The penthouse principle and the order of constituents', in Corum et al. (eds.), *You Take the High Node and I'll Take the Low Node*, Chicago Linguistic Society, Chicago, Ill. 1973, pp. 397–422.

[533] Sledd, J., 'Coordination (faulty) and subordination (upside-down)', in M. Steinmann (ed.), *New Rhetorics*, Charles Scribner's Sons, New York 1967, p. 176–190.

[534] Stalnaker, R., 'Presupposition', in D. Hockney et al. (eds.), *Contemporary Research in Philosophical Logic and Linguistic Semantics*, D. Reidel, Dordrecht 1975, p. 31–41.

[535] Wilson, D., 'Presuppositions on factives', *Linguistic Inquiry* 3 (1972), 405–410.

[536] Wilson, D., *Presuppositions and Non-truth-conditional Semantics*, Academic Press, London 1975.

[537] Wilson, D. and D. Sperber, 'Ordered entailments: an alternative to presuppositional theories', in C. Oh and D. Dineen (eds.), *Syntax and Semantics 11: Presupposition*, Academic Press, New York 1979, pp. 299–323.

[538] Zuber, R., *Structure presuppositionelle de langage*, Dunod, Paris 1972.

CHAPTER 5

[539] Akmajian, A., 'The role of focus in the interpretation of anaphoric expressions', in S. Anderson and P. Kiparsky (eds.), *A Festschrift for Morris Halle*, Holt, Rinehart and Winston, New York 1973.

[540]   Akmajian, A. and R. Jackendoff, 'Coreferentiality and stress', *Linguistic Inquiry* 1 (1970), 124–126.

[541]   Barry, R., 'Topic in Chinese: an overlap of meaning, grammar, and discourse function', *Papers from the Parasession on Functionalism*, Chicago Linguistic Society, Chicago, Ill. 1975, pp. 1–9.

[542]   Beneš, E., 'On two aspects of functional sentence perspective', *Travaux Linguistiques de Prague* 3 (1968), 267–274.

[543]   Chafe, W., 'Givenness, contrastiveness, definiteness, subjects, and topics', in C. Li (ed.), *Subject and Topic*, Academic Press, New York 1976.

[544]   Chomsky, N., *Aspects of the Theory of Syntax*, MIT Press, Cambridge, Ma. 1965.

[545]   Cinque, G., 'The movement-nature of left dislocation', *Linguistic Inquiry* 8 (1977), 397–412.

[546]   Dahl, Ö., *Topic and Comment: A Study in Russian and General Transformational Grammar*, Göteborg 1969.

[547]   Daneš, F., 'Functional sentence perspective and the organization of the text', in F. Daneš (ed.), *Papers on Functional Sentence Perspective*, Mouton, The Hague 1974, and Academia, Prague 1974, pp. 106–128. © Academia, Publishing House of the Czechoslovak Academy of Sciences, 1974.

[548]   Donnellan, K., 'Reference and definite descriptions', *Philosophical Review* 60 (1966), 281–304.

[549]   Donnellan, K., 'Speaker reference, descriptions, and anaphora', in P. Cole (ed.), *Syntax and Semantics, Vol. 9: Pragmatics*, Academic Press, New York 1978, pp. 47–68.

[550]   Firbas, J., 'On defining the theme in functional sentence analysis', *Philologica Praguensia* 8 (1964), 170–176.

[551]   Firbas, J., 'Non-thematic subjects in contemporary English', *Travaux Linguistiques de Prague* 2 (1966), 239–256.

[552]   Firbas, J., 'Some aspects of the Czechoslovak approach to problems of functional sentence perspective', in F. Daneš (ed.), *Papers on Functional Sentence Perspective*, Mouton, The Hague 1974.

[553]   Firbas, J., 'On the thematic and non-thematic section of the sentence', *Style and Text* (1975), pp. 314–334.

[554]   Geach, P., 'Subject and predicate', *Mind* 59 (1950), 461–482.

[555]   Geach, P., *Reference and Generality*, Cornell University Press, Ithaca, N.Y. 1962.

[556]   Goodman, N., 'About', *Mind* 72 (1961), 1–24.

[557]   Grice, P., 'Vacuous names', in D. Davidson and J. Hintikka (eds.), *Words and Objections*, D. Reidel, Dordrecht 1969, pp. 118–145.

[558]   Grimshaw, J., 'Complement selection and the lexicon', *Linguistic Inquiry* 10 (1979), 279–326.

[559]   Gundel, J., 'Left dislocation and the role of topic-comment structure in linguistic theory', *Working Papers in Linguistics* 18 (1975), Ohio State University, Columbus, Ohio.

[560]   Gundel, J., 'Stress, pronominalization, and the given-new distinction', *NELS* 7, North-Eastern Linguistic Society 1976.

[561]   Halliday, M., 'Categories of the theory of grammar', *Word* 17 (1961), 241–292.

[562]   Halliday, M., 'Notes on transitivity and theme in English', *Journal of Linguistics* 3 (1967), 37–81, 199–244; *Journal of Linguistics* 4 (1968), 179–215.

[563] Halliday, M., 'The place of functional sentence perspective in the system of linguistic description', in F. Daneš (ed.), *Papers on Functional Sentence Perspective*, Mouton, The Hague 1974, pp. 43–53.

[564] Heny, F. (ed.), *Ambiguities in Intensional Contexts*, D. Reidel, Dordrecht 1981.

[565] Hintikka, J., 'On the different constructions in terms of the basic epistemological concepts: A survey of some problems and proposals', in R. Olson (ed.), *Contemporary Philosophy in Scandinavia*, Johns Hopkins Press, Baltimore, Md. 1972, pp. 105–122.

[566] Hockett, C., *A Course in Modern Linguistics*, Macmillan, New York 1958.

[567] Hornby, P., 'The psychological subject and predicate', *Cognitive Psychology* 3 (1972), 632–649.

[568] Isard, S., 'Changing the context', in E. Keenan (ed.), *Formal Semantics of Natural Languages*, Cambridge University Press, Cambridge 1974.

[569] Jespersen, O. *The Philosophy of Grammar*, Allen and Unwin, London 1924.

[570] Johnson-Laird, P. and A. Garnham, 'Descriptions and discourse models', *Linguistics and Philosophy* 3 (1980), 371–393.

[571] Kaplan, D., 'DThat', in P. Cole (ed.), *Syntax and Semantics, Vol. 9: Pragmatics*, pp. 221–243.

[572] Karttunen, L., 'Discourse referents', *Indiana University Linguistics Club*, Bloomington, Indiana 1971.

[573] Keenan-Ochs, E., and B. Schieffelin, 'Topics as a Discourse Notion', in C. Li (ed.), *Subject and Topic*, Academic Press, New York 1976.

[574] Keenan-Ochs, E. and B. Schieffelin, 'Foregrounding referents: a reconsideration of left-dislocation in discourse', in H. Thompson et al. (eds.), *Proceedings of the 2nd Annual Meeting of the Berkeley Linguistic Society*, University of California, Berkeley, Ca 1976.

[575] Kripke, S., 'Speaker's reference and semantic referent', *Midwest Studies in Philosophy* 2 (1977), 255–276.

[576] Kuno, S. and E. Kaburaki, 'Empathy and syntax', *Harvard Studies in Syntax and Semantics* 1 (1975), 1–73.

[577] Lakoff, G., *Pronouns and Reference*, Indiana University Linguistics Club, Bloomington, Indiana 1968.

[578] Lakoff, *Irregularity in Syntax*, Holt, Rinehart and Winston, New York 1970.

[579] Lakoff, G., 'The role of deduction in grammar', in C. Fillmore and O. Langendoen (eds.), *Studies in Linguistic Semantics*, Holt, Rinehart and Winston, New York 1971, pp. 63–70.

[580] Li, C. (ed.), *Subject and Topic*, Academic Press, New York 1976.

[581] Mathesius, V., 'On the information-bearing structure of the sentence', transl. from the 1939 original by O. Yokoyama, *Harvard Studies in Syntax and Semantics* 1 (1975).

[582] Mathesius, V., 'On linguistic characterology with illustrations from modern English', in J. Vachek (ed.), *A Prague School Reader in Linguistics*, Indiana University Press, Indiana 1964.

[583] Ochs, E., 'Social foundations of language', in R. Freedle (ed.), *New Directions in Discourse Processing*, Ablex, Norwood, N.J., 1979, pp. 207–221.

[584] Oehrle, R., 'Common problems in the theory of anaphora and the theory

of discourse', in H. Parret, M. Sbisa and J. Verschueren (eds.), *Pragmatics: Possibilities and Limitations*, Benjamins, Amsterdam 1982.

[585] Postal, P. *Crossover Phenomena*, Holt, Rinehart and Winston, New York 1971.

[586] Putnam, H., 'Formalization of the concept "about"', *Philosophy of Science* 25/2 (1958).

[587] Reinhart, T., 'Pragmatics and linguistics: An analysis of sentence topics', *Philosophica* 27 (1981), 53–94.

[588] Richards, K., 'Indirect questions and strange NP's have a common parent', *CLS Book of Squibs*, Chicago Linguistic Society, Chicago 1977, pp. 78–82.

[589] Rodman, R., 'On left dislocation', *Papers in Linguistics* 7 (1974), 437–466.

[590] Ross, J., *Constraints on Variables in Syntax*, Indiana University Linguistics Club, Bloomington, Indiana 1967.

[591] Ross, J., 'Guess!' *CLS* 13, Chicago Linguistic Society, Chicago, Ill. 1977, 515–544.

[592] Sgall, P., 'L'ordre des mots et la semantique', in F. Kiefer (ed.), *Studies in Syntax and Semantics*, Dordrecht 1969, pp. 231–240.

[593] Sgall, P., 'Zur Stellung der Thema-Rhema Gliederung in der Sprachbeschreibung', in F. Daneš (ed.), *Papers on Functional Sentence Perspective*, Mouton, The Hague 1974.

[594] Sgall, P., E. Hajičova, and E. Benešova, *Topic, Focus, and Generative Semantics*, Skriptor Verlag, Kronberg, Taunus 1973.

[595] Smaby, R., 'Ambiguous coreference with quantifiers', in F. Guenthner and S. Smith (eds.), *Formal Semantics and Pragmatics for Natural Languages*, D. Reidel, Dordrecht 1978, pp. 37–75.

[596] Smith, D., 'The Ortcutt connection', in F. Heny (ed.), *Ambiguities in Intensional Contexts*, D. Reidel, Dordrecht 1981, pp. 103–131.

[597] Strawson, 'On referring', *Mind* 59 (1950), 320–344.

[598] Strawson, P., *Individuals*, Methuen & Co., London 1959.

[599] Strawson, P., 'Identifying reference and truth values', *Theoria* 30 (1964).

[600] Weil, H., *De l'ordre des mots dans les langues anciennes comparées aux langues modernes*, Paris 1844; English translation *The Order of Words in the Ancient Languages Compared with That of the Modern Languages*, Boston 1878.

INDEX OF NAMES

311

INDEX OF SUBJECTS

INDEX OF RULES

317

SYNTHESE LANGUAGE LIBRARY

Texts and Studies in Linguistics and Philosophy

Managing Editors:

ELISABET ENGDAHL (University of Wisconsin)
JAAKKO HINTIKKA (Florida State University)
STANLEY PETERS (The University of Texas at Austin)

Editors:

EMMON BACH (University of Massachusetts at Amherst), JOAN BRESNAN
(CSLI, Stanford University), JOHN LYONS (University of Sussex),
JULIUS M. E. MORAVCSIK (Stanford University), PATRICK SUPPES (Stanford
University), DANA SCOTT (Oxford University).

1. Henry Hiż (ed.), *Questions*. 1978.
2. William S. Cooper, *Foundations of Logico-Linguistics. A Unified Theory of Information, Language, and Logic.* 1978.
3. Avishai Margalit (ed.), *Meaning and Use.* 1979.
4. F. Guenthner and S. J. Schmidt (eds.), *Formal Semantics and Pragmatics for Natural Languages.* 1978.
5. Esa Saarinen (ed.), *Game-Theoretical Semantics.* 1978.
6. F. J. Pelletier (ed.), *Mass Terms: Some Philosophical Problems.* 1979.
7. David R. Dowty, *Word Meaning and Montague Grammar. The Semantics of Verbs and Times in Generative Semantics and in Montague's PTQ.* 1979.
8. Alice F. Freed, *The Semantics of English Aspectual Complementation.* 1979.
9. James McCloskey, *Transformational Syntax and Model Theoretic Semantics: A Case Study in Modern Irish.* 1979.
10. John R. Searle, Ferenc Kiefer, and Manfred Bierwisch (eds.), *Speech Act Theory and Pragmatics.* 1980.
11. David R. Dowty, Robert E. Wall, and Stanley Peters, *Introduction to Montague Semantics.* 1981.
12. Frank Heny (ed.), *Ambiguities in Intensional Contexts.* 1981.
13. Wolfgang Klein and Willem Levelt (eds.), *Crossing the Boundaries in Linguistics: Studies Presented to Manfred Bierwisch.* 1981.
14. Zellig S. Harris, *Papers on Syntax*, edited by Henry Hiż. 1981.
15. Pauline Jacobson and Geoffrey K. Pullum (eds.), *The Nature of Syntactic Representation.* 1982.
16. Stanley Peters and Esa Saarinen (eds.), *Processes, Beliefs, and Questions.* 1982.
17. Lauri Carlson, *Dialogue Games. An Approach to Discourse Analysis.* 1983.
18. Lucia Vaina and Jaakko Hintikka (eds.), *Cognitive Constraints on Communication.* 1983.
19. Frank Heny and Barry Richards (eds.), *Linguistic Categories: Auxiliaries and Related Puzzles. Volume One: Categories.* 1983.
20. Frank Heny and Barry Richards (eds.), *Linguistic Categories: Auxiliaries and Related Puzzles. Volume Two: The Scope, Order, and Distribution of English Auxiliary Verbs.* 1983.
21. Robin Cooper, *Quantification and Syntactic Theory.* 1983.